SMASHING
WordPress
Themes

MAKING WORDPRESS BEAUTIFUL

Thord Daniel Hedengren

A John Wiley and Sons, Ltd, Publication

Smashing WordPress Themes is dedicated to the WordPress community.

We're all playing an important part by making free speech easier online. The more people can express their thoughts, dreams, and ideas, the better for everyone. Open source in general, and WordPress in particular, play an important role in the free speech movement.

Keep up the great work, dear community.

Thord Daniel Hedengren

About the Author

Thord Daniel Hedengren is addicted to words, which led him to launch his first online newsletter in 1996. It all went downhill from there, with dozens of Web sites, and a career as an editor and freelancer in both Sweden and abroad.

His international career began with a blog post, which led to a book deal for *Smashing WordPress: Beyond the Blog*, with Wiley Publishing, Inc., and an even stronger voice in the WordPress community. You're now holding Thord's second book.

When not obsessed with words, Thord and his friends build cool Web sites using WordPress at his Web design firm, Odd Alice. He also edits magazines and writes freelance articles for both print and Web publications (in Swedish and English). You can follow everything Thord on `http://tdh.me`.

Thord lives in the land of kings, Sweden.

Contents

x

Introduction

SMASHING WORDPRESS THEMES is all about making your WordPress site look beautiful. But, the beautiful part is a very personal thing, because we all have different preferences. So in essence, my book isn't on Web design, but rather about giving you, dear reader, the tools to build the kind of site that you want to create, using WordPress elements.

A theme is the skin of your WordPress content, your site template so to speak. A huge community of people design and use themes, offering many high-quality designs. With this book, you can now contribute to that community.

As with my previous book, *Smashing WordPress: Beyond the Blog,* this book mainly targets those of you who know a bit about Web development already. If you know some HTML, PHP, CSS, or have fiddled around a bit with WordPress, then this book is for you. If that sounds like Greek to you (or any other language you may not understand), then you should read up a bit before you tackle this. But because even more experienced Web developers need a quick recap at times, you all may find this book a welcome reminder of existing features.

As I write this book, WordPress has reached version 3.0.1, and is rocking the publishing world. Some of the code in this book is based on themes that are available online, but since the Web is an ever-changing entity, the online code may be somewhat different from the examples that you see in this book. Just keep that in mind if things suddenly don't seem to add up.

You can download the example code files from the companion Web site for this book at www.wiley.com/go/smashingwordpressthemes.

Before I wrap this up and let you get started with WordPress theming, here are a few links that you may find interesting.

- Code snippets for this book are available at my Web site at http://tdh.me. Go to Smashing WordPress Themes under "Books." (The companion Web site for this book at www.wiley.com/go/smashingwordpressthemes also contains all the code.)
- Everything Notes related, including themes, plugins, code examples, and so on is available at http://notesblog.com.
- The official WordPress manual, The WordPress Codex, is at http://codex.wordpress.org.

You can also become a fan on my Facebook business Page at http://facebook.com/tdhftw — and follow @tdhedengren on Twitter for the latest from yours truly.

Right! So let's build some cool themes! Welcome to *Smashing WordPress Themes: Making WordPress Beautiful.* I hope you'll enjoy the ride. To properly convey this information, this book is divided into four parts.

PART 1: WHAT ARE WORDPRESS THEMES?

WordPress themes are what make your Web site look good and function well. They are the visual skin, the look and design of your site, what your visitors will see. On the outside, your WordPress site looks and behaves like any other Web site, basically — just working better and looking more gorgeous, hopefully.

The inside of a theme is a completely different beast. It contains stylesheets, template files, and — to the outsider — weird mumbo-jumbo code. You'll find that your theme files are powerful tools that help you control your site's function. It is not just visual bling; it is the actual code that makes it tick, residing on top of the WordPress software platform.

PART II: HACKING A THEME

Just because you're a grand WordPress theme superstar designer doesn't mean you can't look at, and perhaps even use, other people's themes. In fact, that is one of the best ways to learn theming, because you'll get new ideas and find new approaches to problems and situations that you may not have encountered otherwise. It is easy to get caught in the "I have to do everything myself" maelstrom.

You should take advantage of the vast themes community out there in cyberspace. So, I dedicate Part II to working with themes that you have not built yourself.

PART III: BUILDING YOUR OWN THEME

If you want complete control over your WordPress site, build your own theme. Not only does building your own theme make it easier for you to achieve your goals, it is often the best way to keep your site lean and focused on its purpose. After all, while other theme designers may have done a great job building a theme that you can use, the parts of that theme that don't fit your goals will need reworking in some way.

In Part III, I focus on building original themes, with concrete examples and ideas for you to take with you to your own projects. Consider the practical examples as food for thought on how you can solve your own problems as you build your theme, and take inspiration from the solutions herein.

PART IV: TAKING THEMES FURTHER

Whether you create your own theme from scratch, or use and modify someone else's work, sometimes you still do not get the effect you want for your Web site. That's when the wonderful world of WordPress plugins comes into play. You can write your own plugin for release to the WordPress community (for major stuff), or just put it in own your theme's functions.php (for smaller features). Or, simply download someone else's plugin, and save a lot of time.

In this part, I look at the various ways to use plugins to further enhance your WordPress site.

WHAT ARE WORDPRESS THEMES?

1

GETTING STARTED WITH WORDPRESS

WORDPRESS IS A most extraordinary beast. Not only can you run just about any Web site using WordPress as a content management system (CMS), it is also so very easy to get started with. Gone are the days when installing a publishing platform is a bore and a hassle. With quality open-source software, such as WordPress, suddenly you are the one doing the install, not an expensive Web agency or IT consultant.

With WordPress, anyone can get into online publishing. All you need is a domain name and a compatible Web host, and then you're ready to begin.

In this chapter you start by installing WordPress and reviewing a few basics about this software system. I discuss the content of theme folders, and briefly describe the use of posts and Pages, custom taxonomies, and custom posts.

Later in the book, you move on to actually hacking an existing theme, and even build one of your own. Welcome to the wonderful world of online publishing, WordPress-style!

For advanced WordPress programming professionals, go to Part III to build your own WordPress themes.

INSTALLING WORDPRESS IN JUST FIVE MINUTES

WordPress prides itself on something they call the five-minute install. Truth is, it rarely takes five minutes to install WordPress, it is usually a lot faster. But sure, if you consider download time and if your Web host is a slow one, then five minutes may be accurate.

While this book assumes that you know a thing or two about WordPress, it makes sense to go over the install just to be thorough. So here it is; how to install WordPress.

RUNNING WORDPRESS USING A WEB HOST

First, find a Web host that meets the WordPress software requirements. The host needs to run PHP and MySQL, and preferably Apache or Nginx as well, so that you can get permalinks out of the box without any tweaking. Most decent Web hosts will do, but you should go to `http://wordpress.org/about/requirements` to check the latest needs for the current WordPress version, just in case. Ask your Web host if you're uncertain (see Figure 1-1 to download the WordPress software files).

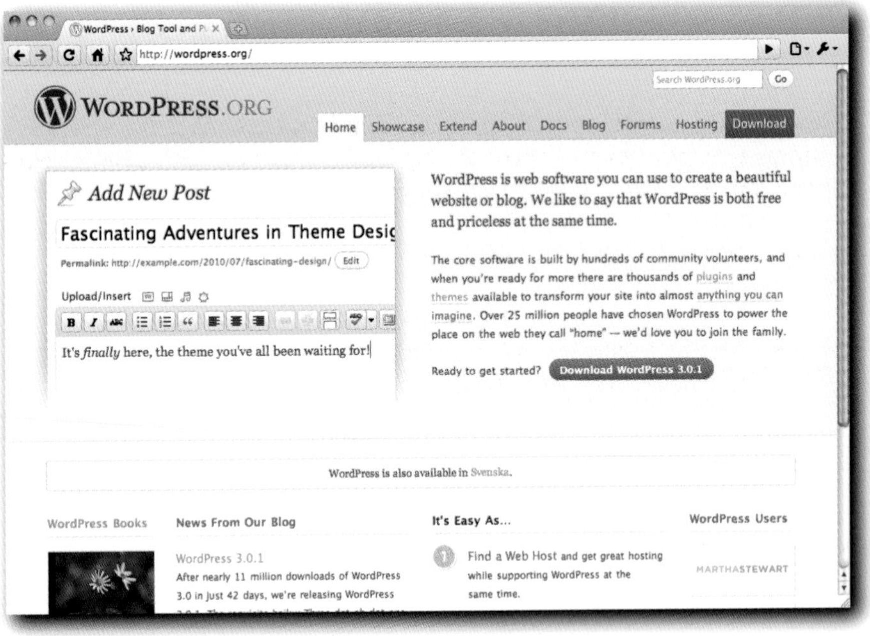

Figure 1-1: Download the WordPress software files at `wordpress.org/download`

Second, you need to set up everything with your Web host. That means that you need to set up a MySQL database and a user with read and write privileges. How you do this will depend on your Web host, so consult their control panel or ask the support staff. Just keep the database name, and the username and password handy; you need them to install WordPress.

Now you can get started! Download the latest software version from `http://wordpress.org/download`. I start by going over the hands-on, edit-everything-yourself install, and then I get to the WordPress guided steps. Start by opening wp-config-sample.php. Find these lines:

```
// ** MySQL settings - You can get this info from your web host ** //
/** The name of the database for WordPress */
define('DB_NAME', 'database_name_here');

/** MySQL database username */
define('DB_USER', 'username_here');

/** MySQL database password */
define('DB_PASSWORD', 'password_here');

/** MySQL hostname */
define('DB_HOST', 'localhost');

/** Database Charset to use in creating database tables. */
define('DB_CHARSET', 'utf8');

/** The Database Collate type. Don't change this if in doubt. */
define('DB_COLLATE', '');
```

This is where you add the database information: the database name, the username, and the password. In some cases, you'll need to swap localhost for a database server if your Web host has one of those. Again, consult your Web host if you're uncertain.

This is how it could look when filled out:

```
// ** MySQL settings - You can get this info from your web host ** //
/** The name of the database for WordPress */
define('DB_NAME', 'swpt_WordPress');

/** MySQL database username */
define('DB_USER', 'kingofkong');

/** MySQL database password */
define('DB_PASSWORD', 'Xgg%4ZZ89QwC');

/** MySQL hostname */
define('DB_HOST', 'localhost');

/** Database Charset to use in creating database tables. */
define('DB_CHARSET', 'utf8');

/** The Database Collate type. Don't change this if in doubt. */
define('DB_COLLATE', '');
```

Now, while that would do it, you should be sure to get the necessary secret keys to help prevent malicious use of your software. You can find these lines in the wp-config-sample.php file:

```
/**#@+
 * Authentication Unique Keys and Salts.
 *
 * Change these to different unique phrases!
 * You can generate these using the {@link https://api.wordpress.org/secret-key/1.1/
 salt/ WordPress.org secret-key service}
 * You can change these at any point in time to invalidate all existing cookies.
 This will force all users to have to log in again.
 *
 * @since 2.6.0
 */
define('AUTH_KEY',          'put your unique phrase here');
define('SECURE_AUTH_KEY',   'put your unique phrase here');
define('LOGGED_IN_KEY',     'put your unique phrase here');
define('NONCE_KEY',         'put your unique phrase here');
define('AUTH_SALT',         'put your unique phrase here');
define('SECURE_AUTH_SALT',  'put your unique phrase here');
define('LOGGED_IN_SALT',    'put your unique phrase here');
define('NONCE_SALT',        'put your unique phrase here');
```

Now, open your favorite Web browser and go to `https://api.wordpress.org/secret-key/1.1/salt`. Here you'll get some random lines of secret keys (as you see in Figure 1-2), different keys with each browser reload. Copy these, and replace the lines in the wp-config-sample.php file. The results could look something like this:

```
/**#@+
 * Authentication Unique Keys and Salts.
 *
 * Change these to different unique phrases!
 * You can generate these using the {@link https://api.wordpress.org/secret-key/1.1/
 salt/ WordPress.org secret-key service}
 * You can change these at any point in time to invalidate all existing cookies.
 This will force all users to have to log in again.
 *
 * @since 2.6.0
 */
define('AUTH_KEY',          '/4t`.1}GnupQ(]XMS}6o6Qcv|.]t{K`v[50DzU~|juF]|z2yoZ
 >Ya$riv)2R];Z');
define('SECURE_AUTH_KEY',   '0S}v/wtac{N-YxX]b_r6`W;cm2FWonA_^2os|XbFz{M<Q;n|e$LrNEy}
 Ft2|0c|N');
define('LOGGED_IN_KEY',     'rZU|=os,q?sFKgru]p=|Ur4;xO=hTZC-TWh@w
 ep2G2I=JFt3?`+(0thNHwif2$|');
define('NONCE_KEY',         '3~Im%^2b3quR]3i=OHxVib-h`npIW4u%]BGq03BgB?8%O@H}76TKLp1|
 ~X/!<xJ-');
define('AUTH_SALT',         'XWLUdK^7SvEd`|XE,SDh`LkP]AvmB=-Aq(~wh.d5q1Zo7@g
 C=H6#|C?O+q+5-8?');
define('SECURE_AUTH_SALT',
 'KM=Qr1FVvY>vEtkvw^vJZC/U#J}-il*BWLn`nZ+%8>6d-F=Pl*sUxT6yNg[t6,4.');
define('LOGGED_IN_SALT',    'GW7z3!E@ rHQv#QPdA_SE?kR3*YBnO.`(,V<_L 0L{O};k}`,t)
 xQ|qN?wFR`d=s');
```

```
define('NONCE_SALT',       '|/R:TYW><?k?`ogGp+N{ge+( )|y-F(J$ff&E#xMnH.
 o|ulrDs=+Uy<A9[FQPsxI');
```

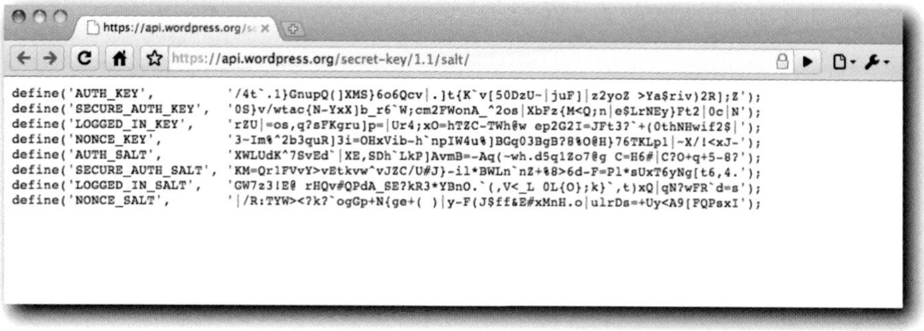

Figure 1-2: The secret keys change with every reload

Finally, you may want to change the default language. I'm Swedish, so I usually launch blogs in Sweden in my native language. A listing of all language files are available at `http://codex.wordpress.org/WordPress_in_Your_Language` in the WordPress Codex. I save these language files for later, and then upload them with all the other WordPress files. For now, all I need to know is the language code. For Swedish, it is `sv_SE`, as I can see from the language filenames listed on the Codex page.

To change the default language, find this section of code:

```
/**
 * WordPress Localized Language, defaults to English.
 *
 * Change this to localize WordPress.  A corresponding MO file for the chosen
 * language must be installed to wp-content/languages. For example, install
 * de.mo to wp-content/languages and set WPLANG to 'de' to enable German
 * language support.
 */
define ('WPLANG', '');
```

All I need to do is type my language code so that WordPress knows to swap the default English language with the one that I pick. After I set the install to use Swedish as the default language, the rest of the process will be in Swedish.

```
/**
 * WordPress Localized Language, defaults to English.
 *
 * Change this to localize WordPress.  A corresponding MO file for the chosen
 * language must be installed to wp-content/languages. For example, install
 * de.mo to wp-content/languages and set WPLANG to 'de' to enable German
 * language support.
 */
define ('WPLANG', 'sv_SE');
```

When you're done, change the filename from wp-config-sample.php to wp-config.php. The sample filename is just a sample, after all.

For more information about localization, see Chapter 6.

But wait! Sometimes all these steps are completely unnecessary. If your host supports it, you can just upload WordPress (which you'll do in the next step, otherwise) and point your Web browser to your URL. A guide takes you through the process. You basically fill out the database details, and that's that. However, you can't change the language this way, so it helps to know your way around the wp-config.php file!

Not everyone feels confident installing WordPress using the Web browser, especially since it involves sending your MySQL username and password unencrypted. It is safer to do the edits in wp-config-sample.php, rename it to wp-config.php, and then upload it using FTP with a secure connection (which your host needs to support). Otherwise, someone could sniff your online traffic and pick up your database username and password.

Now upload the whole thing. Open up your favorite FTP client (if you don't have one, just get Filezilla from `http://filezilla-project.org`) and connect to your Web host. (If that sounds like Greek to you, consult your Web host for help.)

When connected to your Web host with FTP, find the folder in which you want to install WordPress. Upload the WordPress files within the `wordpress` folder, which you got from `http://wordpress.org`. If you changed the default language in wp-config.php, you'll also want to upload the language file. Create a folder called `language` in `wp-content`, and upload the language file to that folder.

After all the files are uploaded, you can install WordPress. Just point your Web browser to the folder where you installed the WordPress files, and you are asked to fill in a name for your blog, as well as the contact e-mail address. Click the Next button and you get an admin username and a password. Now, click the Finish button and then you log in. Do that with your admin username and password, and there you go: you've installed WordPress!

You'll want to review each option in the Settings part of the WordPress admin panel. Just start from the top and make sure that you activate permalinks, since it looks better and search engines like them. I get to the ideal settings later in this chapter, so either wait until then or set everything up the way you see fit for now.

Did it take five minutes? I bet less. Reading this section definitely took longer than installing the software, didn't it?

RUNNING WORDPRESS LOCALLY

You don't actually need a Web host to start using WordPress, at least not for your own testing and development purposes. All you need is a local server environment that is WordPress-compatible, which is a breeze these days. Long gone is the need for an old Linux server in the closet. Instead, you can run WordPress on your Mac or PC using MAMP (that is, Mac, Apache, MySql, and PHP, Perl, or Python) or WAMP (that is, Windows, Apache, MySql, and PHP, Perl, or Python) respectively.

In fact, although several ways exist to run the program locally, both MAMP and WAMP are free to download and use, so I focus on those to get you started.

Setting Up MAMP for your Mac

MAMP is the best solution for running Web sites locally on your Mac. It is free, although there is a Pro version available (and included in the download as well), and it is very easy to use.

First, go to www.mamp.info to download the MAMP package. After you download the software, you have the option to install MAMP or MAMP PRO — you want the former unless you want to pay more for some reason. Just install it like you always do on a Mac, by dropping the program in Applications.

Next, launch MAMP (for the Mac installation, see Figure 1-3), which is in Applications/MAMP unless you've installed it elsewhere.

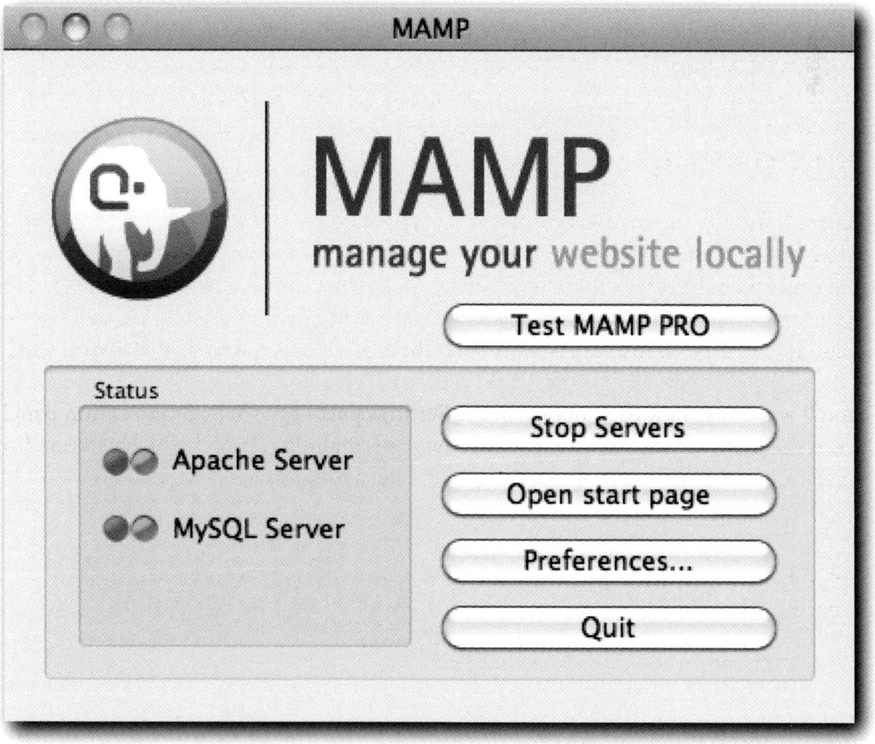

Figure 1-3: Use MAMP to run a Web site locally on your Mac

You might want to go through the settings, but in most cases you can just leave it. It works out of the box. Only change these settings if you know you need to do something particular to your computer setup.

One thing you might want to change is where the `htdocs` folder is located. This folder is your local server root, so to speak. Because it is located under the MAMP folder by default, you may want to move it somewhere else; this is entirely optional and managed in the MAMP settings. You need to open the actual MAMP software to access these settings; there are no links or buttons to the settings panels from the Dashboard widget (see Figure 1-4).

Figure 1-4: The MAMP Dashboard widget

The last thing you need to do, barring actually starting the MAMP server (which is done through the app, or the excellent Dashboard widget), is to create a database for your local install. You'll find a link to PhpMyAdmin on the MAMP start page (Figure 1-5 shows where to create your database), easily reached from the MAMP program, if you forget the URL or accidentally close it. Log in with your MySQL credentials, which you'll find on the MAMP start page in your Web browser.

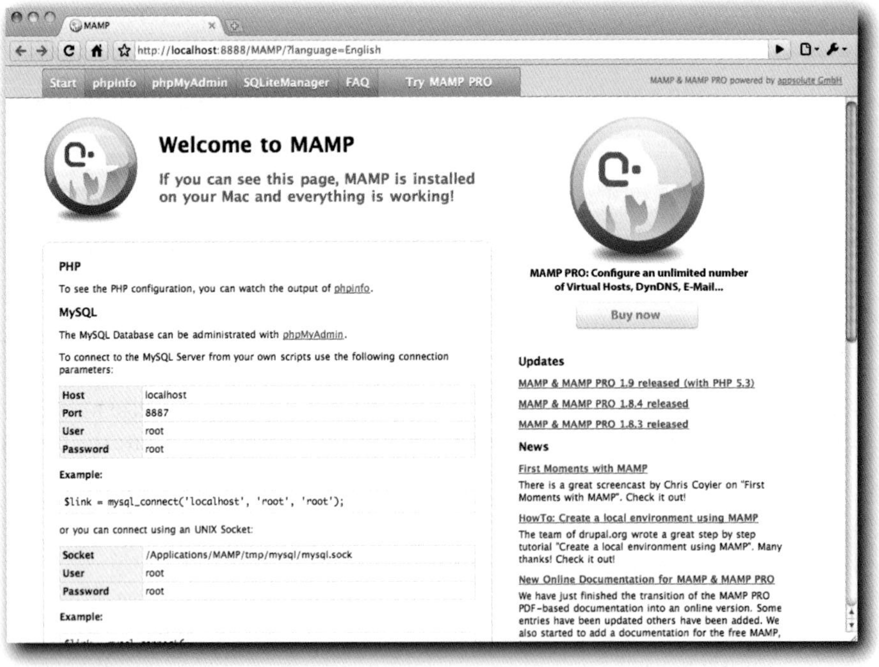

Figure 1-5: The MAMP start page in your default Web browser

In PhpMyAdmin (see Figure 1-6), just create a new database by giving it a name, and then click the Create button.

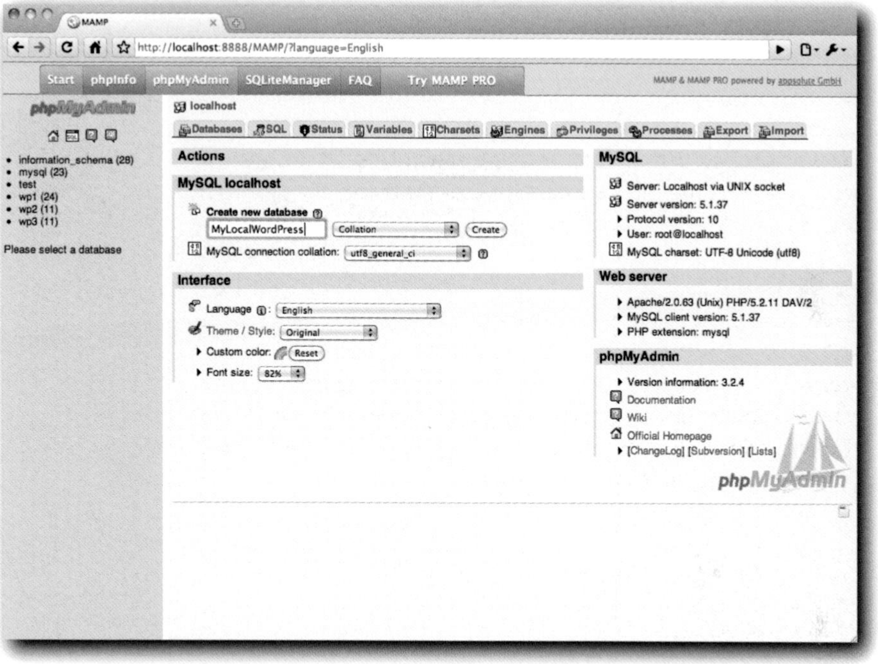

Figure 1-6: PhpMyAdmin home page

That's it! Now you can install WordPress just like you would if this were a normal Web server. Just copy the WordPress files where you want the install, under `htdocs` obviously, and then install it like you usually do.

Setting Up Wampserver for your PC

WampServer is one of several WAMP solutions for Windows PCs. Just like MAMP, it is free to use and simple to install and manage. (As you can see in Figure 1-7, I have the French version.)

To download the WampServer software, go to `http://www.wampserver.com`. It is released under the GPL license and comes as an executable installer file (a dot EXE), so no worries there. Just download it and install it wherever you want.

After you install (and launch, obviously) the software, you see a menu icon on the bottom right of your screen, which gives you access to your Wampserver settings and files. So if you need to hack the php.ini file, for example, you can get to that quickly from here. It is actually pretty neat the way the Wampserver is always at your disposal in this way. What you want to do for now, however, is launch your localhost default page (unlike in Figure 1-8, you may launch your version in English).

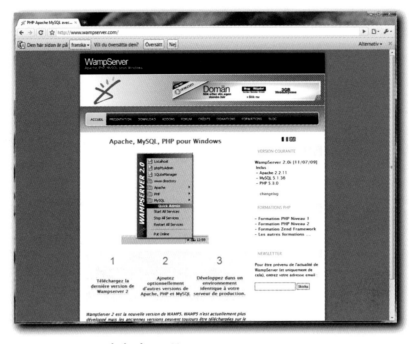

Figure 1-7: Get Wampserver for free for your PC

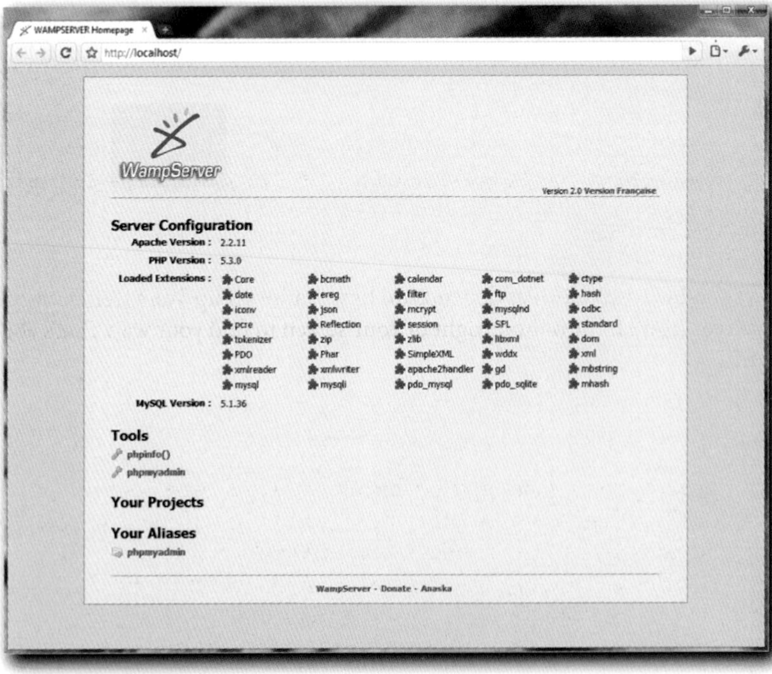

Figure 1-8: The localhost default page

After you launch your Web browser and the localhost page, you can gain quick access to the most necessary information. You can find PhpMyAdmin (to install WordPress on a PC, see Figure 1-9), as well as the phpinfo page, which displays what's running in a nifty manner. PhpMyAdmin works just as it does under MAMP, so all you need to do is to create a database and go from there.

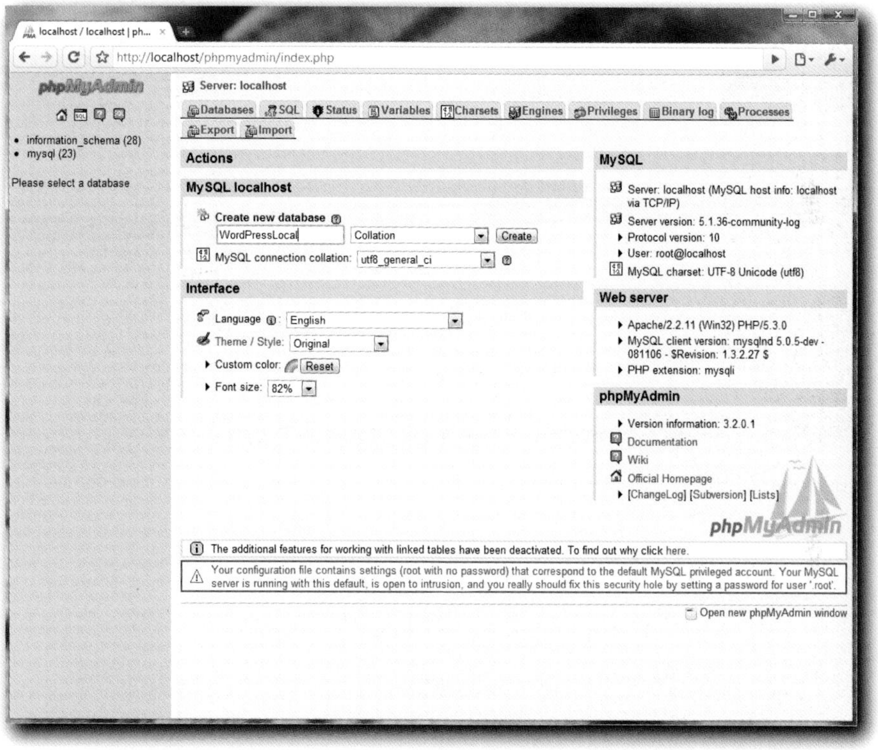

Figure 1-9: PhpMyAdmin, again

Where you actually store your files depends on how you've set up Wampserver. Just look for the Wampserver icon on the bottom right of your screen to find your way. That's about all there is to it!

What About Linux?

As one might guess, there are many options for running a local server under Linux, including the popular LAMP package (Linux, Apache, MySQL, and PHP). If you have Linux installed, chances are that you've already got it under the hood, which actually is true for Mac OS X, as well. If you know what you're doing, you can just use Apache, MySQL, and PHP without relying on any MAMP or Wampserver-like software, but otherwise turn to Google (or any other search engine) to find a solution that fits your Linux distribution of choice.

FINE TUNING YOUR WORDPRESS SETTINGS

You can adjust the site settings in the WordPress admin panel, more specifically in the options found under Settings in the left column. After completing the installation, you may want to take a closer look at them. Go over them all and set up your site according to your needs, with time zones and whatnot. Some of the settings are a bit more important (that is, more crucial) than others, so let's take a closer look at those.

PERMALINKS

First, be sure to enable the permalinks feature, which tells WordPress how the URLs for your posts and Pages will look. You find these settings under Settings, and then Permalinks (Figure 1-10 shows the Permalink Settings screen located in the admin panel). Your actual setup is up to you; just pick settings that you feel make sense. Many theories exist as to what leads to the best rankings in search engines like Google, but I stay clear of those in this book. Research for yourself, but in short, make sure that the post name is in the permalink. See the Codex page on permalinks for more funky options than the suggested defaults: `http://codex. wordpress.org/Using_Permalinks`.

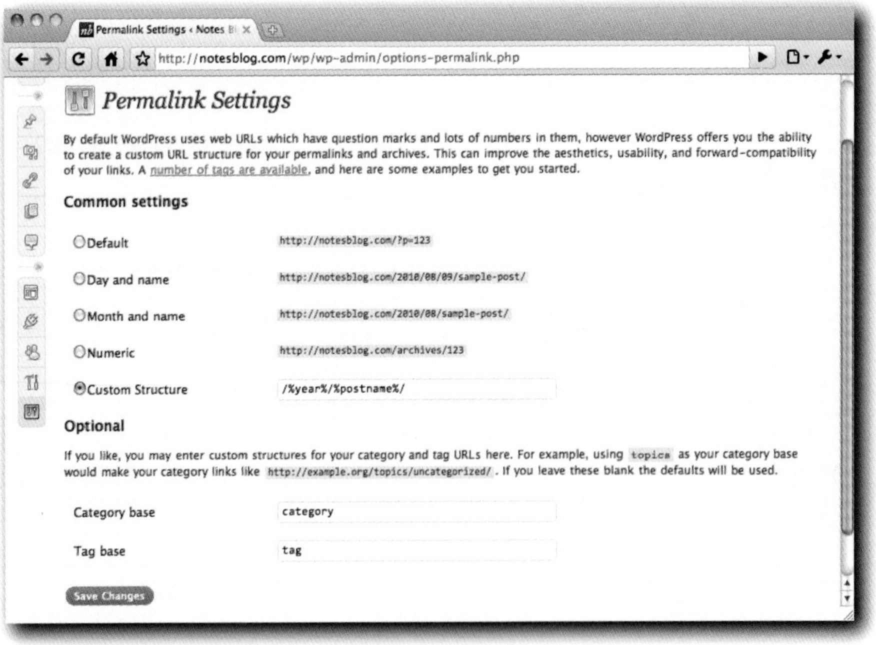

Figure 1-10: The Permalink Settings screen found on a WordPress site

It's worth mentioning here that for the permalink settings to work you need to be able to write to the .htaccess file on your Web host. If WordPress can write to the server, it will create an .htaccess file for you; otherwise, you'll have to do it and make it writeable. If this sounds scary, just follow the instructions on-screen should WordPress not be able to save to the .htaccess file. You'll get a box with the necessary code; just copy and paste it into a text file. Upload that to your WordPress directory (where you've got wp-config.php, among other things); rename it .htaccess, and you'll be fine.

MEDIA SETTINGS AND THE UPLOAD FOLDER

The Media settings are important since they tell your WordPress install how to scale images and manage embeds in your theme. Every image that you upload though the media manager in WordPress, whether it is when writing a post or from the Media Settings screen in the admin panel, is actually saved in up to three sizes. First, there's the thumbnail, which is a small, cropped thumbnail-size version of the image. Then there's the medium-size image, and a large-size one, which are both uncropped versions of the original image, scaled down. These three image sizes are scaled according to the settings on the Media Settings screen (Figure 1-11 is where you specify image dimensions). Make sure that they fit your site. For example, the medium-size image could be used on some Pages where the amount of space is limited, while the large image is the full width available. Take these sizes into consideration when designing your own themes in the future.

Obviously the original image, the one you uploaded, is saved in full size as well. You can add more sizes with themes and plugins, so you're in no way limited to these three sizes. Should the original image be smaller than, say the large image, you won't get one of those, obviously. WordPress only scales down images, never up, since the scaled-up images look bad.

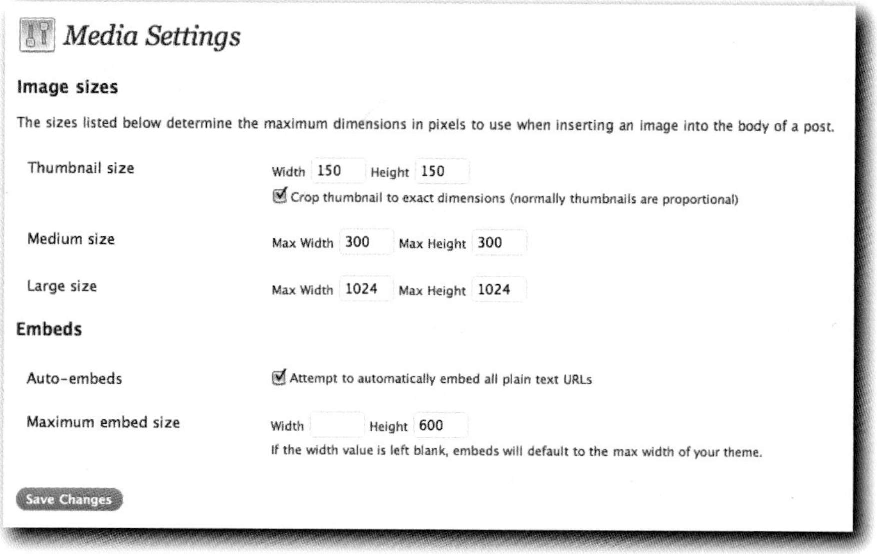

17

Media Settings

Image sizes

The sizes listed below determine the maximum dimensions in pixels to use when inserting an image into the body of a post.

Thumbnail size   Width 150   Height 150
☑ Crop thumbnail to exact dimensions (normally thumbnails are proportional)

Medium size   Max Width 300   Max Height 300

Large size   Max Width 1024   Max Height 1024

Embeds

Auto-embeds   ☑ Attempt to automatically embed all plain text URLs

Maximum embed size   Width   Height 600
If the width value is left blank, embeds will default to the max width of your theme.

Save Changes

Figure 1-11: Media Settings located under Settings in your admin panel

Finally, under the Miscellaneous settings, also found under Settings in the admin panel, you can decide where you want your uploads stored. Usually you won't touch this, but sometimes you may need it. Take a look and remember that the folder that you specify needs to be writable so that WordPress can save your images there. If you ever get an error that your uploads folder isn't working, check these settings.

OTHER NOTEWORTHY SETTINGS

Also check out the General, Writing, Reading, Discussion, and Privacy settings under Settings in the admin panel. The General Settings allow you to change your WordPress tagline, "Just another WordPress site," which may not be what you want to convey. The settings for dates, e-mail, and things like that are all pretty straightforward.

The Reading and Writing settings let you specify how many posts to show per page, whether the front page displays your latest posts or is a static Page, and so on. The Discussion settings page contains information for your comment sections, such as if you allow threaded comments, avatars, and things like that. You can also hide your site from search engines in the Privacy settings. Again, these settings are pretty straightforward, so dig in and get yourself acquainted with your options.

SHAMELESS SELF PROMOTION

For more on the WordPress install, consult the Codex (`http://codex.wordpress.org`). You might also want to get the book *Smashing WordPress: Beyond the Blog* (Wiley Publishing, Inc.), which discusses the install in detail and talks more about securing it, moving it to a different folder, and related items. Incidentally, it is written by yours truly!

WORDPRESS THEME FILES

This book is all about themes, and as such it is important that you get the lingo right from the start. Since you're a WordPress user, you already know that a theme is something of a skin for your WordPress site, containing all the styles necessary to make it look great. The theme can also contain functionality normally associated with plugins, but that's a different matter.

Your theme resides in the `themes` folder, found within the `wp-content` folder, which sits in the root of your WordPress install. Every theme has its own folder, and that theme folder contains a stylesheet, template files, and possibly images and other files needed. The stylesheet is mandatory, the template files are usually necessary, and the rest is icing on the cake (view the theme folders in Figure 1-12). So the essential WordPress theme files are, as follows:

- **Stylesheet file:** Defines the appearance of your theme
- **Template file:** Outputs your content to your Web site
- **Functions.php file:** Allows you to add other new features (such as widget areas)
- **Other files:** Includes images (such as JPEGs) or Java Scripts, for example

Your stylesheet file is named style.css and contains the theme information at the top, in a predetermined format unique to WordPress. Other than that, style.css is a regular stylesheet and you use it as such. That means you can style your links, set your fonts, and do all those things here, or at least import other stylesheets where you do so if you want to put everything in its own stylesheet. The important thing is that your style.css, the primary stylesheet file, contains the theme information.

The template files are PHP files containing the code that outputs content from your Word-Press site. The code is a mixture of PHP, HTML, and the WordPress template tags, which in turn are PHP themselves. I get to that later. What's important is that you know that template files are PHP files used to output your content. That means that the index.php, header.php, footer.php files, and so on in your theme are template files.

Figure 1-12: The default WordPress TwentyTen theme's folder as seen via FTP

Functions.php is one PHP file that is a little different from the others. This little file doesn't display any particular Page or part of your WordPress site (unless you count pages in the admin area, which can be created from functions.php), but rather contains plugin-like functionality, your widget declarations, and related items. In short, while functions.php is a template file, it is also primarily used to add features that you can use globally across your theme.

As I said, the rest is icing on the cake. Most themes contain images, some have JavaScript files, and so on. A theme can contain just about anything that you need, so it isn't limited to the stylesheet and the template files. It is also worth noting that while your theme must reside in a folder in `wp-content/themes`, the theme folder itself can have subfolders. That's handy if you want to put images in one place, stylesheets (but not style.css) in another, and so on.

WORDPRESS AS A CMS

As a regular WordPress user, you may already know how to publish posts and Pages, change current themes and install new ones, and activate plugins. You can drop widgets in their widget areas, and add users with the appropriate capabilities. If you feel uncertain of any of this, you should play around with your WordPress install, publish some posts and Pages, swap a few themes, and use some widgets.

But while a lot of us use WordPress for traditional blogging, you can clearly do a lot more than that. The evolution of the platform is stunning, and you'll soon find that mere blogging is the simplest form of WordPress usage. (Maybe static corporate sites are even simpler, but that really doesn't matter.)

What I want to do is plant the thought that WordPress is a lot more than a blogging platform. It's a CMS, and with WordPress 3.0 or later and the addition of custom post types (which I get to in a little bit), it gets a lot easier to do cool stuff with the platform.

Don't think too much about WordPress' blogging past. It is still a great blogging platform, but it can be so much more. A community, the basis for an e-commerce site, a photo portfolio, a newspaper, an online magazine . . . . All it needs is for you to create the themes for it.

For several versions the WordPress developers have been able to build pretty advanced Web sites using WordPress. That's nothing new, but with the change of the default "Just another WordPress blog" tagline to "Just another WordPress site," both the developers and the platform are telling us that this is something more than just blogging. If you read my book *Smashing WordPress: Beyond the Blog* this is old news to you. I've already shown you that you can build many types of sites with WordPress, and I continue doing that in this book as well.

POSTS, PAGES, AND NEW CUSTOM POST TYPES

As you know, the two primary types of content in WordPress are posts for your typical blog, and Pages, which in the same typical blog is the static content, such as About and Contact pages. Note that Pages is spelled with a capital P; this is to make it clear that it is the Pages in the context of WordPress that is intended, and not a regular page on a Web site.

Posts are used with categories and tags (known as taxonomies), and are in the WordPress content flow (or loop). Posts are obviously ideal for blog posts, but also for news, reviews, tips, and other kinds of content that are updated frequently. (By updated I really mean added to, since you add more posts rather than update your current ones.)

Pages, on the other hand, lack both categories and tags, and are meant just for static content. The About page example on your typical blog applies, as do contact information pages, staff listings, and things like that. Pages are more static; you create them, publish them, and then you might update them once in a while, but that's about it. The idea is that Pages aren't in the content flow in the sense that they show up on the front page like posts traditionally do. Pages stand on their own.

When building WordPress sites you should always consider what parts of the site will be posts and what will be Pages. Need a news section? That's probably a category with a bunch of news posts in it. Want to publish a Google Map with the direction to your office? You should probably do that on a Page since there's no need to update it other than when you move.

TAXONOMIES

Categories and tags are both default examples of taxonomies, as they are ways to file your posts. Taxonomies only work with posts, not with Pages, so you need to keep that in mind.

- **Category:** Hierarchical by nature. That means that you can add a category, and then add a subcategory should you want to. A post can belong to several categories, or just one.
- **Tag:** Basically a keyword that you can add to your post. You type it in (or pick from the suggested ones), and that's it. Tags have no relationship with each other; they just associate the post with the keywords you've added.
- **Custom taxonomy:** An archive distinct from categories and tags that function like tags, but maintain an individual presence.

Both categories and tags are great tools to create new parts of a site. A category called "News" shows all posts associated with it, which gives you a news section. Tags, on the other hand, are better used to link posts together by niche topic, so if you have a bunch of news posts about Google, for example, you'd tag them with "Google," and hence you'll get an archive with all the posts tagged "Google." Basic stuff.

However, you can also create your own taxonomies (Figure 1-13 shows my Artists taxonomy). Sometimes you need more filing options for your posts, and that's when you'll add new taxonomies, in addition to categories and tags. For example, say you run a music site and want to separate the artists from your categories and tags, hence creating an artist archive. You can create a custom taxonomy called "Artists," and tell it to function as a tag. With a few lines of code you end up with a second tag box on the Edit Post screen named "Artists," and you can tag away. The tags in the "Artists" taxonomy are separate from the default tags, which means that you can use them for whatever needs you have. An artist index perhaps?

Creating a custom taxonomy is easy. You just declare it in your theme's functions.php, and then you can start using it. I'll show you how to do this later on. For now you just need to know that you're not tied down to just the default categories and tags for filing your posts — you can add your own rules.

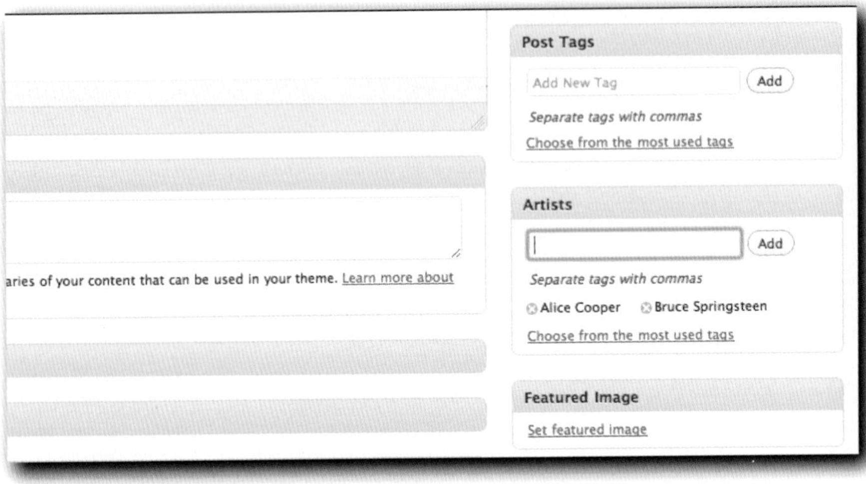

Figure 1-13: A custom taxonomy box for artists on a new post

CUSTOM POST TYPES

Custom taxonomies aren't the only cool feature that can help you take control of your content. Another great tool for making WordPress easier to use, both as a designer and in the backend, is custom post types (Figure 1-14 displays my custom Podcast post). Just as custom taxonomies let you create new taxonomies in addition to the default categories and tags, custom post types let you define new kinds of posts. Or, to put it simply, you can create an additional Posts menu in the WordPress admin panel called anything you like — Podcasts, perhaps — and then create Podcasts posts in it. These posts then can live their own lives on your site, or be included in the regular loop if you prefer.

What's even better, you can control what your new post types will support. Maybe you don't want to be able to add custom fields or an excerpt to your custom post type? Then you can remove these boxes. For you and me, this probably doesn't matter much; we're used to working with WordPress and aren't daunted by a custom fields box on the Edit Post screen. Less WordPress-savvy users, however, might find it stressful to have a lot of boxes to fill with information, despite them not being needed.

Most, if not all, things you can do with custom post types are technically possible with the use of custom fields and a sensible category or tagging setup. However, custom post types mean that you can create a more logical backend for your users, saving them from a bunch of fields and decisions when they really just want to post content.

We use customs post types in projects in Chapter 9.

Figure 1-14: Look at that, a custom post type called Podcasts

THE WORDPRESS CODEX

Your best friend online when working with themes is definitely the WordPress Codex, located at `http://codex.wordpress.org`. That's the documentation wiki for WordPress, and while it is not perfect, it contains information on everything from theme files to template tags, and more (Figure 1-15 shows you the Codex Main Page). If you need to know what a specific code snippet can do, you'll start there. For the basic stuff, you'll find adequate descriptions of what this and that does, and nice lists of functions you can use and so on. However, as your needs grow, you'll find that Google (or whatever search engine you fancy) is necessary. The Codex isn't complete. It is still the go-to place when it comes to finding out what you can do with a specific template tag, for example, but you'll most likely not find every answer there.

If you want to you can help fill in the blanks, add examples to tricky parts, or in any other way help update the Codex. There's a WordPress documentation team that most likely would love to get in touch with you, so get in touch with them if you'd like to help: `http://codex.wordpress.org/Documentation team`. Just like WordPress, the Codex relies on users to participate in the open-source spirit.

Other than the Codex, you'll find great help on the WordPress support forums at `http://wordpress.org/support`. A lot of talented WordPress users are participating there, and chances are someone else already had your problem, so a quick search might very well answer your question.

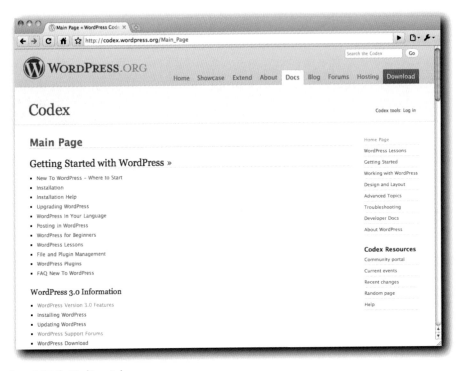

Figure 1-15: The WordPress Codex

WRAPPING IT UP

Right, that's it for the basic stuff. You've got your install up and running, and an overview of theme files and how things work and relate to each other.

In other words, it is time to get your hands dirty and dive into the themes themselves. To build themes you need to know about template tags, the PHP code that WordPress uses to actually output something on the screen for your visitors. If the theme is the skin of a WordPress site, and the template files within the theme is the skeleton, then the template tags are the organs that make everything work. Without them, you'll have no posts or Pages. Sounds like something you need to know about, right?

2

THIS IS A THEME

THE THEME IS what your visitors see, it is the skin for your content, the GUI and design of your Web site. Creating a nice-looking design is one thing, translating it to something that WordPress can interpret is another. That is where the theme and its files come in.

This chapter is all about understanding the theme files, and then doing a few interesting things with them. It is the first step towards further development of your own theme, really.

ABOUT THEMES

I touch this briefly in Chapter 1, so you already know that your theme consists of at least one main stylesheet and some template files. The template files are PHP files containing the code snippets that you need to display your site's content. A few key template files are header.php, index.php, sidebar.php, and footer.php. And the functions.php template file is a bit different from the other ones; it really isn't displaying a part of your site, but rather adds functionality to it.

- **Stylesheet file:** Defines the appearance of your theme, and contains the WordPress-specific theme declaration at the top
- **Template file:** Usually outputs your content to your Web site with the loop
- **Functions.php file:** Allows you to add other new features (such as plugins)
- **Other files:** Like images, Java Scripts, and so on

I rely on the Twenty Ten theme to show off these things in this chapter. Twenty Ten replaced the old default theme, formerly known as Kubrick, in WordPress 3.0; the Twenty Ten theme now ships as the WordPress default theme. It is a nice basis to start building WordPress sites on (see an array of themes in Figure 2-1).

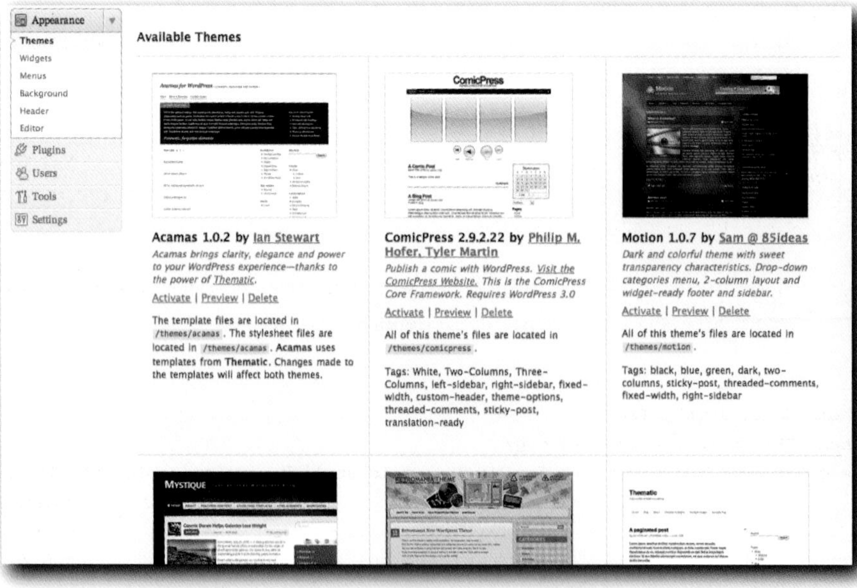

Figure 2-1: The Manage Themes screen in the WordPress admin panel

The loop is what really makes WordPress tick. With PHP, you use it to loop through and output content from the database. You'll find it in most template files that are used to control content. I discuss the loop in more detail later in this chapter, and even further later in the book.

WordPress then knows what to output thanks to template tags. These are actually PHP functions that you can use in your theme to get the result that you want. A lot of them are used within the loop, to output things like post or Page titles, the content, and so on. I go in depth with them later in this chapter as well, especially when I start building themes of our own.

THE STYLESHEET

The stylesheet, or style.css, is the theme file that contains the information of the theme. WordPress reads the top part of this file to discern if the files found in `wp-content/themes` are in fact a theme, or just some random nonsense. This is called the theme declaration.

THEME DECLARATION

The stylesheet, style.css, is necessary for WordPress to understand that your files are in fact a theme. In other words, you need style.css, and you need this data at the very top of that file in this format:

```
/*
Theme Name: The Theme Name Goes Here
Theme URI: http://your-theme-url.com
Description: A description of your theme (basic HTML will work).
Author: Your Name
Version: 1.0
Tags: wordpress.org compatible tags
*/
```

Not all of this is necessary. The "Tags" part is for `wordpress.org` themes directory compatibility, for example. There's more on making your theme `wordpress.org` compatible later on. For now, let's just call it good form.

For comparison's sake, here's the theme declaration for the new default theme (as of WordPress 3.0), Twenty Ten. I get into that in greater detail in Chapter 3.

```
/*
Theme Name: Twenty Ten
Theme URI: http://wordpress.org/
Description: The 2010 theme for WordPress is stylish, customizable, simple, and
  readable -- make it yours with a custom menu, header image, and background. Twenty
  Ten supports six widgetized areas (two in the sidebar, four in the footer) and
  featured images (thumbnails for gallery posts and custom header images for posts
  and pages). It includes stylesheets for print and the admin Visual Editor, special
  styles for posts in the "Asides" and "Gallery" categories, and has an optional
  one-column page template that removes the sidebar.
Author: the WordPress team
Version: 1.1
Tags: black, blue, white, two-columns, fixed-width, custom-header, custom-
  background, threaded-comments, sticky-post, translation-ready, microformats,
  rtl-language-support, editor-style
*/
```

The theme declaration should always be at the very top of your style.css file. Underneath, you can put whatever you want, but this is necessary at the top, otherwise WordPress won't get the information it needs (see the Twenty Ten theme in Figure 2-2).

Figure 2-2: The Twenty Ten theme packed with test content

Just put your regular styles under this, just like you would when using an external stylesheet file. It hardly needs to be said that using an external stylesheet in WordPress is the way to go. Don't put the styles directly in header.php, or things like that, it is bad form.

Now, that doesn't mean that you can't have numerous stylesheets for your theme, it just means that one needs to be called style.css, and that it is prudent to make this the main one. Some people prefer to have their CSS resets in one stylesheet, typography in another, and so on. That is all a matter of taste. You could just as well have everything in your style.css file. Larger sites should be careful not to have too many stylesheets, because you'll need to call them somehow, either in your style.css file or from the HTML header in header.php. Each call is an HTTP request and this puts more strain on your system and could slow down your site. Splitting up your stylesheet into several files for development purposes may be a good idea, although that is a personal preference and you should do what you feel most comfortable with.

The following features are some optional things you can do with style.css. They're optional, and help in various situations, so it is good to know about them. For example, you don't need to add tags meant for the `wordpress.org` themes directory if you have no intention of submitting your theme, and so on.

SET TAGS FOR YOUR THEME

If your theme is included in the `wordpress.org` themes directory, then you can set tags for it in your styles.css file. These tags are predefined and can be found in the theme submission instructions: `http://wordpress.org/extend/themes/about`. Below is the part of the Twenty Ten stylesheet that lists the tags for that particular theme.

```
Tags: black, blue, white, two-columns, fixed-width, custom-header, custom-
  background, threaded-comments, sticky-post, translation-ready, microformats,
  rtl-language-support, editor-style
```

DEFINE A CHILD THEME

In your style.css file, you can define a parent theme that makes your theme a child. I discuss this further in Chapters 3 and 4, but in short, you define the theme that you want WordPress to consider as the parent of your own theme by adding its folder as a parent in your theme's style.css. This means that the theme will revert to its parent theme whenever it lacks some-thing. So if the child theme doesn't have a sidebar.php template but a sidebar is called, it will use the parent theme's sidebar.php instead.

When the child theme has a template, it take priority over the parent theme's template file. This way you can maintain themes with minimal effort if you've got a decent setup. In the following example, you're looking at a dummy theme that relies on the Twenty Ten theme as a parent.

```
/*
Theme Name: Dummy Child Theme
Theme URI: http://dummy-url.com/
Description: This is a dummy theme relying on TwentyTen.
Author: Crash Test Dummy
Version: 1.0
Tags: black, blue, white, two-columns, fixed-width, custom-header, custom-
  background, threaded-comments, sticky-post, translation-ready, microformats,
  rtl-language-support, editor-style
Template: twentyten
*/
```

ADD COMMENTS FOR DEVELOPERS

In your stylesheet file, you can also add some comments to your theme for other developers to see. These comments won't show up in the WordPress admin panel or anything; they are for development purposes only.

Maybe you're using code from someone else and want to credit it, things like that. Just add /*, and then type your comment, ending with */. As you can see from the following example, you can just add your comment to the top, have several lines of code, and add additional comments, as with any stylesheet.

```
/*
Theme Name: Twenty Ten
Theme URI: http://wordpress.org/
Description: The 2010 theme for WordPress is stylish, customizable, simple, and
  readable -- make it yours with a custom menu, header image, and background. Twenty
  Ten supports six widgetized areas (two in the sidebar, four in the footer) and
  featured images (thumbnails for gallery posts and custom header images for posts
  and pages). It includes stylesheets for print and the admin Visual Editor, special
  styles for posts in the "Asides" and "Gallery" categories, and has an optional
  one-column page template that removes the sidebar.
Author: the WordPress team
Version: 1.1
Tags: black, blue, white, two-columns, fixed-width, custom-header, custom-
  background, threaded-comments, sticky-post, translation-ready, microformats,
  rtl-language-support, editor-style

        Here are my theme comments, added to TwentyTen's style.css.
        Some more! Here!

        And a third line with a blank one above.

*/

body { background: #fff; }

/* An additional comment in the file! */

p { font-weight: bold; }
```

That's it for stylesheets; now let's move on to the PHP template files.

THE TEMPLATE FILES AT YOUR DISPOSAL

This link gives an overview of all the template files that you can play with, and what they default back to should they be absent from your theme's folder (http://codex.wordpress.org/template).

The template files are PHP files containing the code snippets needed to display your site's content. A few key template files are header.php, footer.php, index.php, and sidebar.php, as you probably remember (see Figure 2-3 for an overview of these files).

Other possible template files for various parts of your site range from the single-post view (single.php for example, which is used when you view a post) to how a 404 page not found should be displayed (404.php). Figure 2-4 shows a single-post view.

Figure 2-3: A typical theme setup portrayed using the Twenty Ten theme

Figure 2-4: A single post in the Twenty Ten theme, controlled by single.php

The really nice part is that you don't need to use all of these template files, because most of them (although not all) will revert to index.php should they be absent. So you don't need them all, is what I'm saying, although you'll probably want them when you're building advanced sites.

If your theme is lacking a category.php template file, WordPress uses index.php instead. Sometimes there are more than one file to default back to, however, so there is something of a hierarchical order (for an overview of the template file hierarchy, go to `http://codex. wordpress.org/Template_Hierarchy`). For example, if you have a template file for your News category, you can name that one category-news.php. Should it be absent, Word-Press reverts to category.php, and then back to index.php.

You don't need all these template files, you can just as well do everything in index.php with some fancy coding (with conditional tags, I get to that in Chapter 3). In fact, if your site is a simple one, it might not even be all that fancy or hard to pull off. However, this will be a bit messy. Most of the time it is better to split everything up in separate template files than to make index.php do everything at once. It is also a matter of performance, since a massive index.php powering your whole site will mean an unnecessary amount of code being parsed all the time. Utilizing the various template files available is a better choice.

HEADER AND FOOTER TEMPLATE FILES

Besides style.css and index.php (assuming you're not doing a child theme), the two template files that you need in every theme are header.php and footer.php. These two files start and stop WordPress, are easily called (included really) by template tags in every other template file, and make things a lot easier on you.

Think about it, having a file containing the top of your site — from logo and menu to the actual wrapping `div`'s that control the layout — and another file doing the same with the bottom, sure sounds like a good idea, right? It is, and it's not something the WordPress developers thought of first, and it is common practice.

Also, another good thing about having a header.php and a footer.php is so you initiate some stuff in the header section of your theme. WordPress then knows what to do, when to start doing it, and things like that.

The Header Code

The following is the header.php file from the Twenty Ten theme (see the final header in Figure 2-5), which contains a whole lot of stuff you might not actually need, and obviously a bunch of important things as well. Code within /* and */ are commented, as are PHP lines with // in front of them.

Figure 2-5: The Twenty Ten header

```php
<?php
/**
 * The Header for our theme.
 *
 * Displays all of the <head> section and everything up till <div id="main">
 *
 * @package WordPress
 * @subpackage Twenty_Ten
 * @since Twenty Ten 1.0
 */
?><!DOCTYPE html>
<html <?php language_attributes(); ?>>
<head>
<meta charset="<?php bloginfo( 'charset' ); ?>" />
<title><?php
        /*
         * Print the <title> tag based on what is being viewed.
         */
        global $page, $paged;

        wp_title( '|', true, 'right' );

        // Add the blog name.
        bloginfo( 'name' );

        // Add the blog description for the home/front page.
        $site_description = get_bloginfo( 'description', 'display' );
        if ( $site_description && ( is_home() || is_front_page() ) )
                echo " | $site_description";

        // Add a page number if necessary:
        if ( $paged >= 2 || $page >= 2 )
                echo ' | ' . sprintf( __( 'Page %s', 'twentyten' ), max( $paged,
```

```
        $page ) );

            ?></title>
<link rel="profile" href="http://gmpg.org/xfn/11" />
<link rel="stylesheet" type="text/css" media="all" href="<?php bloginfo( 'style-
    sheet_url' ); ?>" />
<link rel="pingback" href="<?php bloginfo( 'pingback_url' ); ?>" />
<?php
        /* We add some JavaScript to pages with the comment form
         * to support sites with threaded comments (when in use).
         */
        if ( is_singular() && get_option( 'thread_comments' ) )
                wp_enqueue_script( 'comment-reply' );

        /* Always have wp_head() just before the closing </head>
         * tag of your theme, or you will break many plugins, which
         * generally use this hook to add elements to <head> such
         * as styles, scripts, and meta tags.
         */
        wp_head();
?>
</head>
```

Now, you don't need all that in your own theme, but some things are important. For example, it is a good idea to include the stylesheet so that your styles will load:

```
<link rel="stylesheet" type="text/css" media="all" href="<?php bloginfo( 'style-
    sheet_url' ); ?>" />
```

Other parts are necessary to validate, like a proper title for example. However, the one really important piece of code here is the one that kicks off WordPress:

```
<?php
        /* We add some JavaScript to pages with the comment form
         * to support sites with threaded comments (when in use).
         */
        if ( is_singular() && get_option( 'thread_comments' ) )
                wp_enqueue_script( 'comment-reply' );

        /* Always have wp_head() just before the closing </head>
         * tag of your theme, or you will break many plugins, which
         * generally use this hook to add elements to <head> such
         * as styles, scripts, and meta tags.
         */
        wp_head();
?>
```

Without that, no WordPress — you need it, it is as simple as that. As the commented part says, you should always put wp_head() just before you close the head tag.

The Footer Code

The same goes for the "I'm done now, thank you very much" message to WordPress found in footer.php. Again, this is the footer.php file from the Twenty Ten theme. It contains a widget area and theme specific stuff. See the Twenty Ten footer in Figure 2-6.

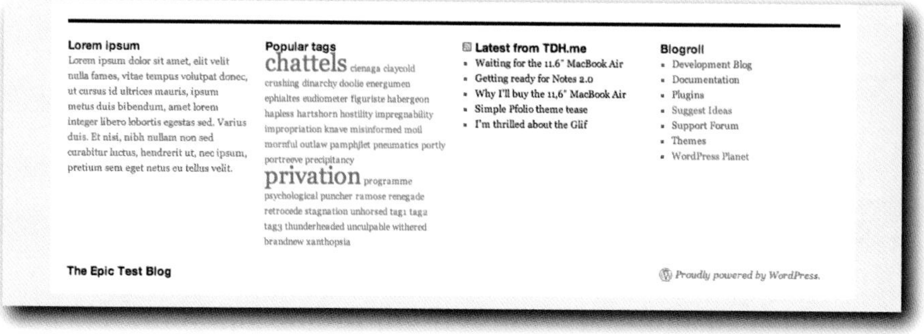

Figure 2-6: The Twenty Ten footer with some content in the widget areas

```php
<?php
/**
 * The template for displaying the footer.
 *
 * Contains the closing of the id=main div and all content
 * after.  Calls sidebar-footer.php for bottom widgets.
 *
 * @package WordPress
 * @subpackage Twenty_Ten
 * @since Twenty Ten 1.0
 */
?>
        </div><!-- #main -->

        <div id="footer" role="contentinfo">
            <div id="colophon">

<?php
        /* A sidebar in the footer? Yep. You can can customize
         * your footer with four columns of widgets.
         */
        get_sidebar( 'footer' );
?>

                <div id="site-info">
                    <a href="<?php echo home_url( '/' ) ?>" title="<?php
  echo esc_attr( get_bloginfo( 'name', 'display' ) ); ?>" rel="home">
                        <?php bloginfo( 'name' ); ?>
                    </a>
                </div><!-- #site-info -->
```

```
<div id="site-generator">
    <?php do_action( 'twentyten_credits' ); ?>
    <a href="<?php echo esc_url( __('http://wordpress.
org/', 'twentyten') ); ?>"
                    title="<?php esc_attr_e('Semantic
Personal Publishing Platform', 'twentyten'); ?>" rel="generator">
                    <?php printf( __('Proudly powered by %s.',
'twentyten'), 'WordPress' ); ?>
    </a>
</div><!-- #site-generator -->

        </div><!-- #colophon -->
    </div><!-- #footer -->

</div><!-- #wrapper -->

<?php
    /* Always have wp_footer() just before the closing </body>
     * tag of your theme, or you will break many plugins, which
     * generally use this hook to reference JavaScript files.
     */

    wp_footer();
?>
</body>
</html>
```

The only important thing here, besides closing all the HTML tags from the header, as well as the body and html tag, is the wp_footer() template tag. This one tells WordPress that the page is done, everything's (hopefully) dandy and it can stop running now. You need it for plugins and other things, and WordPress needs it to stop when it should, so make sure you have it in your theme, just before closing the body tag.

```
<?php
    /* Always have wp_footer() just before the closing </body>
     * tag of your theme, or you will break many plugins, which
     * generally use this hook to reference JavaScript files.
     */

    wp_footer();
?>
```

Both the header.php and footer.php template files can look more or less anyway you'd want. Maybe you prefer tighter header files, or you want to load more stuff, like JavaScript libraries or additional stylesheets (although you could do that from within style.css too, of course) — just do it anyway you like, but make sure that the crucial tags needed to kick off WordPress are there. Likewise, your footer.php will be formed after your needs, both in the actual footer (big or small, full of information or more or less empty — that's your call) and by the fact that WordPress needs to be told when it is done.

THE LOOP AND YOUR CONTENT

Before I go into the template files that control the various parts of your site, I'd like to just touch the essence of what goes in the rest of them, not counting functions.php if that one is present. Most template files in a WordPress theme loads the header, the footer, and the sidebar. This is done with template tags, like this:

```
<?php get_header(); ?>
        THIS IS WHERE THE LOOP OUTPUTS CONTENT.
<?php get_sidebar(); ?>
<?php get_footer(); ?>
```

These three simple little custom PHP tags include the header.php, sidebar.php, and footer.php template files, respectively. They could in fact just as well have been regular PHP includes, which you might be familiar with if you've built sites using PHP before.

Anyway, most of the template files include these files, and the magical little thing that makes WordPress tick: The loop.

WHAT IS THE WORDPRESS LOOP?

The loop, often spelled with a capital L to show that I'm talking about THE loop of loops, is a PHP snippet that pulls your content from the database. It can be a set number of posts (called using a while loop) or just one (fetched using an ID), or it can be a Page. It can also be a custom post type, an archive of posts, an uploaded image, and so on.

The loop is what displays your content. You need it in every template that is meant to pull content from the database and display it. Obviously you can fill your template tags with static content without using the loop, but that doesn't make much sense most of the time, now does it? The whole idea is, after all, to use WordPress as a CMS, not to mimic the HTML files of the old days.

Just to make things a bit more clear, here is a simple template file that first includes the header with `get_header()`, then outputs content using the loop, includes the sidebar.php file with `get_sidebar()`, and finally includes the footer.php file with `get_footer()`.

```
<?php if ( have_posts() ) : while ( have_posts() ) : the_post(); ?>
        <div id="post-<?php the_ID(); ?>" <?php post_class(); ?>>
                <h2><a href="<?php the_permalink(); ?>" title="<?php the_title();
 ?>" rel="bookmark"><?php the_title(); ?></a></h2>
                        <div class="entry">
                            <?php the_content(); ?>
                        </div>
        </div>
<?php endwhile; else: ?>
        <p>Sorry, we've got nothing!</p>
<?php endif; ?>
```

The whole thing starts with a simple `if` clause that checks to see if there are any posts. Then WordPress outputs the posts (with `the_posts`) for as long as there are any using the `while` loop. How many times `while` will loop depends on your WordPress settings and where you are on the site. If you're viewing a category listing and have said that you should display 10 posts per page on the Reading Settings page in the admin panel, WordPress will loop 10 times hence displaying 10 posts. Should there be fewer posts, it'll stop, obviously.

However, you may be on a single-post screen or on a Page, in which case WordPress will just loop once because it knows that you just want a particular post or Page. You'll only get that returned.

Finally, there's an `else` section to output something should there not be anything valid to return.

I work a lot with the loop later on, so this was just a taster to get the principle out there.

THE LOOP TEMPLATE TAG

Prior to WordPress 3.0, you would stick your loop in your template files, such as index.php or single.php. You can still do that, but thanks to the `get_template_part()` template tag you can separate the loop and stick it in its own template file. With `get_template_part()` you can include loop.php (or loop-single.php, for example) in a fashion similar to `get_sidebar()`. This means that you can have one or several loop template files which you call upon when you need theme, further separating design and site layout from code.

I work a lot with `get_template_part()` later in this book. For now, it is enough to be aware that you can include template files containing the loop using `get_template_part()`.

USING THE LOOP IN TEMPLATE FILES

We won't dwell long on this topic since I'll be digging into Twenty Ten in the next chapter, but it might be good to take a quick peek at how the loop is used in template files to control the content on various parts of your site. This could be a single.php (to control your single-post view) or category.php (for your category archive needs), or some other content-related template file in your theme.

Let's take a look at index.php from the Twenty Ten theme. It is the final fallback file for any content view, so it isn't used all that much. That also means that it is pretty general, which suits us perfectly. Here it is:

```php
<?php
/**
 * The main template file.
 *
```

```
 * This is the most generic template file in a WordPress theme
 * and one of the two required files for a theme (the other being style.css).
 * It is used to display a page when nothing more specific matches a query.
 * E.g., it puts together the home page when no home.php file exists.
 * Learn more: http://codex.wordpress.org/Template_Hierarchy
 *
 * @package WordPress
 * @subpackage Twenty_Ten
 * @since Twenty Ten 1.0
 */

get_header(); ?>

                <div id="container">
                        <div id="content" role="main">

                        <?php
                        /* Run the loop to output the posts.
                         * If you want to overload this in a child theme then
   include a file
                         * called loop-index.php and that will be used instead.
                         */
                        get_template_part( 'loop', 'index' );
                        ?>
                        </div><!-- #content -->
                </div><!-- #container -->

<?php get_sidebar(); ?>
<?php get_footer(); ?>
```

The parts above `get_header()` are just comments about what the file is. What you want to be looking at is `get_header()`, which includes header.php, and then go down to the bottom and note `get_sidebar()`, which fetches sidebar.php, as well as `get_footer()` which includes footer.php. The stuff in between, sitting in the `div#container`, is what I'm really interested in here, because this is where you'll find the `get_template_part()` template tag.

```
get_template_part( 'loop', 'index' );
```

This includes the loop template, first looking for loop-index.php, but failing that (Twenty Ten doesn't have that template file), it'll revert to loop.php. And that is where our loop is, hence you've got a working template file relationship here, with all necessary (albeit not possible since loop-index.php is missing, I get to why it is written like this later in the book in Chapter 3) files accounted for.

THE FUNCTIONS.PHP FILE

Functions.php is a special template file that helps you create widget areas (as you see in Figure 2-7), theme option pages for your theme-specific settings, and doubles as something of a plugin for your theme. It can be almost empty, or loaded with functions and cool stuff that add features to the theme. In fact, functions.php needn't even exist for your theme, but that would mean that it isn't widget ready, and you wouldn't want it that way, right?

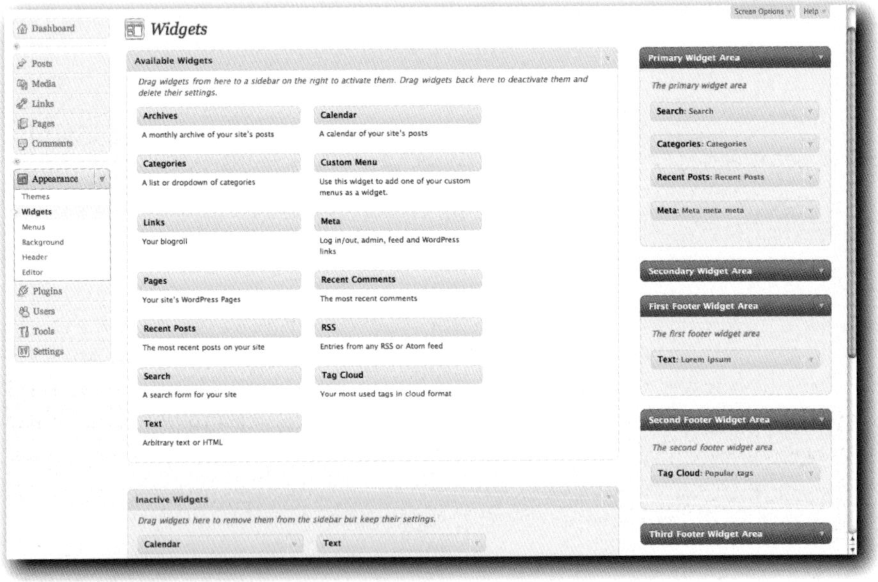

Figure 2-7: Widgets displayed in the WordPress admin panel

Working with functions.php can be a bit daunting if you're not a PHP developer, since most of the code that goes there is pretty advanced stuff for a newbie. Don't fret; you can copy and paste your way through that part, and mastering functions.php isn't at all needed to create good looking or cool WordPress themes. However, if you want to really turbo-charge the functionality of your WordPress site, you'll need to learn, or find someone who can help you with your functions.php file. For now, it's enough if you'll manage to copy and paste your way to declaring and then adding widget areas. I get to that in a little bit as well.

You never need to call on functions.php or include it in any way; if it is there, WordPress will use it. That's the good part. The bad part is that it can get quite messy if you want to do a lot of things on the admin side of things. Let's leave those parts be for now and focus on widgets.

This is the widget code from the Twenty Ten theme, which actually has more than just one widget area, but since they all are pretty much alike, I stick with just one here. The code resides in functions.php, and it needs to be within PHP opening and closing tags, although not necessarily with its own set of those; you can cram several PHP code snippets together if you like.

```php
<?php
// Area 1, located at the top of the sidebar.
register_sidebar( array(
    'name' => __( 'Primary Widget Area', 'twentyten' ),
    'id' => 'primary-widget-area',
    'description' => __( 'The primary widget area', 'twentyten' ),
    'before_widget' => '<li id="%1$s" class="widget-container %2$s">',
    'after_widget' => '</li>',
    'before_title' => '<h3 class="widget-title">',
    'after_title' => '</h3>',
) );
?>
```

The function `register_sidebar` actually doesn't register sidebars per se, it registers widget areas commonly referred to as dynamic sidebars. The first five register widget areas are called Sidebar, Footer A, B, C, and D. With this tiny bit of code, you'll find these in your Widgets settings area in the WordPress admin panel. Obviously you need to add the actual output of the widget area to a template file, otherwise it won't show up anywhere. I get to that later.

The last `register_sidebar` is a bit special in the way it creates the final widget area. Instead of just passing the name to WordPress, you pass a lot more data in an array. The reason for doing this is that widget areas per default are built as lists, using `ul` and `li` tags. In this case, you want a widget area for a submenu that relies on a `div` structure instead, rather than being a list. That's why you need to tell it what to put before each widget in the area, and after, using `before_widget` and `after_widget`.

Functions.php is a powerful tool for those of us who want to do more advanced stuff. You can extend the functionality of your theme tremendously using functions.php. Theoretically you can have a bunch of plugins residing in the template file, adding functionality that way. There's no telling what grand ideas you will realize using functions.php, from settings pages for your theme, to brand new features you haven't thought of yet. Since functions.php essentially lets you run whatever you want (as long as it is PHP), that means that it really has massive potential for theme designers.

Before you go all crazy about the possibilities, do keep in mind that an overly bloated functions.php file will mean longer loading time for your theme. Functionality that isn't theme specific should be kept apart, preferably in a plugin. That way it can extend beyond your theme as well.

USING PAGE TEMPLATES

Page templates are powerful tools for just about any site using WordPress as a CMS. It doesn't matter whether you just have a pretty bloggish simple site, or a full-fledged newspaper running on WordPress, you'll be able to put them to good use either way.

41

So what are Page templates, really? As the name implies, they are special templates for Pages. Pages, with the capital P, are obviously the static pages that you can create in WordPress (as opposed to posts). When creating or editing a Page in WordPress, you'll notice the Template option on the right-hand side of the screen (see Figure 2-8). This is where you pick from your Page templates, on a Page per Page basis.

Figure 2-8: The Page template box is usually found to the right of the screen

CREATING A PAGE TEMPLATE

Creating a Page template is easy. All you need to do is put the following little code snippet at the very top of your new template file, and it then appears as a Page template for your Pages:

```php
<?php
/*
Template Name: My Page Template Title
*/
?>
```

Now, obviously you still need something below that. It could be a different design for a particular Page on your site, or something entirely different. The Page template needn't even contain the loop, maybe you just want to have a Page on your site with content fetched from someplace else, and not the actual Page content? Then this is the way to do it.

You'll create a custom Page template in Chapter 3. For now it is enough to understand that you can add a number of Page template files to your theme that do just about anything by adding those few lines of code.

WHY USE PAGE TEMPLATES?

It can't be said enough: The possibilities of Page templates are huge. You can do a lot of impressive stuff with Page templates if you put your mind to it. It could be anything from portraying your content in the ideal way, to having multiple loops or even content from external services on a Page within WordPress.

Since your Page template isn't limited by the default loop, it means that you can do anything with the loop should you choose to keep it, or just kick it out and do something entirely different with the Page or Pages using the Page template.

Just to get your mind going, here are some ideas as to what you could do with Page templates. Naturally, I do some cool stuff further on, but it never hurts to mull these things over.

- **Create a links Page:** This one's pretty obvious, just output the links from the Links settings in WordPress using the `wp_list_bookmarks()` template tag.
- **Add subsections:** Do custom loops containing the material you need. Sometimes the category or tag browsing just isn't enough, then creating a Page with some custom loops can be the solution.
- **Break your design:** Or rather, break out of it. Your Page template can call a completely different header and footer, and it can contain entirely different objects, or at least CSS classes and IDs. If you need parts of your site to be different, Page templates are an easy enough solution most of the time.
- **Include external content:** Just forget about the loop and use PHP or JavaScript to include external content. Maybe you want to show off your tweets on a dedicated Page on your site? Then just create a Page template suited for it.

The possibilities for Page templates are, if not endless, at least very extensive. Consider what you can do with them when building your site, and you might save yourself some headaches.

UNDERSTANDING TEMPLATE TAGS

Before I dig into the theme files, you need to know a thing or two about template tags. In short, template tags are PHP code snippets that WordPress can read and do things with, such as output the title of your post, link it appropriately to your article, display the content in an appealing way, and so on. For example, you can adjust the output to control how a list is rendered. Just about everything you see on a WordPress site that is actual content is output by template tags.

A commonly used template tag is `the_permalink()`. With it you can output the link to a post, for example. Per default it will output the URL, which means you often use it when linking titles. Combined with `the_title()` you can get the title properly linked.

```
<a href="<?php the_permalink(); ?>"><?php the_title(); ?></a>
```

Sometimes you pass parameters to template tags, such as the `the_bloginfo('name')` example you've seen previously, and at other times you pass the parameters in a different fashion, but always inside the parenthesis of the template tag. You'll get your fill of passing parameters in the coming chapters. For now it is enough to know that the stuff within the parenthesis contain your instructions as to how the template tag should be used. Obviously, not all template tags take parameters, `the_permalink()` is one that doesn't.

WRAPPING IT UP

Now you know what makes a theme tick, and have gotten your hands on some code as well. Let's pick up the pace from here on, shall we?

In Chapter 3, I not only start doing some more advanced stuff, but I also dive into the Twenty Ten theme, adding features and functionality to it. This means that I fiddle with the loop to control the content output, among other things. Twenty Ten is not only a great theme to build WordPress sites with, it is also the perfect learning ground for anyone wanting to get into theming.

That's not all. After I discuss the Twenty Ten, you can get started for real. For now, welcome to the wonderful world of WordPress theming. I think you'll like it.

3

DIGGING INTO THE TWENTY TEN THEME

YOU CAN DO a ton of things with WordPress themes. Up until now, I have really just scratched the surface. In this chapter, I dig a bit deeper and try some functions and features you may find useful, depending on the goals of the site that you're building.

In this chapter, I cover the rest of the basics that I discuss in Chapter 2, and then you get your hands a bit dirty by working with the Twenty Ten theme. You'll learn how to work with the custom menu feature, custom header images, and more. The goal is to show you what you can do with WordPress, what fancy features are within a few lines of code's grasp, and what you'll need plugins or more advanced coding to achieve.

Right, let's go. Bring a shovel.

WORKING WITH THE LOOP

The loop is what makes WordPress tick, looping through your content and outputting the items that meet your criteria. So if you're on a category archive, WordPress loops through all the posts that belong to the selected category and outputs them, but only as many times as are set in the Reading Settings screen on your admin panel (as shown in Figure 3-1). So if you've set WordPress to show ten posts per page, the loop outputs ten posts, and then stops. Obviously the count is for valid outputs. If WordPress stumbles upon something that doesn't belong to said category, the loop just skips it and moves on to the next, until ten posts have been reached. This is something you really should know about since getting control over how many posts you want to display is essential for archive pages.

Figure 3-1: The Reading Settings screen in WordPress admin panel

A LOOP WITH CONTENT

Let's take a closer look at the loop and populate it with some content, something really basic to make it easy to understand. You need to add template tags so that WordPress knows where to output the actual content.

The template tags for the loop:

- `the_title()` for outputting the post title

- `the_permalink()` for linking the post title
- `the_title_attribute()` for the proper link title attribute
- `the_content()` for outputting the content
- `the_ID()` for getting the ID of the post
- `post_class()` to output the correct CSS classes for the post

That's it; so let's have a look.

```php
<?php if ( have_posts() ) : while ( have_posts() ) : the_post(); ?>

        <div id="post-<?php the_ID(); ?>" <?php post_class(); ?>>
            <h2>
                    <a href="<?php the_permalink(); ?>" title="Permalink to
    <?php the_title_attribute(); ?>">
                            <?php the_title(); ?>
                    </a>
            </h2>
            <div class="entry">
                    <?php the_content(); ?>
            </div>
        </div>

<?php endwhile; else: ?>

        <p>Whoa! There's nothing here!</p>

<?php endif; ?>
```

Each post sits in a `div` with an `id` named `post-X` where X is the ID of the post, thanks to `the_ID()`. The `div` also gets a bunch of classes for CSS to use thanks to the `post_class()` template tag, which outputs them automatically. These classes are then used to style posts differently depending on what category, tag, and so forth they are using.

Moving on, you have an `h2` heading in which the post title is located, linked to the post's page. The post title is in the link's title, and is used to output the actual post that the user will see; this is handled with `the_title()`. The link gets the direct link to the post in question from `the_permalink()`.

Finally there's the actual post content, which sits in a `div` of its own here. How the post content will look when output is up to you. If you're using the Read More feature in Word-Press, you get a default "Read the rest of this entry" link; otherwise, you get the whole content of the post in this case, since you're using `the_content()`. An alternative would be to use `the_excerpt()` to either get a machine created excerpt, or get the excerpt added manually in the WordPress admin panel.

That's it. The HTML code that tells the visitor that there are no posts to display is pretty self-explanatory, right? Right.

THE EXTERNAL LOOP.PHP FILE

There's a new template in town, and it is called loop.php. This nifty little thing is meant to make life easier for theme designers. You now have the chance to move the code for the loop from your current template files and include it as an external file, loop.php, instead. Much like how header.php and footer.php work.

The most obvious benefit for using the loop.php file is not having to copy and paste every little change that you make to your loop to every template file in your theme. Instead, you just reference the one file via a template tag. If you need to make changes to the loop, you can update that one file.

The template tag that you use for loop.php is the brand new `get_template_part()`.

```php
<?php get_template_part('loop'); ?>
```

Place this tag where you normally put your loop, and that's that — now your template files include the loop from one central place, just like `get_header()` does with header.php.

However, there's more. Just like the `get_sidebar()` template tag lets you define which sidebar to get, `get_template_part()` can get you a specific loop-X.php template file instead of loop.php.

```php
<?php get_template_part('loop', 'author'); ?>
```

This call looks for loop-author.php first, and then loop.php. That means that you can still have specific loops for specific parts of your site without having to make changes to your main loop.php. In fact, just like theme template files degrade backwards when called for, and end up using index.php if they're out of options, so do the loop template files. If loop-author.php does not exist, WordPress tries loop.php instead. That's why the Twenty Ten theme is using `get_template_part()`, but looking for loop template files that aren't in the theme. This way child theme designers can access them easy enough, without having to alter the actual template file.

To recap, you can put your loop code in loop.php, or in loop-X.php, where X is whatever string parameter you can add to the `get_template_part()` template tag when including the loop template file. I do all that later on.

DO I HAVE TO USE LOOP.PHP?

No, you don't have to use loop.php, and perhaps you shouldn't. While it is a nice way to gain more control over your theme, it also means that it won't work on WordPress versions prior to 3.0. Not all people want to upgrade to the latest version of WordPress, so if you know you're developing a theme for a version prior to 3.0, you can't use `get_template_part()`. What you can do, however, is to include the loop template file using a PHP include function:

```php
<?php include( TEMPLATEPATH . '/loop.php' ); ?>
```

Obviously you'll lose all the nice degrading previously described and everything, but at least your theme will work.

It is my firm belief that everyone should run the latest version of WordPress, if for no other reason than to make sure that the install is secure. If you're building for versions prior to 3.0, they are out of date, so you should try to get them up to speed (and hence be able to use `get_template_part()` and the loop.php template) rather than resort to half-hearted solutions like the one presented in the previous code snippet.

THE TWENTY TEN LOOP

It goes without saying that Twenty Ten uses the `get_template_part()` template tag to include an external loop template.

DISPLAYING POSTS WITH LOOPS

The Twenty Ten theme relies on one mammoth loop.php template file for most (but not all) of its loop needs. It is included in the various template files that needs a loop, such as category.php or archive.php, using get_template_part(). Take a look:

```php
<?php
/**
 * The loop that displays posts.
 *
 * The loop displays the posts and the post content.  See
 * http://codex.wordpress.org/The_Loop to understand it and
 * http://codex.wordpress.org/Template_Tags to understand
 * the tags used in it.
 *
 * This can be overridden in child themes with loop.php or
 * loop-template.php, where 'template' is the loop context
 * requested by a template. For example, loop-index.php would
 * be used if it exists and Iask for the loop with:
 * <code>get_template_part( 'loop', 'index' );</code>
 *
 * @package WordPress
 * @subpackage Twenty_Ten
 * @since Twenty Ten 1.0
 */
?>

<?php /* Display navigation to next/previous pages when applicable */ ?>
<?php if ( $wp_query->max_num_pages > 1 ) : ?>
        <div id="nav-above" class="navigation">
                <div class="nav-previous"><?php next_posts_link( __( '<span
 class="meta-nav">&larr;</span> Older posts', 'twentyten' ) ); ?></div>
                <div class="nav-next"><?php previous_posts_link( __( 'Newer posts
 <span class="meta-nav">&rarr;</span>', 'twentyten' ) ); ?></div>
        </div><!-- #nav-above -->
```

```php
<?php endif; ?>

<?php /* If there are no posts to display, such as an empty archive page */ ?>
<?php if ( ! have_posts() ) : ?>
        <div id="post-0" class="post error404 not-found">
                <h1 class="entry-title">
                        <?php _e( 'Not Found', 'twentyten' ); ?>
                </h1>
                <div class="entry-content">
                        <p><?php _e( 'Apologies, but no results were found for the
 requested archive. Perhaps searching will help find a related post.', 'twentyten'
 ); ?></p>
                        <?php get_search_form(); ?>
                </div><!-- .entry-content -->
        </div><!-- #post-0 -->
<?php endif; ?>

<?php
        /* Start the Loop.
         *
         * In Twenty Ten I use the same loop in multiple contexts.
         * It is broken into three main parts: when I display
         * posts that are in the gallery category, when I'm displaying
         * posts in the asides category, and finally all other posts.
         *
         * Additionally, I sometimes check for whether I am on an
         * archive page, a search page, and so on, allowing for small differences
         * in the loop on each template without actually duplicating
         * the rest of the loop that is shared.
         *
         * Without further ado, the loop:
         */ ?>
<?php while ( have_posts() ) : the_post(); ?>

<?php /* How to display posts in the Gallery category. */ ?>

        <?php if ( in_category( _x('gallery', 'gallery category slug', 'twentyten')
 ) ) : ?>
                <div id="post-<?php the_ID(); ?>" <?php post_class(); ?>>
                        <h2 class="entry-title"><a href="<?php the_permalink(); ?>"
 title="<?php printf( esc_attr__( 'Permalink to %s', 'twentyten' ), the_title_
 attribute( 'echo=0' ) ); ?>" rel="bookmark"><?php the_title(); ?></a></h2>

                        <div class="entry-meta">
                                <?php twentyten_posted_on(); ?>
                        </div><!-- .entry-meta -->

                        <div class="entry-content">
<?php if ( post_password_required() ) : ?>
                                <?php the_content(); ?>
<?php else : ?>
```

```php
                                    <?php
                            $images = get_children( array( 'post_parent'
=> $post->ID, 'post_type' => 'attachment', 'post_mime_type' => 'image', 'orderby'
=> 'menu_order', 'order' => 'ASC', 'numberposts' => 999 ) );
                            if ( $images ) :
                                $total_images = count( $images );
                                $image = array_shift( $images );
                                    $image_img_tag = wp_get_attachment_
image( $image->ID, 'thumbnail' );
                            ?>

                                        <div class="gallery-thumb">
                                            <a class="size-thumbnail"
href="<?php the_permalink(); ?>"><?php echo $image_img_tag; ?></a>
                                        </div><!-- .gallery-thumb -->
                                        <p><em><?php printf( __( 'This
gallery contains <a %1$s>%2$s photos</a>.', 'twentyten' ),
                                                'href="' . get_
permalink() . '" title="' . sprintf( esc_attr__( 'Permalink to %s', 'twentyten' ),
the_title_attribute( 'echo=0' ) ) . '" rel="bookmark"',
                                            $total_images
                                        ); ?></em></p>
                        <?php endif; ?>
                                    <?php the_excerpt(); ?>
<?php endif; ?>
                </div><!-- .entry-content -->

                <div class="entry-utility">
                            <a href="<?php echo get_term_link( _x('gallery',
'gallery category slug', 'twentyten'), 'category' ); ?>" title="<?php esc_attr_e(
'View posts in the Gallery category', 'twentyten' ); ?>"><?php _e( 'More Galler-
ies', 'twentyten' ); ?></a>
                                <span class="meta-sep">|</span>
                                <span class="comments-link"><?php comments_popup_
link( __( 'Leave a comment', 'twentyten' ), __( '1 Comment', 'twentyten' ), __( '%
Comments', 'twentyten' ) ); ?></span>
                                <?php edit_post_link( __( 'Edit', 'twentyten' ),
'<span class="meta-sep">|</span> <span class="edit-link">', '</span>' ); ?>
                </div><!-- .entry-utility -->
            </div><!-- #post-## -->

<?php /* How to display posts in the asides category */ ?>

    <?php elseif ( in_category( _x('asides', 'asides category slug',
'twentyten') ) ) : ?>
            <div id="post-<?php the_ID(); ?>" <?php post_class(); ?>>

                <?php if ( is_archive() || is_search() ) : // Display excerpts for
archives and search. ?>
                    <div class="entry-summary">
                        <?php the_excerpt(); ?>
                    </div><!-- .entry-summary -->
```

```
                    <?php else : ?>
                        <div class="entry-content">
                            <?php the_content( __( 'Continue reading <span
class="meta-nav">&rarr;</span>', 'twentyten' ) ); ?>
                        </div><!-- .entry-content -->
                    <?php endif; ?>

                    <div class="entry-utility">
                        <?php twentyten_posted_on(); ?>
                        <span class="meta-sep">|</span>
                        <span class="comments-link"><?php comments_popup_
link( __( 'Leave a comment', 'twentyten' ), __( '1 Comment', 'twentyten' ), __( '%
Comments', 'twentyten' ) ); ?></span>
                        <?php edit_post_link( __( 'Edit', 'twentyten' ),
'<span class="meta-sep">|</span> <span class="edit-link">', '</span>' ); ?>
                    </div><!-- .entry-utility -->
                </div><!-- #post-## -->

<?php /* How to display all other posts. */ ?>

        <?php else : ?>
            <div id="post-<?php the_ID(); ?>" <?php post_class(); ?>>
                <h2 class="entry-title"><a href="<?php the_permalink(); ?>"
title="<?php printf( esc_attr__( 'Permalink to %s', 'twentyten' ), the_title_
attribute( 'echo=0' ) ); ?>" rel="bookmark"><?php the_title(); ?></a></h2>

                <div class="entry-meta">
                    <?php twentyten_posted_on(); ?>
                </div><!-- .entry-meta -->

        <?php if ( is_archive() || is_search() ) : // Only display excerpts for
archives and search. ?>
                <div class="entry-summary">
                    <?php the_excerpt(); ?>
                </div><!-- .entry-summary -->
        <?php else : ?>
                <div class="entry-content">
                    <?php the_content( __( 'Continue reading <span
class="meta-nav">&rarr;</span>', 'twentyten' ) ); ?>
                    <?php wp_link_pages( array( 'before' => '<div
class="page-link">' . __( 'Pages:', 'twentyten' ), 'after' => '</div>' ) ); ?>
                </div><!-- .entry-content -->
        <?php endif; ?>

                <div class="entry-utility">
                    <?php if ( count( get_the_category() ) ) : ?>
                        <span class="cat-links">
                            <?php printf( __( '<span
class="%1$s">Posted in</span> %2$s', 'twentyten' ), 'entry-utility-prep entry-
utility-prep-cat-links', get_the_category_list( ', ' ) ); ?>
                        </span>
                        <span class="meta-sep">|</span>
```

```php
<?php endif; ?>
<?php
        $tags_list = get_the_tag_list( '', ', ' );
        if ( $tags_list ):
?>
                <span class="tag-links">
                        <?php printf( __( '<span
class="%1$s">Tagged</span> %2$s', 'twentyten' ), 'entry-utility-prep entry-utility-
prep-tag-links', $tags_list ); ?>
                </span>
                <span class="meta-sep">|</span>
        <?php endif; ?>
                <span class="comments-link"><?php comments_popup_
link( __( 'Leave a comment', 'twentyten' ), __( '1 Comment', 'twentyten' ), __( '%
Comments', 'twentyten' ) ); ?></span>
                <?php edit_post_link( __( 'Edit', 'twentyten' ),
'<span class="meta-sep">|</span> <span class="edit-link">', '</span>' ); ?>
        </div><!-- .entry-utility -->
    </div><!-- #post-## -->

        <?php comments_template( '', true ); ?>

    <?php endif; // This was the if statement that broke the loop into three
parts based on categories. ?>

<?php endwhile; // End the loop. Whew. ?>

<?php /* Display navigation to next/previous pages when applicable */ ?>
<?php if (  $wp_query->max_num_pages > 1 ) : ?>
                <div id="nav-below" class="navigation">
                        <div class="nav-previous"><?php next_posts_
link( __( '<span class="meta-nav">&larr;</span> Older posts', 'twentyten' ) ); ?>
</div>
                        <div class="nav-next"><?php previous_posts_
link( __( 'Newer posts <span class="meta-nav">&rarr;</span>', 'twentyten' ) ); ?>
</div>
                </div><!-- #nav-below -->
<?php endif; ?>
```

Wow, that's a lot of looping! Are you ready to write that kind of loop.php file for your upcoming sites?

Luckily you won't have to. In the case of the Twenty Ten, the loop.php template is used to control almost every loop on the site. You don't have to do it that way, and neither should you really, since it makes the file unnecessarily large when you really just need a small part of it. The idea here is to make it easy for child themes to override the loop, because every template file that calls the loop is in fact calling a specific loop (I discuss child themes in Chapter 4). This is from category.php, for example:

```php
<?php get_template_part( 'loop', 'category' ); ?>
```

This code will look for loop-category.php, and then default back to loop.php. In the case of Twenty Ten, it does the latter.

So what part of the code in loop.php would I actually use? Well, since the first two parts are for the Gallery and Asides categories, respectively, I have to go with the loop for all other posts:

```php
<?php /* How to display all other posts. */ ?>

        <?php else : ?>
                <div id="post-<?php the_ID(); ?>" <?php post_class(); ?>>
                        <h2 class="entry-title"><a href="<?php the_permalink(); ?>"
 title="<?php printf( esc_attr__( 'Permalink to %s', 'twentyten' ), the_title_
 attribute( 'echo=0' ) ); ?>" rel="bookmark"><?php the_title(); ?></a></h2>

                        <div class="entry-meta">
                                <?php twentyten_posted_on(); ?>
                        </div><!-- .entry-meta -->

        <?php if ( is_archive() || is_search() ) : // Only display excerpts for
 archives and search. ?>
                        <div class="entry-summary">
                                <?php the_excerpt(); ?>
                        </div><!-- .entry-summary -->
        <?php else : ?>
                        <div class="entry-content">
                                <?php the_content( __( 'Continue reading <span
 class="meta-nav">&rarr;</span>', 'twentyten' ) ); ?>
                                <?php wp_link_pages( array( 'before' => '<div
 class="page-link">' . __( 'Pages:', 'twentyten' ), 'after' => '</div>' ) ); ?>
                        </div><!-- .entry-content -->
        <?php endif; ?>

                        <div class="entry-utility">
                                <?php if ( count( get_the_category() ) ) : ?>
                                        <span class="cat-links">
                                                <?php printf( __( '<span
 class="%1$s">Posted in</span> %2$s', 'twentyten' ), 'entry-utility-prep entry-
 utility-prep-cat-links', get_the_category_list( ', ' ) ); ?>
                                        </span>
                                        <span class="meta-sep">|</span>
                                <?php endif; ?>
                                <?php
                                        $tags_list = get_the_tag_list( '', ', ' );
                                        if ( $tags_list ):
                                ?>
                                        <span class="tag-links">
                                                <?php printf( __( '<span
 class="%1$s">Tagged</span> %2$s', 'twentyten' ), 'entry-utility-prep entry-utility-
 prep-tag-links', $tags_list ); ?>
                                        </span>
```

```
                                        <span class="meta-sep">|</span>
                        <?php endif; ?>
                        <span class="comments-link"><?php comments_popup_
    link( __( 'Leave a comment', 'twentyten' ), __( '1 Comment', 'twentyten' ), __( '%
    Comments', 'twentyten' ) ); ?></span>
                                <?php edit_post_link( __( 'Edit', 'twentyten' ),
      '<span class="meta-sep">|</span> <span class="edit-link">', '</span>' ); ?>
                    </div><!-- .entry-utility -->
            </div><!-- #post-## -->

            <?php comments_template( '', true ); ?>
```

That's basically how the loop.php template works in Twenty Ten. Since the one template file contains almost all the loops that the theme uses, it picks the right loop using conditional tags (which I discuss later in this chapter). The Gallery category check that uses `in_category()` is one of those conditional tags. It only returns true, and hence uses the loop meant for the Gallery category only, if you in fact are in the Gallery category, and so on. It's a bit messy, but again, the whole idea is to make it easy for child theme development on top of Twenty Ten, and then it is nice to have a big loop.php like this to fall back on.

EXAMPLE: LISTING ONLY TITLES IN CATEGORY ARCHIVES

Let's create an alternate loop template for category archives, showing just the title and some post meta data (publishing date and author) for each post. This is stylish and simple, and might fit your site. If nothing else, you'll learn something, which is kind of the point, right?

1. **Find the loop template you need**. Twenty Ten has a category.php file, and that's what's used for category archives as you probably know. A quick look at that reveals this loop inclusion code.

    ```
    get_template_part( 'loop', 'category' );
    ```

    This means that WordPress will look for loop-category.php first, and then fall back to loop.php. Twenty Ten just ships with a single loop.php, which means that you can get to the loop on the category archive pages by creating a loop-category.php file.

2. **Create loop-category.php.** Make a copy of loop.php (don't overwrite it, it is still needed for the rest of the site!) and rename it loop-category.php. Now you've got something like this in a file called loop-category.php:

    ```
    <?php
    /**
     * The loop that displays posts.
     *
     * The loop displays the posts and the post content.  See
     * http://codex.wordpress.org/The_Loop to understand it and
     * http://codex.wordpress.org/Template_Tags to understand
     * the tags used in it.
     *
     * This can be overridden in child themes with loop.php or
     * loop-template.php, where 'template' is the loop context
     * requested by a template. For example, loop-index.php would
    ```

```
 * be used if it exists and I ask for the loop with:
 * <code>get_template_part( 'loop', 'index' );</code>
 *
 * @package WordPress
 * @subpackage Twenty_Ten
 * @since Twenty Ten 1.0
 */
?>

<?php /* Display navigation to next/previous pages when applicable */ ?>
<?php if ( $wp_query->max_num_pages > 1 ) : ?>
        <div id="nav-above" class="navigation">
                <div class="nav-previous"><?php next_posts_link( __( '<span
 class="meta-nav">&larr;</span> Older posts', 'twentyten' ) ); ?></div>
                <div class="nav-next"><?php previous_posts_link( __( 'Newer
 posts <span class="meta-nav">&rarr;</span>', 'twentyten' ) ); ?></div>
        </div><!-- #nav-above -->
<?php endif; ?>

<?php /* If there are no posts to display, such as an empty archive page */ ?>
<?php if ( ! have_posts() ) : ?>
        <div id="post-0" class="post error404 not-found">
                <h1 class="entry-title"><?php _e( 'Not Found', 'twentyten' );
 ?></h1>
                <div class="entry-content">
                        <p><?php _e( 'Apologies, but no results were found for
 the requested archive. Perhaps searching will help find a related post.',
 'twentyten' ); ?></p>
                        <?php get_search_form(); ?>
                </div><!-- .entry-content -->
        </div><!-- #post-0 -->
<?php endif; ?>

<?php
        /* Start the Loop.
         *
         * In Twenty Ten I use the same loop in multiple contexts.
         * It is broken into three main parts: when I display
         * posts that are in the gallery category, when I display
         * posts in the asides category, and finally all other posts.
         *
         * Additionally, I sometimes check for whether I am on an
         * archive page, a search page, etc., allowing for small differences
         * in the loop on each template without actually duplicating
         * the rest of the loop that is shared.
         *
         * Without further ado, the loop:
         */ ?>
<?php while ( have_posts() ) : the_post(); ?>

<?php /* How to display posts in the Gallery category. */ ?>
```

```php
<?php if ( in_category( _x('gallery', 'gallery category slug', 'twen-
tyten') ) ) : ?>
                <div id="post-<?php the_ID(); ?>" <?php post_class(); ?>>
                        <h2 class="entry-title"><a href="<?php the_permalink();
?>" title="<?php printf( esc_attr__( 'Permalink to %s', 'twentyten' ), the_
title_attribute( 'echo=0' ) ); ?>" rel="bookmark"><?php the_title(); ?></a>
</h2>

                    <div class="entry-meta">
                            <?php twentyten_posted_on(); ?>
                    </div><!-- .entry-meta -->

                    <div class="entry-content">
<?php if ( post_password_required() ) : ?>
                            <?php the_content(); ?>
<?php else : ?>
                        <?php
                            $images = get_children( array( 'post_
parent' => $post->ID, 'post_type' => 'attachment', 'post_mime_type' => 'image',
'orderby' => 'menu_order', 'order' => 'ASC', 'numberposts' => 999 ) );
                            if ( $images ) :
                                    $total_images = count( $images
);
                                    $image = array_shift( $images );
                                    $image_img_tag = wp_get_
attachment_image( $image->ID, 'thumbnail' );
                            ?>
                                <div class="gallery-thumb">
                                    <a class="size-thumb-
nail" href="<?php the_permalink(); ?>"><?php echo $image_img_tag; ?></a>
                                </div><!-- .gallery-thumb -->
                                <p><em><?php printf( __( 'This
gallery contains <a %1$s>%2$s photos</a>.', 'twentyten' ),
                                        'href="' .
get_permalink() . '" title="' . sprintf( esc_attr__( 'Permalink to %s',
'twentyten' ), the_title_attribute( 'echo=0' ) ) . '" rel="bookmark"',
                                        $total_images
                                ); ?></em></p>
                        <?php endif; ?>
                                <?php the_excerpt(); ?>
<?php endif; ?>
                    </div><!-- .entry-content -->

                    <div class="entry-utility">
                            <a href="<?php echo get_term_link( _x('gallery',
'gallery category slug', 'twentyten'), 'category' ); ?>" title="<?php esc_
attr_e( 'View posts in the Gallery category', 'twentyten' ); ?>"><?php _e
( 'More Galleries', 'twentyten' ); ?></a>
                            <span class="meta-sep">|</span>
                            <span class="comments-link"><?php comments_
popup_link( __( 'Leave a comment', 'twentyten' ), __( '1 Comment', 'twentyten'
```

```php
), __( '% Comments', 'twentyten' ) ); ?></span>
                                <?php edit_post_link( __( 'Edit', 'twentyten' ),
    '<span class="meta-sep">|</span> <span class="edit-link">', '</span>' ); ?>
                        </div><!-- .entry-utility -->
                    </div><!-- #post-## -->


<?php /* How to display posts in the asides category */ ?>


        <?php elseif ( in_category( _x('asides', 'asides category slug',
    'twentyten') ) ) : ?>
                    <div id="post-<?php the_ID(); ?>" <?php post_class(); ?>>

                    <?php if ( is_archive() || is_search() ) : // Display excerpts
    for archives and search. ?>
                        <div class="entry-summary">
                                <?php the_excerpt(); ?>
                        </div><!-- .entry-summary -->
                    <?php else : ?>
                        <div class="entry-content">
                                <?php the_content( __( 'Continue reading
    <span class="meta-nav">&rarr;</span>', 'twentyten' ) ); ?>
                        </div><!-- .entry-content -->
                    <?php endif; ?>


                        <div class="entry-utility">
                                <?php twentyten_posted_on(); ?>
                                <span class="meta-sep">|</span>
                                <span class="comments-link"><?php comments_
    popup_link( __( 'Leave a comment', 'twentyten' ), __( '1 Comment', 'twentyten'
    ), __( '% Comments', 'twentyten' ) ); ?></span>
                                <?php edit_post_link( __( 'Edit', 'twentyten' ),
    '<span class="meta-sep">|</span> <span class="edit-link">', '</span>' ); ?>
                        </div><!-- .entry-utility -->
                    </div><!-- #post-## -->


<?php /* How to display all other posts. */ ?>


        <?php else : ?>
                <div id="post-<?php the_ID(); ?>" <?php post_class(); ?>>
                        <h2 class="entry-title"><a href="<?php the_permalink();
    ?>" title="<?php printf( esc_attr__( 'Permalink to %s', 'twentyten' ), the_
    title_attribute( 'echo=0' ) ); ?>" rel="bookmark"><?php the_title(); ?></a>
    </h2>


                        <div class="entry-meta">
                                <?php twentyten_posted_on(); ?>
                        </div><!-- .entry-meta -->

        <?php if ( is_archive() || is_search() ) : // Only display excerpts for
    archives and search. ?>
                        <div class="entry-summary">
```

```php
                                    <?php the_excerpt(); ?>
                        </div><!-- .entry-summary -->
            <?php else : ?>
                        <div class="entry-content">
                                    <?php the_content( __( 'Continue reading <span
class="meta-nav">&rarr;</span>', 'twentyten' ) ); ?>
                                    <?php wp_link_pages( array( 'before' => '<div
class="page-link">' . __( 'Pages:', 'twentyten' ), 'after' => '</div>' ) ); ?>
                        </div><!-- .entry-content -->
            <?php endif; ?>

                        <div class="entry-utility">
                                    <?php if ( count( get_the_category() ) ) : ?>
                                        <span class="cat-links">
                                                    <?php printf( __( '<span
class="%1$s">Posted in</span> %2$s', 'twentyten' ), 'entry-utility-prep
entry-utility-prep-cat-links', get_the_category_list( ', ' ) ); ?>
                                        </span>
                                        <span class="meta-sep">|</span>
                                    <?php endif; ?>
                                    <?php
                                        $tags_list = get_the_tag_list( '', ', '
);
                                        if ( $tags_list ):
                                    ?>
                                        <span class="tag-links">
                                                    <?php printf( __( '<span
class="%1$s">Tagged</span> %2$s', 'twentyten' ), 'entry-utility-prep entry-
utility-prep-tag-links', $tags_list ); ?>
                                        </span>
                                        <span class="meta-sep">|</span>
                                    <?php endif; ?>
                                    <span class="comments-link"><?php comments_
popup_link( __( 'Leave a comment', 'twentyten' ), __( '1 Comment', 'twentyten'
), __( '% Comments', 'twentyten' ) ); ?></span>
                                    <?php edit_post_link( __( 'Edit', 'twentyten' ),
'<span class="meta-sep">|</span> <span class="edit-link">', '</span>' ); ?>
                        </div><!-- .entry-utility -->
                </div><!-- #post-## -->

                    <?php comments_template( '', true ); ?>

            <?php endif; // This was the if statement that broke the loop into three
    parts based on categories. ?>

<?php endwhile; // End the loop. Whew. ?>

<?php /* Display navigation to next/previous pages when applicable */ ?>
<?php if (   $wp_query->max_num_pages > 1 ) : ?>
                                    <div id="nav-below" class="navigation">
```

```
                                        <div class="nav-previous"><?php next_
posts_link( __( '<span class="meta-nav">&larr;</span> Older posts', 'twentyten'
) ); ?></div>
                                        <div class="nav-next"><?php previous_
posts_link( __( 'Newer posts <span class="meta-nav">&rarr;</span>', 'twentyten'
) ); ?></div>
                            </div><!-- #nav-below -->
<?php endif; ?>
```

3. **Cut away (almost) everything.** The loop-category.php is way to big! You just want to output the necessary content; no need to have anything related to the Gallery or Asides categories, so start by cutting that away. In fact, you want to get rid of everything that isn't crucial to displaying the posts in the category archives.

```
<?php
/**
 * The loop that displays posts.
 *
 * The loop displays the posts and the post content.  See
 * http://codex.wordpress.org/The_Loop to understand it and
 * http://codex.wordpress.org/Template_Tags to understand
 * the tags used in it.
 *
 * This can be overridden in child themes with loop.php or
 * loop-template.php, where 'template' is the loop context
 * requested by a template. For example, loop-index.php would
 * be used if it exists and I ask for the loop with:
 * <code>get_template_part( 'loop', 'index' );</code>
 *
 * @package WordPress
 * @subpackage Twenty_Ten
 * @since Twenty Ten 1.0
 */
?>


<?php /* Display navigation to next/previous pages when applicable */ ?>
<?php if ( $wp_query->max_num_pages > 1 ) : ?>
        <div id="nav-above" class="navigation">
                <div class="nav-previous"><?php next_posts_link( __( '<span
class="meta-nav">&larr;</span> Older posts', 'twentyten' ) ); ?></div>
                <div class="nav-next"><?php previous_posts_link( __( 'Newer
posts <span class="meta-nav">&rarr;</span>', 'twentyten' ) ); ?></div>
        </div><!-- #nav-above -->
<?php endif; ?>


<?php /* If there are no posts to display, such as an empty archive page */ ?>
<?php if ( ! have_posts() ) : ?>
        <div id="post-0" class="post error404 not-found">
                <h1 class="entry-title"><?php _e( 'Not Found', 'twentyten' );
?></h1>
                <div class="entry-content">
```

```php
                    <p><?php _e( 'Apologies, but no results were found for
  the requested archive. Perhaps searching will help find a related post.',
  'twentyten' ); ?></p>
                        <?php get_search_form(); ?>
                </div><!-- .entry-content -->
        </div><!-- #post-0 -->
<?php endif; ?>


<?php
        /* Start the Loop.
         *
         * In Twenty Ten I use the same loop in multiple contexts.
         * It is broken into three main parts: when I display
         * posts that are in the gallery category, when I display
         * posts in the asides category, and finally all other posts.
         *
         * Additionally, I sometimes check for whether I am on an
         * archive page, a search page, etc., allowing for small differences
         * in the loop on each template without actually duplicating
         * the rest of the loop that is shared.
         *
         * Without further ado, the loop:
         */ ?>
<?php while ( have_posts() ) : the_post(); ?>

                <div id="post-<?php the_ID(); ?>" <?php post_class(); ?>>
                        <h2 class="entry-title"><a href="<?php the_permalink();
  ?>" title="<?php printf( esc_attr__( 'Permalink to %s', 'twentyten' ), the_
  title_attribute( 'echo=0' ) ); ?>" rel="bookmark"><?php the_title(); ?></a></h2>

                        <div class="entry-meta">
                                <?php twentyten_posted_on(); ?>
                        </div><!-- .entry-meta -->
                </div><!-- #post-## -->

                <?php comments_template( '', true ); ?>

<?php endwhile; // End the loop. Whew. ?>

<?php /* Display navigation to next/previous pages when applicable */ ?>
<?php if (  $wp_query->max_num_pages > 1 ) : ?>
                                <div id="nav-below" class="navigation">
                                    <div class="nav-previous"><?php next_
  posts_link( __( '<span class="meta-nav">&larr;</span> Older posts', 'twentyten'
  ) ); ?></div>
                                    <div class="nav-next"><?php previous_
  posts_link( __( 'Newer posts <span class="meta-nav">&rarr;</span>', 'twentyten'
  ) ); ?></div>
                                </div><!-- #nav-below -->
<?php endif; ?>
```

The stuff before and after the actual loop is still there. That's for navigational purposes and what's displayed when the category archive is empty. This is what does the actual post output now:

```php
<?php while ( have_posts() ) : the_post(); ?>

                <div id="post-<?php the_ID(); ?>" <?php post_class(); ?>>
                        <h2 class="entry-title"><a href="<?php the_permalink();
    ?>" title="<?php printf( esc_attr__( 'Permalink to %s', 'twentyten' ), the_
    title_attribute( 'echo=0' ) ); ?>" rel="bookmark"><?php the_title(); ?></a></h2>

                        <div class="entry-meta">
                                <?php twentyten_posted_on(); ?>
                        </div><!-- .entry-meta -->
                </div><!-- #post-## -->

                <?php comments_template( '', true ); ?>

<?php endwhile; // End the loop. Whew. ?>
```

A quick check on a category archive shows us a listing without anything else but a title and some meta data (Figure 3-2 shows this listing). You might want to style it a bit in style.css to make it a little tighter, but it'll do for this example.

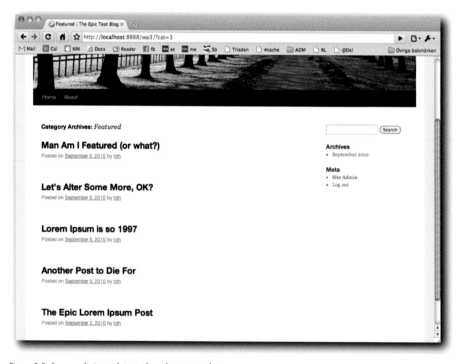

Figure 3-2: Category listing with just title and post meta data

4. **But wait, what about Gallery and Asides?** Yeah, that fancy stuff with thumbnails and asides won't work in category archives anymore, since the loop-category.php is preferred over loop.php, and the custom display code for those two sits there. But you can change that. Let's add the custom display to our loop-category.php. Start by locating this code in loop.php, that's what's doing all the pretty magic.

```php
<?php /* How to display posts in the Gallery category. */ ?>

        <?php if ( in_category( _x('gallery', 'gallery category slug',
    'twentyten') ) ) : ?>
                <div id="post-<?php the_ID(); ?>" <?php post_class(); ?>>
                        <h2 class="entry-title"><a href="<?php the_permalink();
    ?>" title="<?php printf( esc_attr__( 'Permalink to %s', 'twentyten' ), the_
    title_attribute( 'echo=0' ) ); ?>" rel="bookmark"><?php the_title(); ?></a></h2>

                        <div class="entry-meta">
                                <?php twentyten_posted_on(); ?>
                        </div><!-- .entry-meta -->

                        <div class="entry-content">
    <?php if ( post_password_required() ) : ?>
                                <?php the_content(); ?>
    <?php else : ?>
                                <?php
                                        $images = get_children( array( 'post_
    parent' => $post->ID, 'post_type' => 'attachment', 'post_mime_type' => 'image',
    'orderby' => 'menu_order', 'order' => 'ASC', 'numberposts' => 999 ) );
                                        if ( $images ) :
                                                $total_images = count( $images
    );
                                                $image = array_shift( $images );
                                                $image_img_tag = wp_get_attach-
    ment_image( $image->ID, 'thumbnail' );
                                        ?>
                                                <div class="gallery-thumb">
                                                        <a class="size-thumb-
    nail" href="<?php the_permalink(); ?>"><?php echo $image_img_tag; ?></a>
                                                </div><!-- .gallery-thumb -->
                                                <p><em><?php printf( __( 'This
    gallery contains <a %1$s>%2$s photos</a>.', 'twentyten' ),
                                                        'href="' .
    get_permalink() . '" title="' . sprintf( esc_attr__( 'Permalink to %s',
    'twentyten' ), the_title_attribute( 'echo=0' ) ) . '" rel="bookmark"',
                                                        $total_images
                                                ); ?></em></p>
                                <?php endif; ?>
                                        <?php the_excerpt(); ?>
    <?php endif; ?>
                        </div><!-- .entry-content -->
```

```
                                   <div class="entry-utility">
                                           <a href="<?php echo get_term_link( _x('gallery',
                      'gallery category slug', 'twentyten'), 'category' ); ?>" title="<?php esc_
                      attr_e( 'View posts in the Gallery category', 'twentyten' ); ?>"><?php _e(
                      'More Galleries', 'twentyten' ); ?></a>
                                               <span class="meta-sep">|</span>
                                               <span class="comments-link"><?php comments_
                      popup_link( __( 'Leave a comment', 'twentyten' ), __( '1 Comment', 'twentyten'
                      ), __( '% Comments', 'twentyten' ) ); ?></span>
                                           <?php edit_post_link( __( 'Edit', 'twentyten' ),
                      '<span class="meta-sep">|</span> <span class="edit-link">', '</span>' ); ?>
                                       </div><!-- .entry-utility -->
                                   </div><!-- #post-## -->


<?php /* How to display posts in the asides category */ ?>


              <?php elseif ( in_category( _x('asides', 'asides category slug',
           'twentyten') ) ) : ?>
                          <div id="post-<?php the_ID(); ?>" <?php post_class(); ?>>

                               <?php if ( is_archive() || is_search() ) : // Display excerpts
           for archives and search. ?>
                                   <div class="entry-summary">
                                       <?php the_excerpt(); ?>
                                   </div><!-- .entry-summary -->
                              <?php else : ?>
                                   <div class="entry-content">
                                       <?php the_content( __( 'Continue reading <span
           class="meta-nav">&rarr;</span>', 'twentyten' ) ); ?>
                                   </div><!-- .entry-content -->
                              <?php endif; ?>

                                   <div class="entry-utility">
                                           <?php twentyten_posted_on(); ?>
                                           <span class="meta-sep">|</span>
                                           <span class="comments-link"><?php comments_
           popup_link( __( 'Leave a comment', 'twentyten' ), __( '1 Comment', 'twentyten'
           ), __( '% Comments', 'twentyten' ) ); ?></span>
                                           <?php edit_post_link( __( 'Edit', 'twentyten' ),
           '<span class="meta-sep">|</span> <span class="edit-link">', '</span>' ); ?>
                                   </div><!-- .entry-utility -->
                               </div><!-- #post-## -->
```

Copy it, and insert it right after the loop starts, which is here:

```
<?php while ( have_posts() ) : the_post(); ?>
```

Then go down to where your newly added code ends, before the old code begins, and add this code snippet in between:

```
<?php /* How to display all other posts in category listings. */ ?>

        <?php else : ?>
```

The first line is obviously just for documentation purposes; it helps us find our way in the file. It's the `else` part that is important.

After that is our old code that displays the title and the post meta. This just needs one more little addition, and that is the ending of the `if` clause you started when you added the code for the Gallery and Asides types of posts. You want to add the `endif` just after the `comments_template()` call, and before the `endwhile`, which wraps up the whole loop.

```php
<?php endif; // This was the if statement that broke the loop into three
parts based on categories. ?>
```

That's it; now it works! The Gallery and Asides category archives will behave as they do in Twenty Ten, and all other category archives will just list a title and a post meta, like they did after Step 3. In the case of mixed archives where posts belong to more than one category, they will be managed individually, as shown in Figure 3-3.

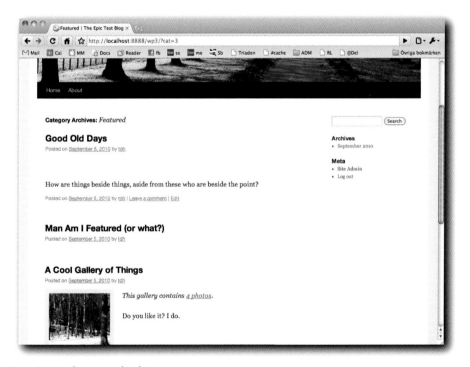

Figure 3-3: Mixed category archive listing

Here's the final loop-category.php code with our Gallery and Asides additions:

```php
<?php
/**
 * The loop that displays posts.
 *
 * The loop displays the posts and the post content.  See
```

```
 * http://codex.wordpress.org/The_Loop to understand it and
 * http://codex.wordpress.org/Template_Tags to understand
 * the tags used in it.
 *
 * This can be overridden in child themes with loop.php or
 * loop-template.php, where 'template' is the loop context
 * requested by a template. For example, loop-index.php would
 * be used if it exists and I ask for the loop with:
 * <code>get_template_part( 'loop', 'index' );</code>
 *
 * @package WordPress
 * @subpackage Twenty_Ten
 * @since Twenty Ten 1.0
 */
?>

<?php /* Display navigation to next/previous pages when applicable */ ?>
<?php if ( $wp_query->max_num_pages > 1 ) : ?>
        <div id="nav-above" class="navigation">
                <div class="nav-previous"><?php next_posts_link( __( '<span
 class="meta-nav">&larr;</span> Older posts', 'twentyten' ) ); ?></div>
                <div class="nav-next"><?php previous_posts_link( __( 'Newer posts
 <span class="meta-nav">&rarr;</span>', 'twentyten' ) ); ?></div>
        </div><!-- #nav-above -->
<?php endif; ?>
```

```
<?php /* If there are no posts to display, such as an empty archive page */ ?>
<?php if ( ! have_posts() ) : ?>
        <div id="post-0" class="post error404 not-found">
                <h1 class="entry-title"><?php _e( 'Not Found', 'twentyten' ); ?>
 </h1>
                <div class="entry-content">
                        <p><?php _e( 'Apologies, but no results were found for the
 requested archive. Perhaps searching will help find a related post.', 'twentyten'
 ); ?></p>
                        <?php get_search_form(); ?>
                </div><!-- .entry-content -->
        </div><!-- #post-0 -->
<?php endif; ?>

<?php
        /* Start the Loop.
         *
         * In Twenty Ten I use the same loop in multiple contexts.
         * It is broken into three main parts: when I display
         * posts that are in the gallery category, when I display
         * posts in the asides category, and finally all other posts.
         *
         * Additionally, I sometimes check for whether I am on an
         * archive page, a search page, etc., allowing for small differences
```

```
         * in the loop on each template without actually duplicating
         * the rest of the loop that is shared.
         *
         * Without further ado, the loop:
         */ ?>
<?php while ( have_posts() ) : the_post(); ?>

<?php /* How to display posts in the Gallery category. */ ?>

       <?php if ( in_category( _x('gallery', 'gallery category slug', 'twentyten')
   ) ) : ?>
              <div id="post-<?php the_ID(); ?>" <?php post_class(); ?>>
                    <h2 class="entry-title"><a href="<?php the_permalink(); ?>"
  title="<?php printf( esc_attr__( 'Permalink to %s', 'twentyten' ), the_title_
  attribute( 'echo=0' ) ); ?>" rel="bookmark"><?php the_title(); ?></a></h2>

                    <div class="entry-meta">
                          <?php twentyten_posted_on(); ?>
                    </div><!-- .entry-meta -->

                    <div class="entry-content">
<?php if ( post_password_required() ) : ?>
                          <?php the_content(); ?>
<?php else : ?>
                          <?php
                                $images = get_children( array( 'post_parent'
  => $post->ID, 'post_type' => 'attachment', 'post_mime_type' => 'image', 'orderby'
  => 'menu_order', 'order' => 'ASC', 'numberposts' => 999 ) );
                                if ( $images ) :
                                     $total_images = count( $images );
                                     $image = array_shift( $images );
                                     $image_img_tag = wp_get_attachment_
  image( $image->ID, 'thumbnail' );
                                ?>
                                     <div class="gallery-thumb">
                                          <a class="size-thumbnail"
  href="<?php the_permalink(); ?>"><?php echo $image_img_tag; ?></a>
                                     </div><!-- .gallery-thumb -->
                                     <p><em><?php printf( __( 'This
  gallery contains <a %1$s>%2$s photos</a>.', 'twentyten' ),
                                          'href="' . get_
  permalink() . '" title="' . sprintf( esc_attr__( 'Permalink to %s', 'twentyten' ),
  the_title_attribute( 'echo=0' ) ) . '" rel="bookmark"',
                                          $total_images
                                     ); ?></em></p>
                          <?php endif; ?>
                                <?php the_excerpt(); ?>
<?php endif; ?>
                    </div><!-- .entry-content -->

                    <div class="entry-utility">
```

```php
                                 <a href="<?php echo get_term_link( _x('gallery',
        'gallery category slug', 'twentyten'), 'category' ); ?>" title="<?php esc_attr_e(
        'View posts in the Gallery category', 'twentyten' ); ?>"><?php _e( 'More Galler-
        ies', 'twentyten' ); ?></a>
                                 <span class="meta-sep">|</span>
                                 <span class="comments-link"><?php comments_popup_
        link( __( 'Leave a comment', 'twentyten' ), __( '1 Comment', 'twentyten' ), __( '%
        Comments', 'twentyten' ) ); ?></span>
                                 <?php edit_post_link( __( 'Edit', 'twentyten' ),
        '<span class="meta-sep">|</span> <span class="edit-link">', '</span>' ); ?>
                         </div><!-- .entry-utility -->
                 </div><!-- #post-## -->

<?php /* How to display posts in the asides category */ ?>

        <?php elseif ( in_category( _x('asides', 'asides category slug', 'twen-
        tyten') ) ) : ?>
                 <div id="post-<?php the_ID(); ?>" <?php post_class(); ?>>

                 <?php if ( is_archive() || is_search() ) : // Display excerpts for
        archives and search. ?>
                         <div class="entry-summary">
                                 <?php the_excerpt(); ?>
                         </div><!-- .entry-summary -->
                 <?php else : ?>
                         <div class="entry-content">
                                 <?php the_content( __( 'Continue reading <span
        class="meta-nav">&rarr;</span>', 'twentyten' ) ); ?>
                         </div><!-- .entry-content -->
                 <?php endif; ?>

                 <div class="entry-utility">
                         <?php twentyten_posted_on(); ?>
                         <span class="meta-sep">|</span>
                         <span class="comments-link"><?php comments_popup_
        link( __( 'Leave a comment', 'twentyten' ), __( '1 Comment', 'twentyten' ), __( '%
        Comments', 'twentyten' ) ); ?></span>
                                 <?php edit_post_link( __( 'Edit', 'twentyten' ),
        '<span class="meta-sep">|</span> <span class="edit-link">', '</span>' ); ?>
                         </div><!-- .entry-utility -->
                 </div><!-- #post-## -->

<?php /* How to display all other posts in category listings. */ ?>

        <?php else : ?>

                 <div id="post-<?php the_ID(); ?>" <?php post_class(); ?>>
                         <h2 class="entry-title"><a href="<?php the_permalink(); ?>"
        title="<?php printf( esc_attr__( 'Permalink to %s', 'twentyten' ), the_title_
        attribute( 'echo=0' ) ); ?>" rel="bookmark"><?php the_title(); ?></a></h2>
```

68

```php
                        <div class="entry-meta">
                                <?php twentyten_posted_on(); ?>
                        </div><!-- .entry-meta -->
                </div><!-- #post-## -->

                <?php comments_template( '', true ); ?>

        <?php endif; // This was the if statement that broke the loop into three
parts based on categories. ?>

<?php endwhile; // End the loop. Whew. ?>

<?php /* Display navigation to next/previous pages when applicable */ ?>
<?php if (  $wp_query->max_num_pages > 1 ) : ?>
                                <div id="nav-below" class="navigation">
                                        <div class="nav-previous"><?php next_posts_
link( __( '<span class="meta-nav">&larr;</span> Older posts', 'twentyten' ) ); ?>
</div>
                                        <div class="nav-next"><?php previous_posts_
link( __( 'Newer posts <span class="meta-nav">&rarr;</span>', 'twentyten' ) ); ?>
</div>
                                </div><!-- #nav-below -->
<?php endif; ?>
```

WORKING WITH TEMPLATE TAGS

We touched on template tags in Chapter 2, but just briefly. When working with your own themes, or just changing existing themes, you need to know how to work with template tags in particular, as well as conditional tags, which I discuss later in this chapter.

All of the template tags are listed in the WordPress Codex (see Figure 3-4) for your viewing pleasure (`http://codex.wordpress.org/Template_Tags`). You'll be using this page frequently since it is the best reference available, aside perhaps from the actual WordPress files should you enjoy digging into them.

The template tags all work differently, although there are obvious similarities. A lot of them take the same kind of parameters, and you pass them in similar ways. This means that as soon as you understand how template tags work, you can start using them all.

PASSING PARAMETERS

While most template tags have a default output, sometimes that's not exactly what you want. That's why you want to pass parameters to the template tag so that it does what you want. Parameters are your way of telling the template tag what it should and shouldn't do.

Before moving on, remember that not all template tags will take a parameter. Sometimes the template tag just does one thing, and then you won't need to pass anything to it. Just use it as is, with no parameters.

Figure 3-4: The template tags page in the Codex

There are two primary ways to pass parameters to the template tag, but before you can do that you need to know which parameters the template tag can take. After all, they aren't psychic beings that know exactly what you want! A listing of which parameters the template tag of your choice can take is available in the WordPress Codex page on template tags. Just click the one you want and you'll get a description with examples and everything.

Function-style parameters

Now, the first way to pass parameters to the template tag is often referred to as function-style parameter. A simple and commonly used template tag is `bloginfo()`, often used to output the name of your site. This is handy if you don't want to manually change the name of the site in your template files since it will pick up the site title from the General Settings screen in the WordPress admin panel.

```
<?php bloginfo('name'); ?>
```

What you find within the single quotes is the parameter, 'name' in this case. The `bloginfo()` template tag outputs the site's name. If I want the URL instead, I pass 'url' to `bloginfo()`, which means that I replace name in the previous code example with url.

```
<?php bloginfo('url'); ?>
```

Some template tags take several parameters at once, like `the_date()`, which outputs the date. It will work on its own, without any parameters, but you can get more control by adding more. In the following code snippet, I get the date output within h1 tags.

```php
<?php the_title('<h1>', '</h1>'); ?>
```

You recognize `the_title()` from previous examples I'm sure; it outputs a post (or Page) title. As you can , you've got two parts within the parenthesis, which are each within their own single quotes. Each one contains a parameter. The first one is the `h1` tag, which is what goes before the output (again, the post or Page title), and the second one is what comes after. Obviously you want to close our `h1` tag here. What you get is the title outputted within `h1` tags.

There's actually a third parameter that you can pass to `the_title()`, located last. It is a Boolean parameter, which means it is either TRUE or FALSE, defaulting to TRUE. The only thing it does is control whether `the_date()` should print the content on the screen (TRUE), or just store it for use in a PHP script (FALSE). Since it is located last you won't need to declare it, it just defaults to the default value (again, TRUE), but if it were located in the middle of everything, you would have to pass it as well so that you wouldn't disrupt the order of things. In fact, the order in which you pass the arguments is very important, so get it right.

Let's say I wanted to set that last parameter to FALSE. This is how I would do that:

```php
<?php the_title('<h1>', '</h1>', FALSE); ?>
```

Notice the absence of single quotes around the Boolean parameter. TRUE or FALSE values don't need that.

Query-style parameters

The second way you can pass parameters to a template tag is usually used when there are a ton of options. Let's take a look at `wp_tag_cloud()`, a template tag that outputs a tag cloud. The default values will get the job done well enough, but perhaps you want to make some changes to the output. For example, maybe you don't like the default number of tags, which is 45. Let's say you want 30 instead. Now, `wp_tag_cloud()` has 13 possible values you can fill. If that was to be managed with the function-style parameter explained in the previous section, that would be quite a string now, wouldn't it? Luckily, query-style template tags let you change the value of one argument no matter where in the order it is.

```php
<?php wp_tag_cloud('number=30'); ?>
```

See that, a quick look at the `wp_tag_cloud()` page in the Codex told you that the argument you want to change is called number in this case, and then you just add it and tell the template tag which value you want. Simple, huh?

So what about changing several values then? It's almost as easy. Suppose you want to change the order of the tags from the default value, which is by name, to how many posts are using the tags instead. A quick check at the Codex page tells you to use orderby and change that from name (which is the default) to count.

```php
<?php wp_tag_cloud('number=30&orderby=count'); ?>
```

A simple ampersand (&) separates the two arguments, and that's that! You can add several arguments just by separating them with ampersands. You don't need to pass these parameters in any particular order, but it is a good idea to follow the one in the Codex since it will make the code easier to read over time.

But what if you need to pass an ampersand as a parameter? That won't work with this method, obviously, because the template tag would think it was supposed to take another argument since ampersands are used as separators. The way around that is to pass the arguments in an array. Here's the previous example with the added argument separator, which controls what goes between the tags in the tag cloud, and the parameter • which is HTML for a bullet.

```
<?php $params = array('number'    => 30,
                      'orderby'   => 'count',
                      'separator' => '&bull;' );
wp_tag_cloud($params); ?>
```

This looks a bit different. The array wants you to connect argument with parameter using the => arrow, and then keep both the argument and the parameter inside single quotes of their own. At least when they're not Booleans (TRUE or FALSE) or integers (a whole number) no single quotes are needed. In the preceding example, the parameter for number is an integer (30). You separate them with a comma, as you can see at the end of each line. All these arguments are stored in `$param`, which then is passed to `wp_tag_cloud()` at the end.

Did that mess with your head? Don't worry about it; I get into more practical examples later on.

Now you know how to use template tags. This means that you're ready to do cooler things with your themes and control the output of content better.

ABOUT STRINGS, BOOLEANS, AND INTEGERS

A string is a line of text, and can consist of one or several words. It is common that template tags takes strings as parameters. Strings are passed within single quotes.

A Boolean is either TRUE or FALSE. The parameters can also be passed as true or false, as well as 1 (which is TRUE) or 0 (which is FALSE).

Finally, an integer is a whole number, which could be 14, 2, -3, 1, and so on. You can pass integers with or without single quotes, it doesn't matter.

FINDING THE TEMPLATE TAG YOU WANT

Knowing which template tag is the right one isn't always that easy. The best way is to read up on them all, but keeping them all fresh in mind is, of course, a bit much to ask. Luckily they are grouped by naming conventions so that it is a bit easier to find them, as you've no doubt discovered on the Template Tags page in the WordPress Codex. With this in mind, you can narrow down the possible template tags for what you want to achieve, making it easier to find the right one.

For example, all `wp_list_XXX()` template tags behave the same way. So if you've figured out how `wp_list_pages()` work, you'll have no problem using `wp_list_book marks()`. This can also help you find the right template tag, since you might have used `wp_list_pages()` before and you know you want a similar styled listing of links. Seeing that there is a `wp_list_bookmarks()` should point you in the right direction.

Looking at themes is another great way of learning which template tags do what. Putting template tags to work is still the best way to master them, and that is also how you'll learn enough to quickly decide which template tag is right for your current problem.

A FEW WORDS ABOUT LOCALIZATION

Before moving on, sometimes you'll see `__()` around parameters in the code, or perhaps `_e()`. These notations are for localization purposes, and help the software find the strings that can be translated. They are always within PHP tags. So if you write `<?php __('This can be translated', locale); ?>` this means that the text "This can be translated" can be translated with the use of language files.

You've seen this in the Twenty Ten files. It is a fully localized theme, where locale from the preceding example is twentyten. That means that the translation is unique to the theme. It is important to set a suitable locale to make sure there are no language conflicts. There's more on theme localization later in the book; for now it is enough to understand what these `__()` and `_e()` notations represent.

73

CONDITIONAL CONTENT WITH CONDITIONAL TAGS

Wouldn't it be handy to be able to check whether you're on a particular section of your site? For example, if you're on a Page, post, or perhaps a category archive, you can output one thing, and if you're not you can output another? Well, you can, thanks to conditional tags that check whether a condition is met. If it is, it returns true (and you can perform one action), and if it is not, it returns false (and you can do something else).

Conditional tags perform a range of functions, from checking whether you're on the front page, on a single post or in a specific category, to if the post type is hierarchical, if a post has an excerpt, and so on. In short, whenever you need to check a condition that relates to a location on your site, you can look for an appropriate conditional tag. You'll find them all in the WordPress Codex, at `http://codex.wordpress.org/Conditional_Tags`.

WORKING WITH CONDITIONAL TAGS

Some knowledge of PHP is useful when working with conditional tags. Not that it is complicated, but if you're less experienced with this code, it may be a bit daunting. That being said, simpler things might very well be achieved by copy and pasting your way.

Try a quick check to see if you're on a single-post page. If you are, you'll output a short text snippet. The conditional tag that you use is `is_single()`.

```php
<?php if (is_single()) {
        echo 'Whoa nelly, this is a single post page!';
} ?>
```

This outputs the text Whoa nelly, this is a single post page! if the page where the code is executed is a single-post page (the Twenty Ten theme in Figure 3-5). Now, this isn't a book about PHP, but it might be good to know that `echo` outputs things, simple text, or HTML code for that matter.

Figure: 3-5: Here's a regular single post using the Twenty Ten theme

Let's say you want to output an ad block on the home page only. You can use `is_home()` for this:

```php
<?php if (is_home()) { ?>

        <div class="ad-block">
                <a href="http://tdh.me" title="Buy the book!">
                        Did you know I wrote another book as well?<br />
                        <strong>Get Smashing WordPress: Beyond the Blog</strong>
                </a>
        </div>

<?php } ?>
```

Since the ad block contains a bunch of HTML code, you don't use the `echo` function here. Instead, just interrupt the PHP snippet and resume it after the HTML code.

But what if you want the ad block above to be on the home page and also on Archives? Then you need both `is_home()` and `archive()`. You can list several conditions by separating them with double pipes, like this.

```php
<?php if (is_home() || is_archive()) { ?>

        <div class="ad-block">
                <a href="http://tdh.me" title="Buy the book!">
                        Did you know I wrote another book as well?<br />
                        <strong>Get Smashing WordPress: Beyond the
                        Blog</strong>
                </a>
        </div>

<?php } ?>
```

Hang on, what about the rest of the site where you've got no ads? How about outputting informational text there instead, rather than outputting nothing at all, which is the case right now. Yes, do that:

```php
<?php if (is_home() || is_archive()) { ?>

        <div class="ad-block">
                <a href="http://tdh.me" title="Buy the book!">
                        Did you know I wrote another book as well?<br />
                        <strong>Get Smashing WordPress: Beyond the
                        Blog</strong>
                </a>
        </div>

<?php } else { ?>

        <div class="ad-block">
                Want to <a href="/advertise" title="Advertise here!">advertise
                here?</a>
        </div>

<?php } ?>
```

The added `else` part will be used if the conditions within the first `if` part aren't met.

Finally, it may be useful to be able to do things when conditions are NOT met. That's easy; just add an exclamation mark (!) in front of the conditional tag, like so:

```php
<?php if (!is_home()) { ?>

        <p>This paragraph will show up everywhere except on the home page.</p>

<?php } ?>
```

The preceding code outputs the paragraph everywhere except on the home page.

EXAMPLE: ADDING CONDITIONAL SIDEBARS

Sometimes you want different content in your sidebar depending on where you are on your site. It is not uncommon to have one type of content in your sidebar when on posts or archives, but another when on a Page. The following example shows how to handle that.

1. **Save the old sidebar.php.** Find sidebar.php in your theme and rename it OLD_sidebar. php. This way you can revert to the old code anytime you want, which might be a good idea if you are trying this with a theme that you've downloaded.

2. **Create a new sidebar.php.** You'll do this from the ground up, so create a brand new file and name it sidebar.php.

3. **Get the typical sidebar stuff in there.** Let's assume that your theme follows decent WordPress nomenclature. That means that the following code should get your new sidebar to show up where it should be. If it does not, just copy the classes from OLD_ sidebar.php.

```
<ul id="sidebar">

        <!-- This is where the sidebar content goes -->

</ul>
```

4. **Check if it's a Page.** Use the following code to check if you are on a Page.

```
<ul id="sidebar">

        <?php if (is_page()) { ?>

                <!-- Stuff here will show up when viewing a Page -->

        <?php } ?>

    </ul>
```

Now you have a simple `if` clause with the conditional tag `is_page()`. If that returns TRUE, whatever's within the `if` clause will be returned. Right now, it is just commented HTML code, so you won't see anything. This is where you want the sidebar content for your Pages.

5. **Handle the rest of the site.** Use a similar technique for the rest of the site.

```
<ul id="sidebar">

        <?php if (is_page()) { ?>

                <!-- Stuff here will show up when viewing a Page -->

        <?php } else { ?>

                <!-- The rest of the site will show this, and not the stuff
```

```
    above -->

        <?php } ?>

</ul>
```

So, if `is_page()` is TRUE (which means you are on a Page), you get the first comment, and if it is not, you get the second comment.

6. **Get some content in there!** You can put whatever content you like instead of each of these two comments. It could be template tags listing content, advertisements, widget areas, or whatever:

```
<?php register_sidebars(); ?>
```

In the preceding example, a single Page just shows links to other Pages (via `wp_list_pages()`, a template tag), whereas the rest of the site gets a category listing (with `wp_list_categories()`, another template tag), a simple linked image, and then some links from the `wp_list_bookmarks()` template tag.

ENABLING FEATURES IN FUNCTIONS.PHP

Before I move on, I need to talk a little bit about enabling features in functions.php. This beautiful little template file is what adds the ability to post thumbnails, add menu support, enable custom backgrounds and headers, and so on. While all these features work with WordPress 3.0 and later (some actually came in earlier versions), you can't use them unless you enable them in functions.php. I provide examples for these features later in this chapter.

ADD THE ADD_THEME_SUPPORT TEMPLATE TAG

The template tag that you use is `add_theme_support()` and it is prudent to add all your feature enabling early in functions.php so that it is easy to scan the code for what's enabled and what's not.

The `add_theme_support()` enables

- **Custom headers**: Using the parameter `custom-header`
- **Custom backgrounds**: Using the parameter `custom-background`
- **Post thumbnails**: Using the parameter `post-thumbnails`
- **Menus**: Using the parameter `menus`
- **Automatic feed links**: Using the parameter `automatic-feed-links`
- **Editor styles**: Using the parameter `editor-style`

PASS THE CORRECT PARAMETERS

It is really easy to enable a feature for use with `add_theme_support()`. All you need to do is define the features you want to add by passing the appropriate parameter to `add_theme_support()` in functions.php, and it is ready for your use.

```php
<?php
        add_theme_support('custom-header');
        add_theme_support('custom-background');
        add_theme_support('post-thumbnails');
        add_theme_support('menus');
        add_theme_support('automatic-feed-links');
        add_theme_support('editor-style');
?>
```

This code would add theme support for all of the features mentioned in the preceding list.

Remember that just because you have added theme support for a feature, it doesn't mean that it actually shows up somewhere. Take post thumbnails, for example, which need to be output somewhere in your theme's template files as well (using the_post_thumbnail(), a template tag). However, not enabling the feature means that it won't work at all, and in the post thumbnail's case, your users won't be able to pick images to use as post thumbnails at all, even if you have the appropriate template tag in your theme.

It might sound like a good idea to always enable all these features, but I recommend against this. After all, why have WordPress show custom header panels in the admin panel if the theme won't actually show them? Enable the features you need, and add the rest as needed.

ADDING WIDGETS USING TEMPLATE FILES

Widget areas, often referred to as dynamic sidebars (despite not being sidebars all the time), are a theme designer's best friend when developing for clients. These drag-and-drop areas make it easy for anyone to add functionality, info boxes, and what not, just by dropping widgets where you want them. Through plugins, you can extend the available widget functionality almost indefinitely, so having widget areas is a sure way to make a site more flexible.

Adding widgets is easy enough. The code needed is split in two parts. The widget declaration, which adds the widget areas under Widgets in the WordPress admin panel, is in your theme's functions.php file (see the Widgets settings in Figure 3-6).

The second part is the code snippet that you put in your template files, where you want the widget area to appear. This means that if you want a widget area beside your logo located in the header.php template, for example, you'll add it to that particular place in header.php.

DEFINE WIDGET AREAS

As stated, you define widget areas in your theme's functions.php. This file can contain a bunch of items, and if you're looking at the Twenty Ten theme, you'll notice that it can be quite extensive.

When defining widget areas, you're actually registering sidebars with register_sidebars(). Despite the name, a widget area can be anything, not just a sidebar; this is something inherited from WordPress' past.

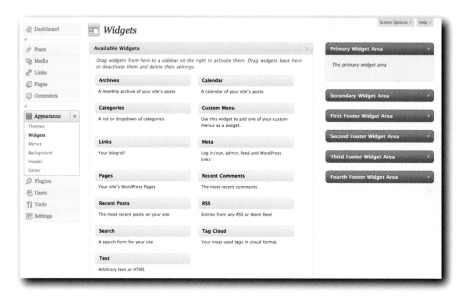

Figure 3-6: The Widgets settings in the admin panel

Adding the `register_sidebars()` tag to your functions.php file automatically registers a widget area called Sidebar:

```php
<?php register_sidebars(); ?>
```

Your functions.php file is often full with other things, so you will probably not need the opening and closing PHP snippets around `register_sidebars()`.

So what if you want a widget area named Footer? Try this code to pass information to `register_sidebars()`:

```php
<?php
        register_sidebar(array('name'=>'Sidebar'));
        register_sidebar(array('name'=>'Footer'));
?>
```

There are two ways for this to occur: one being passed the name Sidebar (which is the default, but since I'm naming them manually, I should name this one too), and one getting the name Footer.

You obviously can change the name of a widget area by passing a parameter to the name argument, so what other things can you control? The WordPress Codex page for `register_sidebars()` tells you to pass data to the following arguments:

- **name** is the name of the widget area
- **id** is the widget area ID
- **before_widget** is the code that goes before a widget in the widget area

- **after_widget** is the code that goes after a widget in the widget area
- **before_title** is the code that goes before the title (if the widget has one) of widgets
- **after_title** is the code that goes after the title (if the widget has one) of widgets

The default values are simple enough, and if you've hacked themes before you know them well enough. Widgets go inside li tags, and their titles are wrapped in h2 headings with the class widgettitle for easy access via CSS. By passing other values to the arguments via an array, you can get more control over how widgets behave in a particular widget area.

To see it in action, check out the Twenty Ten theme's functions.php; they're making some alterations there. Another example is the Notes Blog Core Theme (get it from http:// notesblog.com), which features a bunch of widget options. The following code is cropped and altered to fit our purpose and shows how you can mix default widget settings with more custom options.

```php
<?php
register_sidebar(array('name'=>'Sidebar'));
        register_sidebar(array('name'=>'Footer'));
        register_sidebar(array(
                'name' => 'Submenu',
                'id' => 'submenu',
                'description' => 'The submenu area, empty by default',
                'before_widget' => '<div class="submenu-nav">',
                'after_widget' => '</div>',
                'before_title' => '<span class="widgettitle">',
                'after_title' => '</span>'
        ));
?>
```

You'll recognize the top of this widget declaration, which gives you the areas Sidebar and Footer with default settings. Below that, however, is a slightly more complicated widget called Submenu. This one has special settings for wrapping widgets in a div rather than an li (and should per definition not sit in a ul, which is common practice). It also puts a span with the class widgettitle around any potential headings through the before_title and after_title arguments.

ADD WIDGET AREAS TO THE TEMPLATE FILES

Right, so now you know how to define widget areas. The only thing you need to know is how to add them to your template files so that they show up where you want them to. This is even easier thanks to the dynamic_sidebar() function. Just add the following to whichever template file you want to display your widget area in:

```php
<?php dynamic_sidebar('Sidebar'); ?>
```

As indicated in the first line of code, the dynamic_sidebar() that you want to show is the one called Sidebar. If you want to show one named Footer instead, just swap the name:

```php
<?php dynamic_sidebar('Footer'); ?>
```

Simple, right? Just pop in the name of the widget area you want to use in dynamic_sidebar() and you're good to go. And, again, just to clarify: This isn't just for sidebars, but for widget areas in general.

So what about that placeholder content then? Well, consider this code:

```php
<?php if ( !dynamic_sidebar('Footer') ) : ?>

    <li>

            <h2>Hey there!</h2>
            <p>This is just a placeholder. You need to drop some widgets
            here!</p>
    </li>


<?php endif; ?>
```

When there are no widgets in the widget area, Footer in this case, an li containing an h2 heading and a paragraph will show up, telling people to drop widgets in the widget area. But as soon as someone actually does, the placeholder code will disappear and only the widgets remain. In other words, if you've got nothing as placeholder text, then nothing will be visible until you drop a widget in the area. This is worth thinking about if you want to make certain parts of a theme easy to customize.

PUT WIDGETS TO GOOD USE

So what's the purpose of stepping away from the default values? Well, it would depend on the theme obviously, but the Submenu example shown earlier is actually a sound one, at least in principle, since you now have support for menus in WordPress and having submenus is even better. While WordPress recommends that widget areas are in ul blocks with every widget enclosed in an li that might not always be suitable. And even if it is, perhaps you have one widget area that would benefit greatly from a different class on the heading, or perhaps even on the li items for some reason? You'll know it when you need it.

Widgets, in general, are great. The fact that they are drag-and-drop features makes them easy to use. You don't need to be an experienced WordPress user to manage widgets, and if that isn't enough, the ease with which you can add features through the use of plugins that offer widgets is hard to match.

In short, when looking at the parts of a site that isn't all about the posts and Pages, but still need to be dynamic, widgets are often the way to go.

EXAMPLE: ADDING A NEW WIDGET AREA

In this example, you put your newfound knowledge of widgets to the test by adding a new widget area to a theme (Figure 3-7 and 3-8 shows the before and after views). Which theme?

81

Any theme!

Figure 3-7: This is how the Widgets screen looks if you have no widget areas defined in functions.php

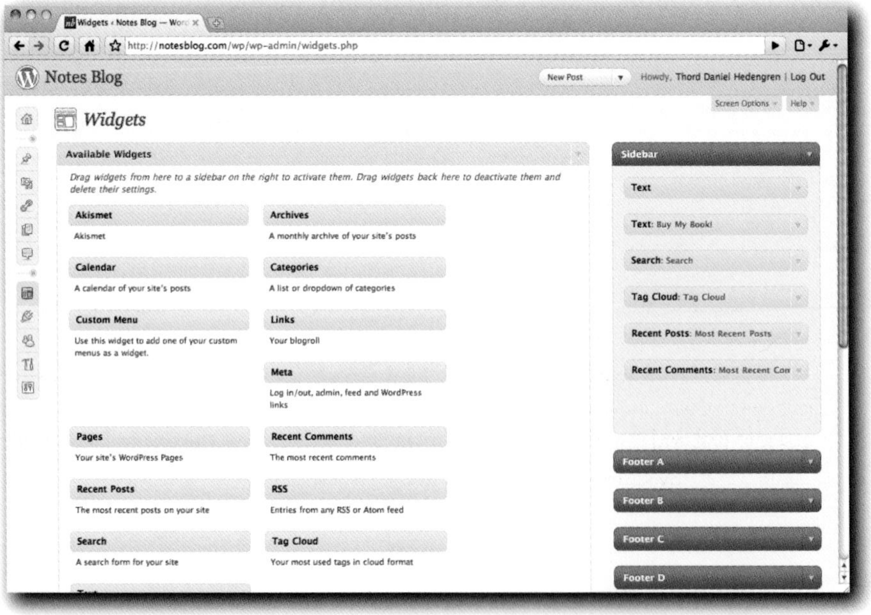

Figure 3-8: By comparison, the Twenty Ten theme's Widgets screen, obviously with widgets defined in functions.php

1. **Open functions.php.** The widget declaration is in functions.php, which is located in your theme's folder. If there isn't one, which is highly unlikely, you need to create it yourself. Just create an empty file and name it functions.php.

2. Find the widget area declaration. Add a widget area called Hypothetical (you can call it anything you'd like if you're doing this on a theme that you'll want to actually use). You need to find the widget declarations in functions.php. They contain `register_sidebar()` and you need to add an extra line to it.

3. Add the new widget area. Assume the widget declarations in your theme looks like this:

```
register_sidebar(array('name'=>'Sidebar'));
    register_sidebar(array('name'=>'Footer'));
```

Now just add another line where you use `register_sidebar()` to add your widget area called Hypothetical. (Note that every widget area ends with a semicolon.)

```
register_sidebar(array('name'=>'Sidebar'));
    register_sidebar(array('name'=>'Footer'));
    register_sidebar(array('name'=>'Hypothetical'));
```

4. But wait, you need another widget area! This one is called Obsessive and needs some special attention in terms of classes for the `li` and `h2` elements that wrap around each widget, and widget heading, respectively. Just add that below your Hypothetical widget area from Step 3:

```
register_sidebar(array('name'=>'Sidebar'));
    register_sidebar(array('name'=>'Footer'));
    register_sidebar(array('name'=>'Hypothetical'));
        register_sidebar(array(
                'name' => Obsessive,
                'id' => 'obsessive-widget-area',
                'description' => 'Widget area for obsessive things',
                'before_widget' => '<li class="widget-obsessive">',
                'after_widget' => '</li>',
                'before_title' => '<h2 class="widget-title">',
                'after_title' => '</h2>',
        ));
```

To achieve the special `li` and `h2` elements, you pass several parameters to the relevant arguments in the array. To top it off, you also add an ID and a description.

5. Add the widget areas to the templates. Now that you've created your widget areas, you need to display them somewhere on your site. To do that, open whatever template file you feel fits, and just add the following code for the first widget area, the one called Hypothetical.

```
<?php if ( !dynamic_sidebar('Hypothetical') ) : ?>

        <li>
                <h2>Whoa!</h2>
                <p>You need to drop some widgets here mate.</p>
        </li>

<?php endif; ?>
```

If you forget to drop widgets in the Hypothetical widget area, that placeholder text is sure to get your attention, right?

83

Moving on, the Obsessive widget area should also show up somewhere. However, you may not always be obsessive enough to show something in that part of the site. So when there are no widgets in the area, it shouldn't say anything. In other words, it's OK if the Obsessive widget area is empty sometimes:

```
<?php dynamic_sidebar('Obsessive'); ?>
```

There you go; it's as easy as that to add two widget areas to any theme.

THE POWER OF CUSTOM PAGE TEMPLATES

Pages, the static part of your WordPress site's content that's been there since forever, are in fact a great tool when building more advanced sites. The traditional blog uses Pages for static content like information about the site, advertisement rates, policies, and similar items. This is all well and good, but consider this: Some sites consist primarily of static content. That's Pages for you, and there's more. Since you can apply Page templates as custom templates in your theme, to your Pages that means that you can do pretty cool stuff just by creating a template and inserting the code there.

With some creative coding in Page templates you can build just about anything with Word-Press. Create the Page in your admin panel, add the necessary content to it, and do all the funky stuff in the template. Include an outside script, offer alternate content to display — in short: Pages are one potentially powerful ally in creating The Site.

CREATE A CUSTOM PAGE TEMPLATE

A theme can have any number of Page templates. The template file hierarchy indicates that the first thing WordPress will look for is an assigned Page template, which you choose in the Edit Page screen of the admin panel. Obviously your theme will need at least one Page template for this control to show up (as you see in Figure 3-9, click the arrow to select a template).

After that, you have page-X.php where it first checks to see if X is the Page slug, and then if it is the Page ID. Moving on, WordPress tries to use the generic page.php, and finally uses index.php. That's all well and good, and sometimes it might be handy to do your custom stuff in a dedicated Page template using the slug or ID version, but more often you create a Page template that you can pick for several Pages, if you want to, manually in the WordPress admin panel.

So how do you create a Page template? First, you need a few lines of code at the very top of your Page template file so that WordPress knows that it is supposed to let you pick it in the admin panel:

```
<?php
/*
Template Name: My Brand New Page Template
*/
?>
```

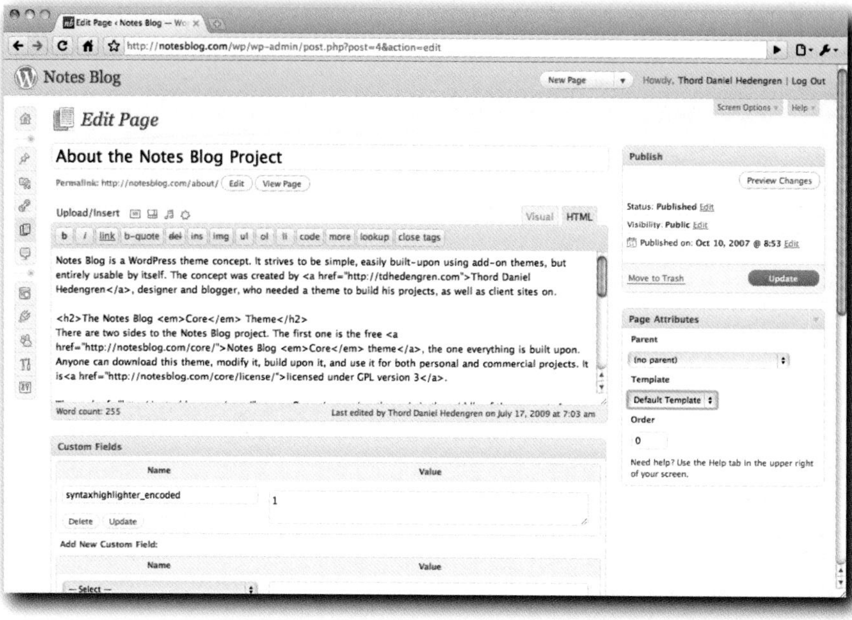

Figure: 3-9: Pick a Page template (in the box in the right column)

Obviously you'll name your Page template something more descriptive. This is what you see in the Page template drop-down box on the Edit Page screen (in the admin panel).

Below these few lines of code, type your actual Page template. How this looks depends entirely on what you want to do. Perhaps you just want to alter some things from your regular page. php template, in which case you'd just copy the contents of that file, paste it in your Page template file, and make your changes.

But hang on, what should your Page template file be called? This is up to you; my-page-template.php works as long as it sits in your theme folder and has the necessary Page template code at the very top of the file. However, it might be a good idea to name your Page template file something in the lines of pagetemplate-my-page-template.php. By having "pagetemplate-" before the actual Page template filename, it will be easier to find the file when working with the theme, especially if you have several Page templates. You shouldn't just put "page-" in front of the actual Page template filename because WordPress will try and apply it to a slug if you do. Stick with "pagetemplate-" or something similar.

EXAMPLE: CREATING AN ARCHIVES PAGE TEMPLATE

In this example, you create an Archives Page template so that you can set up a Page showing the latest posts, a tag cloud, and all our categories easily. You display these using template tags like `wp_list_categories()` for categories, `wp_tag_cloud()` for tags, and `wp_get_archives()` for a monthly post list.

1. **Find your theme of choice.** That's right, this works with any theme out there. Go with the Notes Blog Core theme, available at `http://notesblog.com/core`, for this example. You can apply this to just about any theme though (including the Twenty Ten).

2. **Copy page.php and rename it page-archives.php.** To make it easy to see that the template file is a Page template, name it page-X, where X is "archives," in this case. You want to base this Page template on the basic page.php template, so just copy the contents of that one to a file named page-archives.php.

3. **Make it a Page template.** At the very top of page-archives.php, add the code snippet that tells WordPress that this is a Page template. Name it "Archives," since that's what it is.

```php
<?php
/*
Template Name: Archives
*/
?>
```

4. **Add the archive goodness.** Keep the loop around in this template to make it easy to alter the text at the very top of the archives page, should you want to. Find the loop, and then find the `the_content` tag. Below it, add the archives code, which is this:

```php
<h2><?php _e('Browse by Month:", "notesblog");?></h2>
<ul>
    <?php wp_get_archives('type=monthly'); ?>
</ul>
<h2><?php _e("Browse by Category:", "notesblog");?></h2>
<ul>
    <?php wp_list_categories('title_li='); ?>
</ul>
<h2><?php _e("Browse by Tag:", "notesblog");?></h2>
<?php wp_tag_cloud('smallest=8&largest=28&number=0&orderby=name&order=ASC'); ?>
```

What you have here is an h2 heading that is localized so that translated versions of the theme can edit it. Then there's a ul list block that outputs the monthly archive links. Next, another h2 and a category list in its own ul block. Finally you've got an h2 heading and then the tag cloud, and that's about it.

Just for clarity's sake, here's the full page-archives.php, which is now done:

```php
<?php
/*
Template Name: Archives
*/
?>

<?php get_header(); ?>

        <div id="content" class="widecolumn">
```

```php
<?php if (have_posts()) : while (have_posts()) : the_post(); ?>

                        <div id="post-<?php the_ID(); ?>" <?php post_class();
?>>

                            <h1><?php the_title(); ?></h1>
                            <div class="entry">
                                <?php the_content(); ?>
                                <h2><?php _e("Browse by Month:", "notes-
blog");?></h2>

                                <ul>
                                    <?php wp_get_
archives('type=monthly'); ?>
                                </ul>
                                <h2><?php _e("Browse by Category:",
"notesblog");?></h2>

                                <ul>
                                    <?php wp_list_
categories('title_li='); ?>
                                </ul>
                                <h2><?php _e("Browse by Tag:", "notes-
blog");?></h2>

                                <?php wp_tag_cloud('smallest=8&largest=2
8&number=0&orderby=name&order=ASC'); ?>
                            </div>
                        </div>

                <?php endwhile; ?>
            <?php endif; ?>

            </div>

<?php get_sidebar(); ?>
<?php get_footer(); ?>
```

5. **Upload page-archives.php to your theme folder.** You obviously need to upload the Page template to use it, so do that now. Place it in your theme's `wp-content/themes` folder.

6. **Create the Page in WordPress.** You need to create a Page for your archives in WordPress. For this example, keep it simple and call it Archives (see Figure 3-10), and make sure that it gets the permalink "archives" since that will look good. A short blurb in the content area introduces the visitor to your Archives Page. Above all, it shows the archives functionality since it is output where `the_content()` is, and you put your archives code below it.

7. **Pick the Archives template and admire your work.** The only thing left to do is to pick the Archives template in the drop-down box to the right on your Edit Page screen. Save the Archives Page (as in Figure 3-11), and it will use your template, which means that it will include and output the code from page-archives.php.

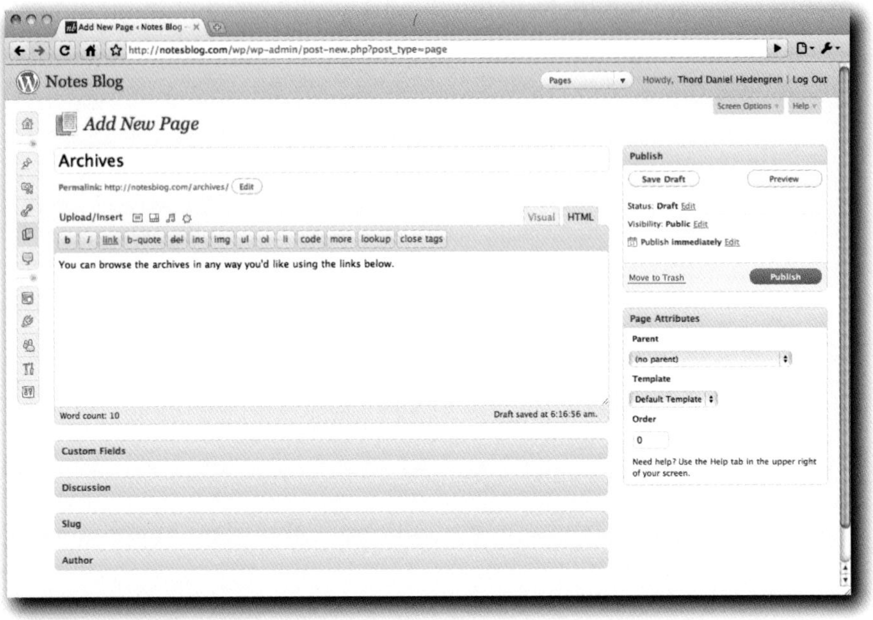

Figure 3-10: Create the Archives Page

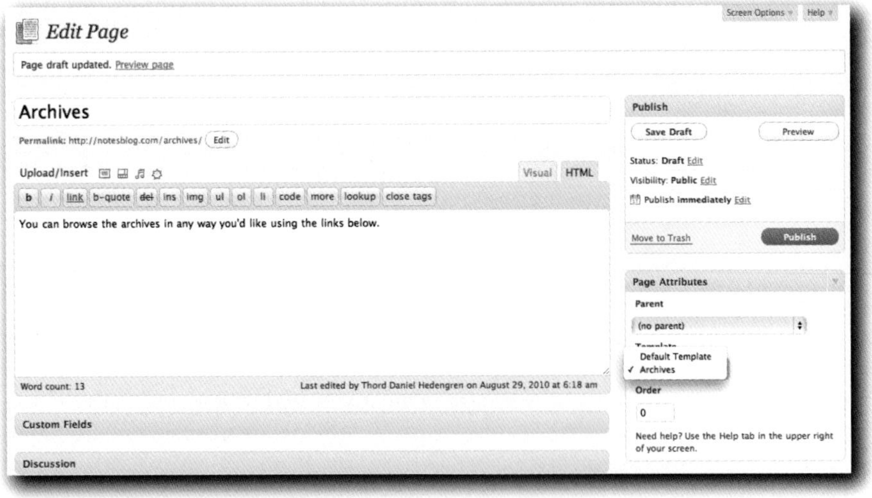

Figure 3-11: Select the Archives Page template

Figure 3-12 shows you what you have created, pretty simple, huh?

Figure 3-12: The somewhat unstyled end result on notesblog.com/archives/

FINDING YOUR WAY WITH CUSTOM MENUS

As of WordPress 3.0, you can create menus from the admin panel. This fancy little thing can be likened to a widget area, but for menus created on the Menus interface in WordPress admin panel, under Appearance, if your theme supports it. I'm likening them with widget areas for two reasons:

- As with widget areas (also known as dynamic sidebars), you define them in functions.php and then add the defined areas to your theme's template files.
- Managing the actual menus in the admin panel is fairly similar to widget management.

There's also the fact that your Menus (as in menus created with Menus in the admin panel — yes, it's the pages/Pages semantics all over again) will work perfectly well on a lot of widget areas thanks to the Menus widget (see Figure 3-13). That's right. You can create a menu using Menus and drop it in any widget area, using said widget.

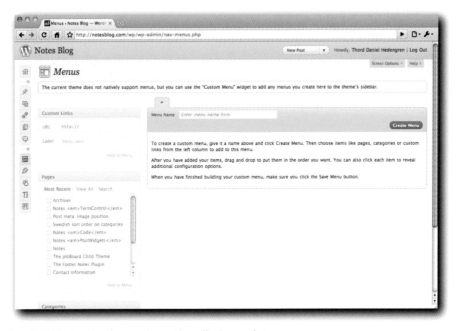

Figure 3-13: The Menus interface on a theme with no official support for it

Before you get to the actual code for adding this feature, remember that Menus are WordPress 3.0 and later only. If you need to support older versions, you can't use it. If you still want to add it, check whether the function exists, just like when you include widget areas.

If you do use the Menus feature on an older version of WordPress, it will degrade to display-ing Pages with `wp_list_pages()`. While your menu could very well consist of just links to Pages, that is not always the case. If you're building menus for your site and need to keep it backwards compatible, you should stay clear of the Menus feature. After all, you can't just not show a navigational element, and more often than not you don't want that list of Pages that `wp_list_pages()` will get you. Better to use a traditional widget area and make sure that the use of the menu widget element (see Figure 3-14) will look good for your 3.0 users.

DECLARE A MENU AREA

As with widget areas, you need to define menu areas in your theme's functions.php. The code is simple enough:

```
function register_menus() {
        register_nav_menu( 'top-navigation', __( 'Top Navigation' ) );
}


add_action( 'init', 'register_menus' );
```

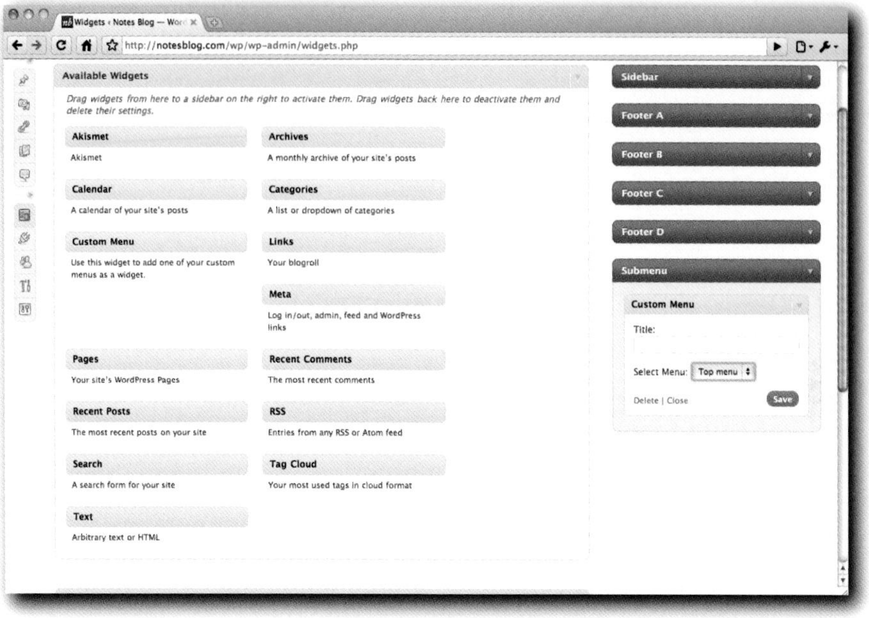

Figure 3-14: A Custom Menu widget on the Available Widgets screen of your admin panel

This adds a menu called Top Navigation to your theme, for use on the Menus screen in the admin panel. The last line actually adds the functionality; without it nothing will happen.

As with widget areas, you can add several menu areas at once. The following code adds areas meant for both the sidebar and the footer. You need to declare these in an array; the preceding code will only work with a single menu.

```
function register_menus() {
        register_nav_menus(
                array(
                        'top-navigation' => __( 'Top Navigation' ),
                        'side-menu' => __( 'Side Menu' ),
                        'bottom-navigation' => __( 'Bottom Navigation' ),)
                );
        }

add_action( 'init', 'register_menus' );
```

That's it! The only thing left is to actually add the menu areas to your theme's template files.

ADD A MENU AREA TO YOUR TEMPLATE FILES

As you would expect, there's a template tag for adding a menu area to your theme. The template tag is called `wp_nav_menu()`, and if you have only one menu added, it will output that, otherwise default to a list of Pages via `wp_list_pages()`.

Obviously you want to control which menu goes where, so you have to let `wp_nav_menu()` know. Starting with the menu called Top Navigation in the previous example, pass the theme location parameter from your declaration to `wp_nav_menu()`, hence telling WordPress which menu area you want it to output.

```php
<?php wp_nav_menu( array( 'theme_location' => 'top-navigation' ) ); ?>
```

Adding a menu to this area using the Menu admin panel will output it, enclosed in a `div` with the CSS class `menu`. That's default output, but you can control that. Suppose your sidebar menu from above wants to sit in an `li` instead, because it is enclosed in a `ul#sidebar` item.

```php
<?php wp_nav_menu( array(
        'container'                     => 'li',
        'container_class'       => 'menu-sidebar',
        'theme_location'        => 'top-navigation'
) ); ?>
```

As you can see, the code uses a different class for this one in order to style it differently. You can also add an ID and control what goes before and after the actual menu within the area, to name a few things. Something that might be handy is a different fallback tag, since `wp_list_pages()` might not be ideal at all times. Have it output your categories instead, using `wp_list_categories()`:

```php
<?php wp_nav_menu( array(
        'container'                     => 'li',
        'container_class'       => 'menu-sidebar',
        'fallback_cb'       => 'wp_list_categories',
        'theme_location'        => 'top-navigation'
) ); ?>
```

Pretty neat, huh?

EXAMPLE: ADDING A MENU AREA

In this example you add an area for menus in a theme? It's really simple, and you can throw out any hard-pressed custom menu solutions you may have found or created over the years.

1. **Declare the menu.** Call this menu "Main Menu" and give it the location name "main-menu" since that just makes sense. The former is what you see in the admin panel, the latter will be used with the `wp_nav_menus()` tag in the template files. The last line adds the functionality. Oh, and you use the array format here despite not needing to. This makes it easy for you to add more menus, if you want to.

```php
<?php
        function register_menus() {
                register_nav_menus(
                        array(
                                'main-menu' => __( 'Main Menu' )
```

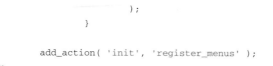

```
                                   );
                }

        add_action( 'init', 'register_menus' );
    ?>
```

2. **Create a menu.** Now create a menu so that you have something to output. In the admin panel, click Appearance, and then Menus. Just fill it with something suitable. Perhaps add a Page, a category, and a custom link to some other site that you have.

3. **Add wp_nav_menus().** Right, so now you add your spanking new menu to your theme. You'll use it in header.php, but you can put it anywhere of course.

```
<?php wp_nav_menu( array( 'theme_location' => 'main-menu' ) ); ?>
```

That's it!

4. **A bit short and simple, right?** Let's add another menu area for good measure, adding to the code in functions.php:

```
<?php
        function register_menus() {
                register_nav_menus(
                        array(
                                'main-menu' => __( 'Main Menu' ),
                                'footer-menu' => __( 'Footer Menu' )
                        );
                }

        add_action( 'init', 'register_menus' );
    ?>
```

Now add this to your footer.php file (but again, you could use it anywhere). Because you want this menu to behave slightly differently, give it another CSS class:

```
<?php wp_nav_menu( array(
        'container_class'        => 'menu-footer',
        'theme_location'         => 'top-navigation'
) ); ?>
```

Obviously you can style this in style.css (or any other stylesheet that you might be loading), so just make the type bold for good measure:

```
.menu-footer {
        font-weight:bold;
        }
```

Still simple; still easy to work with.

CHANGING YOUR HEADER IMAGE

The feature that allows you to change the header image (Figure 3-15 shows the default image in the Twenty Ten theme) has been created a ton of times in the past, but with WordPress version 3.0, you actually have a custom header function to work with. This is primarily aimed at simpler sites where changing the image header is the only customization needed, but it could come in handy when building larger sites as well.

Figure 3-15: The header image as it is used in the Twenty Ten theme

Adding custom headers is simple enough, and done in functions.php. First you define the data for the header with four constants. Then you write two functions: one for theme view and one for admin panel view. Finally you enable the whole thing with `add_custom_image_header()` with said functions passed as parameters.

DEFINE THE HEADER IN FUNCTIONS.PHP

The basic definition of the header listed in the Codex are these:

```php
<?php
    define('HEADER_TEXTCOLOR', 'ffffff');
    define('HEADER_IMAGE', '%s/images/default_header.jpg');
        // %s is the template dir uri
    define('HEADER_IMAGE_WIDTH', 775);
        // use width and height appropriate for your theme
    define('HEADER_IMAGE_HEIGHT', 200);
?>
```

However, I do not recommend the second line in the preceding code snippet, which fetches the default header image from your theme's directory. By using the following line instead, you fetch the default image using `get_bloginfo()` and its parameter `stylesheet_directory`.

```php
define('HEADER_IMAGE', get_bloginfo('stylesheet_directory') .
'/images/banner.jpg');
```

Now, WordPress will use the stylesheet directory rather than the theme's directory, which means that if you're building a child theme based on this particular parent theme, it looks in the child theme's directory, since that is where the primary stylesheet sits. Obviously you can just go with the default lines if you know that you'll never build a child theme upon your theme. The second example works either way, so you may as well use it.

DISPLAY THE HEADER IN YOUR THEME

The functions that show the header image are simple enough, and are passed to `add_custom_image_header()` in the end. First, you need one to display the image in your

94

theme, which you attach to the `wp_head` action hook — basically when WordPress starts to load your site. What you put in the function is a CSS that will then output the header image.

```php
<?php
    function site_header_style() {
        ?><style type="text/css">
            #header {
                background: url(<?php header_image(); ?>);
            }
        </style><?php
    }
?>
```

Note that you need to step out of PHP for a bit unless you want to echo the whole stylesheet part. Obviously you could make this as advanced as you'd like, with lots of styles and nifty stuff.

The second function shows the header image in the admin panel. Here you just add width and height to a pre-defined CSS ID called `#headerimg`, which is what you use to display the header in the custom header admin panel. There is little point in messing with this function, but obviously you can.

```php
<?php
    function admin_header_style() {
        ?><style type="text/css">
            #headimg {
                width: <?php echo HEADER_IMAGE_WIDTH; ?>px;
                height: <?php echo HEADER_IMAGE_HEIGHT; ?>px;
            }
        </style><?php
    }
?>
```

Last but not least, you need to enable the whole thing and pass these two functions as parameters using `add_custom_image_header()`. The first parameter is the function that the theme uses to display the header, and the second parameter is used in the admin panel.

```php
add_custom_image_header('site_header_style', 'admin_header_style');
```

The whole thing would look like this in functions.php:

```php
<?php
    define('HEADER_TEXTCOLOR', 'ffffff');
    define('HEADER_IMAGE', get_bloginfo('stylesheet_directory') . '/images/
banner.jpg');
    define('HEADER_IMAGE_WIDTH', 775);
    define('HEADER_IMAGE_HEIGHT', 200);
```

```php
// The site header function
function site_header_style() {
    ?><style type="text/css">
        #header {
            background: url(<?php header_image(); ?>);
        }
    </style><?php
}

// The admin header function
function admin_header_style() {
    ?><style type="text/css">
        #headimg {
            width: <?php echo HEADER_IMAGE_WIDTH; ?>px;
            height: <?php echo HEADER_IMAGE_HEIGHT; ?>px;
        }
    </style><?php
}

// Enable!
add_custom_image_header('site_header_style', 'admin_header_style');
?>
```

EXAMPLE: ADDING A CUSTOM HEADER

In this example, you add a custom header to a theme; any theme that doesn't support it already will do. You do the whole thing in functions.php, so open that.

1. **Define text color and default header.** You need to add four constants to make sure that the custom header feature will work. Start by defining the text color and the default image, adding it to functions.php.

```php
<?php
    define('HEADER_TEXTCOLOR', 'ffffff');
    define('HEADER_IMAGE', get_bloginfo('stylesheet_directory') . '/img/
header-default.jpg');
?>
```

2. **Set the image width and height.** You want to decide the header image's width and height. This is important because the admin panel will scale to this should you upload something larger. This example is 940 pixels wide and 130 pixels high, but you should obviously make sure this suits the header area in your theme.

```php
<?php
    define('HEADER_TEXTCOLOR', 'ffffff');
    define('HEADER_IMAGE', get_bloginfo('stylesheet_directory') . '/img/
header-default.jpg');
    define('HEADER_IMAGE_WIDTH', 940);
    define('HEADER_IMAGE_HEIGHT', 130);
?>
```

3. **Add some header style for your theme.** The following code adds the header image, using a function that you later can include when enabling the feature.

```php
<?php
        define('HEADER_TEXTCOLOR', 'ffffff');
        define('HEADER_IMAGE', get_bloginfo('stylesheet_directory') . '/img/
    header-default.jpg');
        define('HEADER_IMAGE_WIDTH', 940);
        define('HEADER_IMAGE_HEIGHT', 130);


        // The site header function
        function site_header_style() {
            ?><style type="text/css">
                div#header {
                    background: url(<?php header_image(); ?>);
                }
            </style><?php
        }
?>
```

This code adds your new header image as a background image to div#header; obviously your theme may have another element where you'd like the header to show up. You might also want to add some borders or other CSS to make it fit into your theme of choice.

4. **And some style for the admin.** You need another function for display in the admin panel. You can just set width and height to the ID #headerimg since that's what's used in admin.

```php
<?php
        define('HEADER_TEXTCOLOR', 'ffffff');
        define('HEADER_IMAGE', get_bloginfo('stylesheet_directory') . '/img/
    header-default.jpg');
        define('HEADER_IMAGE_WIDTH', 940);
        define('HEADER_IMAGE_HEIGHT', 130);


        // The site header function
        function site_header_style() {
            ?><style type="text/css">
                div#header {
                    background: url(<?php header_image(); ?>);
                }
            </style><?php
        }


        // The admin header function
        function admin_header_style() {
            ?><style type="text/css">
                #headimg {
                    width: <?php echo HEADER_IMAGE_WIDTH; ?>px;
                    height: <?php echo HEADER_IMAGE_HEIGHT; ?>px;
                }
            </style><?php
        }
?>
```

97

5. **Enable the whole thing.** Let's wrap this up by enabling the custom header feature. You do that with `add_custom_header_image()` to which you pass first the function for the header in our theme, and then the function for use in the admin panel.

```php
<?php
        define('HEADER_TEXTCOLOR', 'ffffff');
        define('HEADER_IMAGE', get_bloginfo('stylesheet_directory') . '/img/
header-default.jpg');
        define('HEADER_IMAGE_WIDTH', 940);
        define('HEADER_IMAGE_HEIGHT', 130);

        // The site header function
        function site_header_style() {
            ?><style type="text/css">
                div#header {
                    background: url(<?php header_image(); ?>);
                }
            </style><?php
        }

        // The admin header function
        function admin_header_style() {
            ?><style type="text/css">
                #headimg {
                    width: <?php echo HEADER_IMAGE_WIDTH; ?>px;
                    height: <?php echo HEADER_IMAGE_HEIGHT; ?>px;
                }
            </style><?php
        }

        // Enable!
        add_custom_image_header('site_header_style', 'admin_header_style');

?>
```

ADJUSTING YOUR SITE BACKGROUND

The custom background feature is another handy little item you can use from your theme. It lets you alter the background image or color of a site. In fact, what it does alter is the stylesheet for the `body` tag, so it might not work as expected if your theme has a lot of styling in the `body` already.

Adding the feature is almost ridiculously simple. Just add the following tag to functions.php and the panel pops up in the admin panel, and that's it. Yes, that's right, this tiny template tag, along with the feature activation tag that you add to the code, outputs the necessary style code, and so on, in your theme. Assuming your theme doesn't do something that nulls out the included styles, it should just work.

```php
<?php
        // Enable custom backgrounds
        add_theme_support('custom-background');

        // Activate the admin panels
        add_custom_background();
?>
```

This attaches the stylesheet code to the `wp_head` action hook. The only thing left to do is make sure that your theme has the template tag `body_class()` in your body tag. It works much like `post_class()` does for your post container (usually a `div`), adding styles that gives you additional control. This line should be in your theme's header.php, otherwise you should replace your body tag with it:

```
<body <?php body_class(); ?>>
```

You can get the nitty-gritty details in the Codex `http://codex.wordpress.org/Function_Reference/add_custom_background`, but most likely you don't want to mess with anything here. Just embrace the simplicity of this feature; you'll have plenty of time to pull your hair out over annoying features later on!

WRAPPING IT UP

By now you should have a better idea of what you can do with themes, what features are just around the corner, and so on. The knowledge of how you work with template tags and pass parameters to them will make it a lot easier when looking up things online for your projects, and conditional tags will make your themes more flexible.

From here on I mix practical with conceptual, putting what you've learned to good use. You've got the basics now, so it's time to start doing things, beginning with child themes. Child themes are a wonderful way to work with themes, further separating the code from the design. That's up next!

II

HACKING A THEME

PART

4

USING CHILD THEMES

SO YOU THINK you know all you need to know about theming to get your hands dirty, eh? In a way you do. Now you can hack away at just about any theme, which you did in Part I; but, there is more to it still.

Theme design is comprised of many elements. You've got your template tags, conditional tags, custom post types and taxonomies, custom backgrounds and headers, widget areas, and so on.

These things are cool, and important for the theme designer to know. A veritable key to the themes universe, as well as to a beautiful and feature-rich WordPress site.

But what is often overlooked, and ironically the most important thing that can save you time and headaches, are child themes. If you want to design a WordPress theme by altering an existing one, you can take it to the next level with a child theme.

THE CHILD THEME CONCEPT

As the name implies, child themes rely on another theme that serves as a parent for the child. The child theme borrows everything from the parent, unless the child theme contains the necessary code itself. So in other words, if your child theme has a single.php template file, it'll use that, but if it doesn't, it'll use the one from the parent theme.

WHY ARE CHILD THEMES SO GREAT?

First of all, it depends on what you're trying to do. Child themes are not always the solution, especially if you're looking at heavyweight sites with tons of visitors and every byte counts, and costs money. Since a child theme often overrides parts of its parent theme, this may result in some code overhead. It is worth keeping in mind when deciding if a project should use a child theme or not.

That aside, the brilliant part of a child theme is that you can move all your code into a single theme: the parent theme folder. In other words, your original theme (that is, the parent) acts as a framework that contains all the core functionality, such as the content loops (although you can override those too, of course), basic markup, template files, and so on. In short, everything that is tied to features within WordPress sits in the parent theme. Whenever a new feature is rolled out in a new version of the software, you change it in your parent theme, leaving the child theme unaffected and saving you time. The same applies for bugs and other changes you may need to change over time. This is especially true if you have several sites sharing the same parent theme, which I get to in a bit.

Another way to use child themes is when you download a theme that you want to change. Put the change in the child theme and let the parent theme author worry about keeping it up to date. This leaves you with just making sure that updates are applied properly. When you update the parent theme, none of your own edits will be overwritten, which is the case if you hack the theme itself. Because your work sits in the child theme, it isn't affected by an update to the parent. This, incidentally, is the only sound way to hack a theme, if you plan on following its development cycle.

So what you've got is two ways to work with child themes. If you've found a theme you like that you want to alter a bit, you put your changes in a child theme and continue to update the parent. Or, if you've developed a theme of your own that you plan to use as a basis, the parent theme, that is, to several sites (I discuss this later in this chapter), then you're responsible for the parent theme updates. When applying these updates, you'll be rolling out your new features automatically. Figure 4-1 shows a site that uses three child themes.

Figure 4-1: The Thematic theme with a few child themes

Get them from http://themeshaper.com

HOW CHILD THEMES WORK

Child themes are easy to create, as long as you grasp the basics (see Figure 4-2 for an overview of child themes and template files). You are building a theme that consists of, in its most minimal form, a style.css template file. A child theme can also contain any other template files, including functions.php, as well as images, Java Scripts, and so on. In all, it is a regular theme, with the exception that it needs a parent theme.

The files in the child theme sit in a folder, just like all other themes. Template files are created and built in the same way. Really, you need to understand that a child theme is, in every way, a WordPress theme. The only difference is that it isn't complete by itself. It needs its parent.

Every file in a child theme automatically overrides its namesake in the parent theme (except functions.php, which I get to in a bit). That means that if you have a category template (being category.php) in your child theme, and also in your parent theme, the child theme file will be used. WordPress checks the child theme for templates first, and then the parent.

You could have a template file for everything in your child theme, essentially making your parent theme unnecessary. I probably don't have to point out how unnecessary that is, as the whole point for using a child theme is to separate child theme changes from the parent theme. You could liken it to how you separate PHP and HTML code from CSS styles with an external stylesheet.

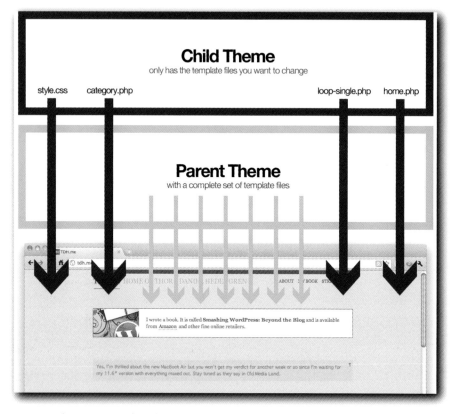

Figure 4-2: A schematic overview of how child themes work

CREATING A CHILD THEME

Creating a child theme is easy, which is a good thing since you'll have your hands full building cool sites as it is. The only file you need to create is style.css, but most likely you'll want to add a couple of template files as well. Anyway, style.css is the only mandatory one, and it is actually just one puny little extra line of code needed to tell WordPress that this is a child theme:

```
Template: my-template-theme-of-choice
```

Just swap "my-template-theme-of-choice" to whichever theme you'd like to use as a parent theme. Do keep in mind that you want to type the parent theme's folder name here, not the actual name! So for Twenty Ten, you don't type **Twenty Ten** (the theme name) but rather the folder name, which is `twentyten`. If you're uncertain what the folder is, just check `wp-content/themes` to find out. Assuming your parent theme is actually uploaded to that folder, that is. It needs to be, after all.

That little template line goes in the familiar top block of style.css in your theme declaration. In the following code, I've added it to a dummy child theme header, just to show it in its right element.

```
/*
Theme Name: My Dummy Child Theme
Theme URI: http://my-dummy-url.com
Description: My dummy theme description for my dummy child theme.
Author: My Name
Author URI: http://my-url.com/
Template: twentyten
Version: 1.0
*/
```

That's that, actually. With a style.css in a folder, uploaded to your `wp-content/themes` folder just like any other theme, along with the parent theme also residing in the themes folder, you're ready to go. You'll find your child theme in the WordPress admin panel under Appearance settings in Themes. You activate it there, just like any other theme.

GETTING PARENT THEME STYLES INTO A CHILD THEME

However, you probably want one more thing in your style.css, besides any extra styles for your child theme. Template files in child themes override the ones in the parent theme. So your child theme loads its style.css file, and not the one in the parent theme. You'll then lose all the styles from the parent theme, which is probably not what you want to happen.

Luckily there is an easy way to remedy that: Just import the parent theme's stylesheet first into your child theme's style.css, but place it after the theme header.

```
/*
Theme Name: My Dummy Child Theme
Theme URI: http://my-dummy-url.com
Description: My dummy theme description for my dummy child theme.
Author: My Name
Author URI: http://my-url.com/
Template: twentyten
Version: 1.0
*/
```

```
@import url('../twentyten/style.css');
```

Now you can add whatever styles you need for your child below the `@import` rule. Load your parent theme's stylesheet first to make sure that you have a basis to work on. Simple and neat. If your parent theme is built around several stylesheets, you may need to import them too, either in the child theme's style.css, or in its header.php (if you add one).

FINDING IMAGES IN CHILD THEMES

Another thing worth knowing before you build a child theme for real is how WordPress finds images that reside in the child theme's folder. Normally you use the `bloginfo()` template tag with the `template_directory` parameter to find your theme's folder when including images in you template files.

```
<img src="<?php bloginfo('template_directory'); ?>/image.jpg" alt="Alt texts are
    nice" />
```

You can do that in your child theme as well, but it will actually lead to your parent theme's folder. It is, after all, the parent theme directory. Although it may seem a bit confusing, it does make sense.

Now, you want to be able to include images in your child theme as well, and output them in the same easy fashion that you're used to. That's why I resort to the `stylesheet_direc-tory` parameter instead. The following code tells `bloginfo()` to look for where the primary stylesheet sits (which is style.css, of course), and points us to the child theme's folder.

```
<img src="<?php bloginfo('stylesheet_directory'); ?>/image.jpg" alt="Alt texts are
    nice" />
```

That you can pull images from both your child theme folder (and subdirectories within it) and your parent theme's folder (again, subdirectories too) can be very handy, so keep it in mind.

FUNCTIONS AND CHILD THEMES

The functions.php template file is the only one that doesn't behave like the rest of the flock, and it should come as no surprise that it is functions.php. Your child theme can have a functions.php file that contains just about whatever you want as usual, but it won't actually replace the file in your parent theme. Rather, if there is a functions.php file in a child theme, WordPress loads it first, before loading functions.php in the parent theme. Yes, both files are loaded. The file in the child theme goes first.

What does this mean? Well, first of all, if you need to do away with any function in the parent theme's functions.php, you can deregister that function. This one removes the custom Read more feature `twentyten_excerpt_more` in the Twenty Ten theme for example.

```
remove_filter( 'excerpt_more', 'twentyten_excerpt_more' );
```

You could also take said function and make it do something else. Let's just change the text that is output when you use the Read more feature. This code snippet works in a child theme using Twenty Ten as a parent theme because it will change its function (`twentyten_excerpt_more` mentioned above). It starts with a function, which I apply to the action hook `excerpt_more` that is already present in the Twenty Ten theme. However, since Twenty Ten already has a function attached to that (that is, `twentyten_excerpt_more`), I need to deregister that before registering our brand new one, called `custom_excerpt_more`.

```
// The kind of function I want
function custom_excerpt_more($more){
        return '<a href="'. get_permalink() . '">' . get_the_title() . '  is
    over here!</a>';
}
```

```
// Remove the default twentyten_excerpt_more from the excerpt_more hook
remove_filter( 'excerpt_more', 'twentyten_excerpt_more' );

// Add our new function from above, custom_excerpt_more, to the excerpt_more hook
add_filter ('excerpt_more', 'custom_excerpt_more' );
```

Not very hard at all, right?

So your child theme's functions.php file won't actually overwrite the functions in the parent theme's functions.php unless you want it to. That means that you can keep them around (probably a good idea more often than not). Or, you can load them up with new stuff that fits your child theme better. And you can add new functions to the child theme's functions.php, completely independent of the parent theme. You don't have to do things with the parent theme's functions at all, you can do new stuff too.

EXAMPLE: CREATING A SIMPLE CHILD THEME

Now you can put your spanking new knowledge to good work by creating a simple child theme for the Twenty Ten theme (Figure 4-3 shows the default WordPress theme). This child theme won't change much, just move the sidebar from the right-hand side, to the left-, for this particular project.

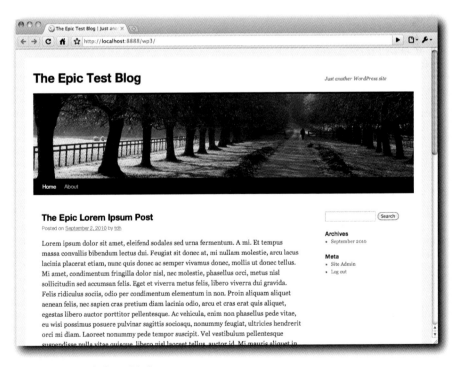

Figure 4-3: Twenty Ten fresh out of the box

1. **Create the child theme.** Create a folder for your child theme and name it Twenty Ten Left Sidebar. Name the folder `twentyten-ls`, that way it will be easy to find in your FTP software in the future, sitting next to the Twenty Ten folder.

   Every child theme needs a style.css file with the theme information, so create a brand new file. Get the necessary theme header information into it, along with the `import` rule that loads the Twenty Ten stylesheet. You want that too, after all.

```
/*
Theme Name: Twenty Ten Left Sidebar
Theme URI: http://tdh.me/wordpress/
Description: A simple child theme for Twenty Ten that moves the side column to
  the left.
Author: Thord Daniel Hedengren
Author URI: http://tdh.me/
Template: twentyten
Version: 1.0
.

        This here is just to show that you can add a comment
        here as well. Fancy huh?

.
*/


/* Import the Twenty Ten stylesheet */
    @import url('../twentyten/style.css');
```

2. **Find the elements to change.** Right, so you want the sidebar on the left rather than on the right. This is a simple positioning issue that you can address in your style.css file in the child theme, but you still need to figure out what you want to change. Depending on your Web browser, you'll want to use different kinds of tools to inspect the code (for example, Firebug for Firefox, the Inspect Element right-click command in Chrome and Safari, and so on). Use whatever you usually use to inspect HTML files from your Web browser.

   Some inspection shows that the content area (found in Figure 4-4) is controlled by `div#container`, and the right column (found in Figure 4-5) uses `div#primary` for positioning. Actually, `div#secondary` is used as well according to the code, so add that in there too.

Figure 4-4: The content area is positioned by `div#container`

Figure 4-5: The side column is positioned by `div#primary`

3. **Add the necessary styles.** You're ready to add the necessary styles, so go back to style.css in your child theme. All you need to do is change the floating on `div#container` to `right`, and `div#primary` to `left` to achieve what you want. You'll add the styling after the import rule.

```
/*
Theme Name: Twenty Ten Left Sidebar
Theme URI: http://tdh.me/wordpress/
Description: A simple child theme for Twenty Ten that moves the side column to
   the left.
Author: Thord Daniel Hedengren
Author URI: http://tdh.me/
Template: twentyten
Version: 1.0
.

        This here is just to show that you can add a comment
        here as well. Fancy huh?

.
*/

/* Import the Twenty Ten stylesheet */
@import url('../twentyten/style.css');

/* Move the content column to the right */
div#container { float:right; }

/* Move the side column to the left */
   div#primary, div#secondary { float:left; }
```

4. **Activate the child theme.** After saving and uploading your child theme, it appears in the WordPress admin panel, under Appearance settings in Themes. If you want a nice thumbnail image, you'll have to add a screenshot.png in your child theme's folder, as well.

   Activate, and voila! The right column is now on the left (as you can see in Figure 4-6), and it will stay there even when Twenty Ten, your parent theme, is updated as all the changes you've made sit in a child theme.

Figure 4-6: Twenty Ten Left Sidebar really does have the sidebar to the left

THE PERFECT TWENTY TEN PROJECT

Since child themes work best when you don't have to make dramatic alterations to the parent themes, you should consider what you want to build and how that fits with Twenty Ten. Not all sites are ideal, so compare your goal with Twenty Ten and decide whether it is suitable or not.

A few things to think about include:

- Is the main layout similar?
- Is the content flow similar?
- Is this the ideal way to deliver the content?
- Can I fit all the ads, promotional messages, and similar blocks that I need?
- Do I need the extra features, such as custom headers and such, or is that something I need to remove?
- Will I need to overwrite a lot of files in my child theme?

Any child theme should consist of as little code as possible, from the stylesheet to actual PHP and HTML in the template files. The less you need to override in your child theme, the better. That's why it is sometimes a better idea to build your own parent theme, and then use child themes on top of that.

TWENTY TEN AND CHILD THEMES

Using Twenty Ten as the parent theme for child themes is a good idea for several reasons. First of all, the theme is pretty clean and sweet design-wise, although you may disagree. However, the fact that it is so clean makes it easy to make minor changes to, and you get all those features as a bonus. That means that minimal child theming lets you change the look and feel of the theme, while maintaining the custom header image functionality, for example.

Second, Twenty Ten is the default theme in WordPress 3.0, which means that it is widespread. While it might not be the default theme forever, you can expect a majority of users will have it in their themes folder. If you intend to release your child theme in the wild, and not just keep it for yourself, then that's a good thing.

Third, as the default theme, a ton of eyes have reviewed it during its development. So it showcases WordPress functions in a good and modern way. If that's not enough for you, the mere number of comments in the code will help you learn theming. Among those things that actually matter for child theming is the `get_template_part()` usage for fetching the loop, which I've talked about before.

These are the things that make Twenty Ten suitable to build child themes upon. You can hack it straight up if you'd like, fork it into a different theme and be happy with that, but that would mean that you'd miss out on the automatic updates to the theme. Child themes are always the way to go in these cases. So unless you're making drastic alterations, you should go with a child theme setup.

EXAMPLE: ADDING A SECOND SIDEBAR

You've been idle long enough; it's time to do something cool with Twenty Ten, like add an additional sidebar with its very own widget area of course. You'll add it to the left column since a lot of people like tri-column designs. And you'll do it as a child theme, naturally.

1. **Create the child theme.** To create the child theme, which you can call Twenty Ten Tr, create a folder called `twentyten-tri`, drop it in `wp-content/themes`, and add a style.css file with the following content:

```
/*
Theme Name: Twenty Ten Tri
Theme URI: http://tdh.me/wordpress/twentyten-tri/
Description: A child theme for Twenty Ten that adds an extra sidebar.
Author: Thord Daniel Hedengren
Author URI: http://tdh.me/
Template: twentyten
Version: 1.0
.

        As made famous by the wonderful book
        Smashing WordPress Themes: Making WordPress Beautiful

.
*/
```

```
/* Import the Twenty Ten stylesheet */
   @import url('../twentyten/style.css');
```

2. **Add another widget area.** The left sidebar needs a widget area. To add that, you need to create a functions.php for the child theme as well. This one will load first, in addition to the parent theme's functions.php file, so the widget area will just be added.

```php
<?php
        register_sidebar( array(
                'name' => __( 'Left Widget Area', 'twentyten' ),
                'id' => 'left-widget-area',
                'description' => __( 'The left hand sidebar widget area',
    'twentyten' ),
                'before_widget' => '<li id="%1$s" class="widget-container
    %2$s">',
                'after_widget' => '</li>',
                'before_title' => '<h3 class="widget-title">',
                'after_title' => '</h3>',
        ) );
    ?>
```

The widget code comes from Twenty Ten's functions.php and the right widget area in particular, since you want to retain the same style to the left. Name the widget area Left Widget Area (shown in the right column in Figure 4-7).

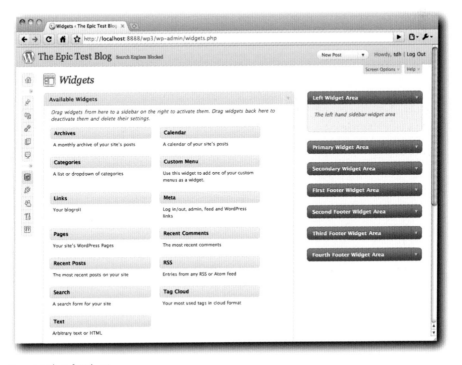

Figure 4-7: The Left Widget Area

115

3. **Create the left sidebar template file.** You need something to show in the left-hand widget area. That's why you'll create a file called sidebar-left.php for your child theme, containing everything you need to output the Left Widget Area. This is what's in it, based on the code from Twenty Ten's own sidebar.php to keep it in the same style.

```php
<?php
/* The left hand sidebar, called with get_sidebar('left') in header.php */
?>

                <div id="leftsidebar" class="widget-area" role="complementary">
                    <ul class="xoxo">

<?php if ( ! dynamic_sidebar( 'left-widget-area' ) ) : ?>

                        <li>
                                Hey buddy, you need to get some widget in here!
                        </li>

                    <?php endif; // end left widget area ?>
                    </ul>
                </div><!-- #leftsidebar .widget-area -->
```

Why is it called sidebar-left.php, then? That's so that you can call it with the get_sidebar() template tag, and just pass the parameter 'left' to it. You could also have called it sidebar-arthur.php and pass the parameter 'arthur', but that doesn't make as much sense, now does it?

4. **Add a new header.php.** The easiest way to get the left column into every template is to copy header.php from Twenty Ten into your child theme. Then you'll just add get_sidebar('left') after div#main and hence get it included before the content and right sidebar.

```php
<?php
/**
 * The Header for our theme.
 *
 * Displays all of the <head> section and everything up till <div id="main">
 *
 * @package WordPress
 * @subpackage Twenty_Ten
 * @since Twenty Ten 1.0
 */
?><!DOCTYPE html>
<html <?php language_attributes(); ?>>
<head>
<meta charset="<?php bloginfo( 'charset' ); ?>" />
<title><?php
        /*
         * Print the <title> tag based on what is being viewed.
         */
        global $page, $paged;
```

```php
        wp_title( '|', true, 'right' );

        // Add the blog name.
        bloginfo( 'name' );

        // Add the blog description for the home/front page.
        $site_description = get_bloginfo( 'description', 'display' );
        if ( $site_description && ( is_home() || is_front_page() ) )
                echo " | $site_description";

        // Add a page number if necessary:
        if ( $paged >= 2 || $page >= 2 )
                echo ' | ' . sprintf( __( 'Page %s', 'twentyten' ), max( $paged,
$page ) );

        ?></title>
<link rel="profile" href="http://gmpg.org/xfn/11" />
<link rel="stylesheet" type="text/css" media="all" href="<?php bloginfo( 'style-
sheet_url' ); ?>" />
<link rel="pingback" href="<?php bloginfo( 'pingback_url' ); ?>" />
<?php
        /* I add some JavaScript to pages with the comment form
         * to support sites with threaded comments (when in use).
         */
        if ( is_singular() && get_option( 'thread_comments' ) )
                wp_enqueue_script( 'comment-reply' );

        /* Always have wp_head() just before the closing </head>
         * tag of your theme, or you will break many plugins, which
         * generally use this hook to add elements to <head> such
         * as styles, scripts, and meta tags.
         */
        wp_head();
?>
</head>

<body <?php body_class(); ?>>
<div id="wrapper" class="hfeed">
        <div id="header">
                <div id="masthead">
                        <div id="branding" role="banner">
                                <?php $heading_tag = ( is_home() || is_front_
page() ) ? 'h1' : 'div'; ?>
                                <<?php echo $heading_tag; ?> id="site-title">
                                        <span>
                                                <a href="<?php echo home_url(
'/' ); ?>" title="<?php echo esc_attr( get_bloginfo( 'name', 'display' ) ); ?>"
rel="home"><?php bloginfo( 'name' ); ?></a>
                                        </span>
                                </<?php echo $heading_tag; ?>>
                                <div id="site-description"><?php bloginfo(
```

```
'description' ); ?></div>

                              <?php
                                    // Check if this is a post or page, if
it has a thumbnail, and if it's a big one
                                    if ( is_singular() &&
                                          has_post_thumbnail(
$post->ID ) &&
                                          ( /* $src, $width,
$height */ $image = wp_get_attachment_image_src( get_post_thumbnail_id(
$post->ID ), 'post-thumbnail' ) ) &&
                                          $image[1] >= HEADER_
IMAGE_WIDTH ) :
                                          // Houston, I have a new header
image!
                                          echo get_the_post_thumbnail(
$post->ID, 'post-thumbnail' );
                                    else : ?>
                                          <img src="<?php header_image();
?>" width="<?php echo HEADER_IMAGE_WIDTH; ?>" height="<?php echo HEADER_IMAGE_
HEIGHT; ?>" alt="" />
                                    <?php endif; ?>
                        </div><!-- #branding -->

                        <div id="access" role="navigation">
                          <?php /*  Allow screen readers / text browsers to skip
the navigation menu and get right to the good stuff */ ?>
                              <div class="skip-link screen-reader-text"><a
href="#content" title="<?php esc_attr_e( 'Skip to content', 'twentyten' );
?>"><?php _e( 'Skip to content', 'twentyten' ); ?></a></div>
                              <?php /* Our navigation menu.  If one isn't
filled out, wp_nav_menu falls back to wp_page_menu.  The menu assiged to the
primary position is the one used.  If none is assigned, the menu with the
lowest ID is used.   */ ?>
                              <?php wp_nav_menu( array( 'container_class' =>
'menu-header', 'theme_location' => 'primary' ) ); ?>
                        </div><!-- #access -->
                  </div><!-- #masthead -->
            </div><!-- #header -->

            <div id="main">

                  <?php get_sidebar('left'); ?>
```

Now you get a simple output (from the default widget area content defined in sidebar-left.php). Figure 4-8 shows that the widget is not yet where you intend it to be.

I assume that you've activated the child theme, so do that. I discuss this earlier in this chapter in our simple child theme example.

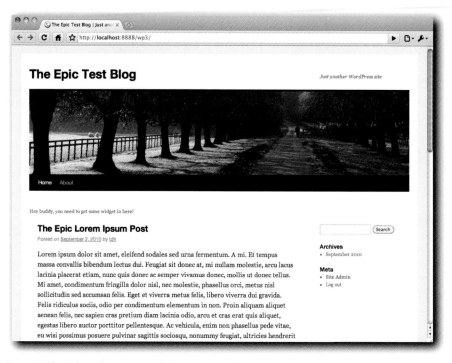

Figure 4-8: The sidebar ends up on top, not looking too good at the moment

5. **Style it with style.** Right, so now the sidebar shows up, and it will look and behave just like the right-hand sidebar does. You pass it in sidebar-left.php. However, you need it to use the correct width, and you want it to float left — now it just sits on top of everything looking sad. That's why you use `#leftsidebar` for the `div`. This is in style.css (in the child theme) and will take care of the first problem.

```
#leftsidebar {
        float: left;
        width: 220px;
}
```

Now you've got your sidebar floating to the left of the content (Figure 4-9 shows that the widget is in the left column), but the content in turn is pushing down the right sidebar.

Next you need to fix the `div#container` element since that has a 100% width and aligns with the right sidebar using negative margin. That won't work on the left column, so you have to set the width (in pixels) for `div#container` so that it'll work with the left side.

```
#container {
        width: 720px;
}
```

The container is set to 720 pixels width. Full width is 940 pixels, removing 220 pixels for the left sidebar container gives you 720 pixels. You don't need to worry about the right sidebar since that is still managed with a negative margin to the right in the original Twenty Ten stylesheet (Figure 4-10 shows your intended result).

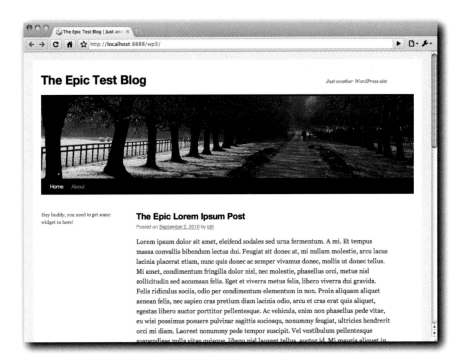

Figure 4-9: The content pushes down the right sidebar

Figure 4-10: Both sidebars aligned with the content

There you go, the sidebars are aligned! Take a look at the full style.css from your child theme.

```
/*
Theme Name: Twenty Ten Tri
Theme URI: http://tdh.me/wordpress/twentyten-tri/
Description: A child theme for Twenty Ten that adds an extra sidebar.
Author: Thord Daniel Hedengren
Author URI: http://tdh.me/
Template: twentyten
Version: 1.0
.

        As made famous by the wonderful book
        Smashing WordPress Themes: Making WordPress Beautiful

.
*/

/* Import the Twenty Ten stylesheet */
@import url('../twentyten/style.css');

/* Left Widget Area */
#leftsidebar {
        float: left;
        width: 220px;
}

/* Main content container fix */
#container {
        width: 720px; /* max width is 940px,
  subtract for #leftsidebar */
}
```

All that's left to do is to drop some widgets in there, but you already know how to do that, right?

Get the complete child theme from http://tdh.me/ wordpress/twentyten-tri.

USING CHILD THEMES IN MULTIPLE NETWORK SITES

Since any template file within a child theme takes precedence over its namesake in the parent theme, you can get a pretty nifty setup. This is especially true if you want to use the same parent theme across a network of sites.

Child themes are especially great when you have multiple sites in a network that share a common code base. With a parent theme in the middle, each site will have its own child theme and hence its own distinctive style. But, whenever you want to roll out new features on your sites, you can just add them to the parent theme. The new features then instantly deploy in all your other sites (for example, on your network).

This means that when you have a network of sites, build a parent theme that fits your needs in terms of ad spots, content, and so on. Then you just use child themes to make each site stand on its own. The sooner you convert to it, the better for you. Then you don't have to update several themes, just one, when it comes to code and basic features. I bet traditional blog networks would've loved this feature back in the day!

WRAPPING IT UP

Considering a child theme setup for your WordPress sites, especially if you're looking at a whole lot of them, is not only prudent, it is also a must if you want to streamline your work. And, as if that isn't enough, child themes are the preferred way to alter themes since hacking them will have your changes overwritten in updates.

In other words, you should learn to work with child themes and use them when appropriate. Now you know how, so there's really nothing stopping you.

So with the child theme knowledge close at hand, how do you choose the correct theme to work with, if you don't want to build your own from scratch? Let's find out. Turn the page to the next chapter.

5

CHOOSING A THEME

IT IS ALWAYS a good idea to play around with other people's themes. Whether you're seeking to find a perfect theme to build upon, or just to learn more about WordPress software, is really beside the point. By trying new themes, you gain a greater understanding of how themes work and how you can address various issues.

This chapter is all about choosing new themes, what you should think about, and what you should definitely avoid.

PICKING THE RIGHT THEME

Finding themes is easy enough: tons of sites offer them for free or for a fee, and there's the `wordpress.org` themes directory as well. The problem is finding the right theme, that perfect one that you are looking for. This is actually a serious matter for a lot of WordPress users out there, which is why blog posts picking nice-looking themes are both popular and common. Chances are you still haven't found the perfect theme (see one interesting example in Figure 5-1). After all, design is very much a matter of personal preference, and then there's your vision for the site that you need the theme for to consider as well.

Figure 5-1: Autofocus+ is actually a paid Thematic child theme, buy it from `http://fthrwght.com/autofocus`

The fact that you're reading this book tells me that you're not afraid to get your hands dirty (with code at least). This means that you're at an advantage compared to most WordPress users. Should you not find the perfect theme, you can always create your own, or modify one that has the basics right, but just needs a little work to fit your needs.

What I find to be a nice theme may not be your flavor at all (Figure 5-2 is an example of one popular theme), which means that it is really hard to give any actual advice on the subject. So that's why I made a list. It is not complete, and your mileage will vary, but it does contain some things to think about. When you're selecting a theme that you aim to release to the community, make sure that you can answer these questions, and more.

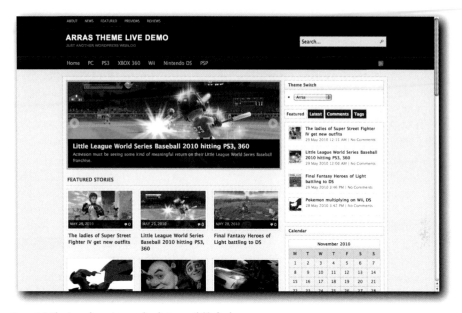

Figure 5-2: The Arras theme is a popular choice, available for free at `http://arrastheme.com`

DESIGN ISSUES

- **Does the theme look good?** Get a theme that you like, or at least one that appeals to your target audience, if that is important to you. Your personal site might not suffer from using a quirky design that people either love or hate, but it might be a completely different matter if you intend to promote a product or a cause.

- **Does the theme support custom headers?** If not, can you add it easily if you want it? While it is easy enough to add the custom header functionality, it just won't fit in every theme. If you feel you need that functionality and it isn't supported out of the box, figure out how and where you'll add it visually before committing to the theme.

- **Does the theme support custom backgrounds?** If not, can you add them easily if you want, and can you do it in such a fashion that it doesn't look silly when used? Not all themes look good with a custom background. Extremely visual themes can suffer since the various elements might be tightly knit together to deliver a certain look and feel. If you want to be able to use custom backgrounds, make sure that it will be aesthetically appealing when you do.

- **Is the theme easy to modify, in terms of logos, colors, type, and so on?** Luckily, most theme authors know by now that they shouldn't hardcode the CSS styles into the various elements in the template files, but rather should rely on CSS classes and ID's which you can easily get to through style.css (or similar), so this is more an issue of having a decent layout and nomenclature. Can you, for example, change all link colors easily or do you need to make the same color change in a lot of places? A decent CSS layout will do. Another aspect here are theme options, where you may be able to make some if not all modifications in terms of colors and logos.

125

LAYOUT ISSUES

- **Is the main layout what you're looking for?** Is the layout following a column grid that you can work with? Is there enough space for your content? If not, find another one to save time.

- **Does the content flow the way you'd like?** Pay attention to how posts can be portrayed (such as, is there support for attachments). Does the archive treat the content the way you want? Luckily, it is pretty easy to alter these things, but this could be a factor, especially if your content is all images and you need to be able to display them properly.

- **Is the theme localized?** Can you add your own translations to it without hacking the template files? If you need to translate the theme of your choice, then you should go for one that is localized from the start. This will narrow your scope quite a lot, unfortunately, but perhaps you can help push the theme designer into adding localization support to the theme in question, or help him do it yourself? If you need to localize the theme, you should do it with language files and not by translating every text snippet in the template files. For more information on localization, see Chapter 6.

- **Does the theme have all the widget areas that you like?** If not, is there room to add them without too much of a hassle? The same goes for ad spots really, if you know you need to fit in particular ad sizes, then make sure there is room to add them. Widgets are a nice way of doing that.

DEVELOPMENT ISSUES

- **Does the theme have all the necessary template files?** If not, can you add the missing files should you want to use it anyway?

- **Is the theme easy to build child themes upon?** Can you change the look and feel easily with a child theme? It helps if the theme uses `get_template_part()` and the loop templates. This is obviously only an issue if you intend to use the theme as a parent theme.

- **What about menu support?** Are there menu areas, and if not, do menus display in widget areas where you might want to add them? This is fairly easy to add, luckily, both menu areas and the necessary styling of the Menu widget should you resort to that.

- **Is the code in the theme's files well-structured?** Can you find your way in it easily? If not, then alterations and changes will take more time, and chances are the theme's quality is lacking.

- **Does your site load quickly with the theme enabled?** Get a lightweight theme if you can, both users and search engines like speed.

- **Speaking of which, is the theme well-designed in terms of search engine optimization?** SEO is a huge topic, but you should make sure that the fundamentals are in, such as post and Page titles in the title tag, proper meta descriptions, and such. Luckily Word-Press takes care of most of this, and there are plugins that can help as well.

- **Does the theme validate?** Some claim that search engines like that too, and it's the right thing to do. It may also help make sure that future Web browsers will read the markup correctly. Check it at `http://validator.w3.org`.

- **Does the theme rely on any outside scripts or services?** This could be JavaScripts hosted with Google, font replacement scripts, as well as inclusion from sites like Facebook or services like DISQUS. Using outside scripts and services increase load times, and not all of them degrade nicely when the service you're relying on is experiencing problems. You need to be wary with too many outside scripts and services, and should definitely be careful not to rely too much on them.

- **Does the theme work in all major Web browsers?** It should, fixing that is often tedious work. What Web browsers you need to support is entirely up to you. Consult your demographic information to see what your needs are.

- **What about mobile devices, is there any built-in support for that?** If not, that's OK. You can use plugins that can help, but it sure is a bonus.

- **Is the theme ready for common plugins, such as Subscribe to Comments?** You can add support for these things easily enough yourself, but it can be a bonus if there's built-in stylings and such from the start.

- **Is the theme licensed under GPL? Does that matter to you?** This is a complicated issue, and if you're doing work for a company then consult the legal department to avoid any problems. All themes found on `wordpress.org` are licensed under a GPL-compliant license.

- **Does the theme author support the theme?** If you intend to use the theme as a parent theme, or as is, then it is obviously a good thing if the theme author is active in support forums. It is also good if the theme is in active development since that probably means that it will be updated when WordPress gets new features.

THEME FRAMEWORKS

Any theme can serve as your theme framework. Some theme authors push this, making their themes sound more like frameworks than others. They might be, depending on how well they fit your needs. Just because a theme isn't labeled as a theme framework doesn't mean it won't serve as one. There is no "framework template tag" or anything like that — themes are themes.

Some themes are more suitable as Web site frameworks than others. Always pick the framework most suited to your site's needs. For example, a theme created to display photographs probably won't have the text support and features you want to run your newspaper site. In this case, you're better off picking something more aligned to text.

You'll note that I use the term framework loosely. The purpose of a framework is to make development easier, which saves time and possibly money (and headaches). Any theme that saves me time developing the site I'm after that can serve as a robust starting point, and perhaps even as a parent theme for my projects, is a framework. It is a matter of what you need, nothing else. One popular framework is The Hybrid theme (at `http://theme hybrid.com`). Check out these two Web sites that use The Hybrid theme as a framework: Lero9 (at `http://lero9.co.nz`) and Daisy Olsen (at `http://daisyolsen.com`).

WHAT IS A GOOD FRAMEWORK, THEN?

Despite the arguments over what constitutes a framework, most of the time you'll find a lot of common denominators. While the needs of your sites should determine your choice of a framework theme, you have technical things to consider as well. Some themes might be so niched to their primary functions and vision that they lack some features that you might need, which makes them unsuitable as frameworks. Others are so feature-filled that they become bulky and hard to manage, which might be good at some point, but certainly not in all situations.

You want your theme framework to be lightweight, good at what it does, but not necessarily do everything. That adds overhead, and you don't want that. This means that themes filled with extra functionality that calls the database a lot should be avoided, since every call makes the site a little bit slower and unless you need it, it shouldn't be there. This is especially true if you intend to use the theme as a parent theme (Figure 5-3 shows a good parent theme example), and not just build upon it.

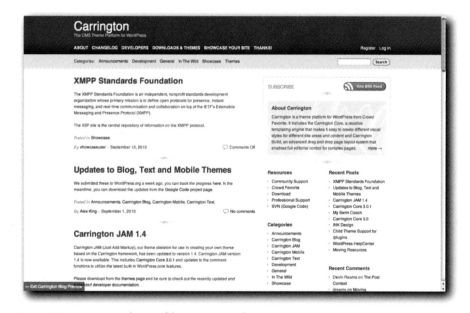

Figure 5-3: Carrington is a popular suite of themes: Carrington Blog, at `http://carringtontheme.com`

Source: www.carringtontheme.com

On the other hand, you want your theme framework to be complete. That means that it should handle everything that is default in WordPress, from posts and Pages, to attachments and author archives. All those features should be presented in a decent manner, making it easy for you to work with them. You might not need a particular template on one project, but it may be necessary on the next. Since theme frameworks are meant to ease the development of sites, it is important that all the default stuff is there. That way you can focus on creating the features that are unique to your new site.

A decent theme framework also needs to manage all the CSS classes used by default in WordPress, as well as possibly your primary set of plugins. The more of that you can include in your framework, the better. At the very least, you want support for image placement, captions, and similar items (Figure 5-4 shows an effective framework). All themes following the themes checklist earlier in this chapter should comply. Whether they look good or not is a completely different matter.

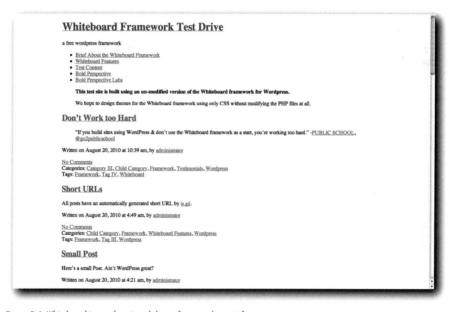

Figure 5-4: Whiteboard is a truly stripped theme framework, get it from `http://whiteboardframework.com`

CREATE YOUR OWN FRAMEWORK

One way to make sure that you get the features and setup that you need from your theme framework is to create it yourself. This is a particularly good idea if you intend to embrace the child theme concept fully, and need to publish a series of sites that share functionality. That way, you can roll out new sites faster by just creating child themes to your theme framework.

COMMERCIAL THEMES

Not all WordPress themes are available for free; some will cost money. While you could debate if this is something good or bad for the WordPress community and what it means for the GPL license, the fact is that you can find lots of high quality themes out there for a small amount of money. These themes are either sold as they are, or as part of what's being offered to members of a themes club or such. Check out Figure 5-5 if you are looking for a newspaper-style theme.

The commercial themes often come with support from the theme developers, which obviously can come in handy. That also means that the themes will be updated with new versions of WordPress, not something you can count on with a free theme that someone created in their free time. Sometimes you get what you pay for, or rather, you'll get more if you pay since theme licenses usually won't set you back very much.

Figure 5-5: Advanced Newspaper is a newspaper theme, available from http://gabfirethemes.com

However, you should remember that while buying a commercial theme may make your site stand out a bit more than when you're rolling the default WordPress theme, others can buy the same theme (Figure 5-6 shows one such popular commercial theme). If you want to have a truly unique theme, you'll need to design and develop it yourself, or commission it from a designer. The price for unique themes depends on who you want to hire; up and coming designers might settle for a few hundred dollars, while the professionals will set you back thousands of dollars. It all depends on what you want and what your needs are for your custom theme.

I see absolutely nothing wrong with going with a commercial theme, whether it is a license from a themes club, or a privately commissioned, unique site. The former is especially useful if you find a theme you like and then want to tweak it to your needs. You'll have to do some work yourself to get it to look and feel the way you like, while a commissioned theme will be tailored to your needs from the start.

If nothing else, a commercial theme is something to consider. But given the fact that you're reading this book, chances are you may want to build a theme yourself. If that is the case and you want to take a shortcut towards launching a WordPress-powered site, finding a commercial theme close to what you want to achieve and building upon it like a framework, with child themes, may be a good place to start.

Figure 5-6: Mimbo Pro is a popular choice, available from `http://prothemedesign.com`

THE OFFICIAL THEMES DIRECTORY

The official Free Themes Directory for WordPress themes is located on `http://wordpress.org/extend/themes`. All themes found here (see Figure 5-7) have a GPL-compatible license and can be auto-updated from within WordPress. Users can rate them, and you'll find all kinds of necessary information about the theme. All themes from the `wordpress.org` Free Themes Directory are free to download, of course.

Themes on this site comply with the WordPress standards (at the time of submission). You'll be notified from within the WordPress admin panel when a new version of your theme is available from the `wordpress.org` directory.

Another nice thing about the wordpress.org themes directory is that it resides in every WordPress install out there. Assuming your Web host supports it (which they should; complain otherwise) you can install brand new themes from within the Appearance section of the WordPress admin panel. Just click Add New and browse the `wordpress.org` themes directory. Pretty sweet.

Figure 5-7: The wordpress.org themes directory, found at `http://wordpress.org/extend/themes`

This all sounds good of course, but there are some flaws. The most obvious one is that the theme author may have his own page for the theme, where he offers the theme files. This means that unless the theme author remembers to update the theme on `wordpress.org`, you won't be notified of the new version, nor will you be able to auto-update from within your WordPress admin panel. Granted, most theme authors keep their themes up to date on `wordpress.org`, but you might want to keep in mind that this is a manual thing and that means that mistakes can happen.

The issue of what versions of WordPress the theme has been tested on is also a concern. Often the themes' information says that it has been tested up to a specific version, which may very well be several steps older than the one you're running. This doesn't mean that the theme doesn't work with the most recent version of WordPress; it just says that it hasn't been tested with it. This is something the theme author manages from within his theme files. Unless he or she has a reason to update the theme, this information won't be updated. But, if the theme hasn't been tested with your version of WordPress, give it a go anyway — it might work!

Finally, a few words about commercial themes on `wordpress.org`, or the lack of them rather. There is a link page to some themes marketplaces (`http://wordpress.org/extend/themes/commercial`), but that's about it. If you want to buy commercial themes you'll have to do that elsewhere. Figure 5-8 shows the commercial themes listing from `wordpress.org`.

Figure 5-8: Commercial GPL-compliant themes promoted, but not sold, on `wordpress.org`

THINGS TO BE WARY ABOUT

Thousands of WordPress themes are available online, which is a good thing. WordPress is a very popular and widespread publishing platform and that alone means that tons of themes, and plugins for that matters, are created and sometimes released. Most are free, but some will cost you money. This is a good thing, but there are things to be wary about.

The most important thing to watch out for are themes containing malicious links. The theme author might not be as nice as you'd expect from someone who is kind enough to release his or her theme for free online. Sneaky links to malicious Web sites, or just plain old text links to play search engines like Google, can suddenly appear on your site because the theme you downloaded and activated have them in strategic places. Even worse, there might be malicious code within the theme files. Themes downloaded from the themes directory on `wordpress.org` should be free of this, but you can't be too careful, of course.

The following questions might help you choose the right theme, or at least avoid going with the wrong one.

- Is it full of ugly hacks and perhaps deprecated functionality, or does it appear to be coded in a good and modern way? Using template tags and standards of recent versions of WordPress will make sure that the theme will work in the future as well.
- Is it backwards compatible, or is it created for a particular version of WordPress only? While you should always endeavor to run the latest version of WordPress, sometimes it may not be possible.

- Is the theme hosted on wordpress.org so that you can get automatic updates, or does the theme author supply them on his site? How will you know when the theme is updated? Is there a mailing list? This is important if you intend to build child themes on top of the theme. If you intend to use the theme as a base and modify it directly, then this point obviously becomes moot.
- Is there support, paid or pro bono, available for the theme should you need it?

Consider these things before going with a particular theme that you've found online and you'll make things easier on yourself and your site in the future.

Obviously none of these things matter if you decide to just build upon the theme you've downloaded. Then you'll be on your own anyway, and paid support or auto-updates from wordpress.org aren't interesting to you.

WRAPPING IT UP

Finding the perfect theme is difficult. Whether you're looking for something to build upon, either with child themes or as a basis for your own theme, or you actually want something that you're content with as it is, you'll find that the vast numbers of themes make it hard to find the perfect one. In fact, I'd wager you won't find the perfect theme on wordpress.org or anywhere else online, since your needs and your preference most likely differs from everybody else's. Then again, you might get close enough!

Utilizing the number of themes out there is both a great way to get started with theming and a wonderful course when you're looking to learn something new. If you know you're after a particular feature, find a theme that does it. Analyze how it is done by looking through the template files to get inspiration for how to add it to your theme.

But enough of that for now. It's time to start building your own themes.

BUILDING YOUR OWN THEME

6

PLANNING THE THEME

HOPEFULLY YOU'LL BUILD plenty of themes over the coming weeks, months, and years. This chapter is all about that: what to consider before you begin, site goals that can make it easier to plan for the long run, and checklists for stuff you just can't forget about, such as required template files and basics for good framework design. Whether you're looking to release your theme for anyone to download, or just want to build a cool site for yourself, your clients, or other projects, these are things to consider.

This chapter starts with a look at what it takes to build a useful theme. And then, when you're done with that, you get into more niched themes (that is, themes that focus on static content, images, or a magazine-inspired design). Good times ahead!

PLAN BEFORE YOU BUILD

Before you create a brand new theme from scratch, make things as easy as possible for yourself. Establish a plan before you get carried away building your theme files and designing a layout. There are many ways to plan a theme, but I tend to go about it in this way.

THE SITE CONCEPT STAGE

At the concept stage, I want to answer the following questions:

- What is the primary goal for this theme?
- Do I need to build it up for later use, or can I just get it out there in the minimum amount of time?
- Do I want to release this theme to the general public at some point?
- Do I need outside help to create this theme?

The second and third questions are all about how I should tackle the code when it comes to that. If speed is of the essence, I don't want to worry about making the theme easy to build other sites on (at least not at this stage). Yet, if I do plan to use the theme as a parent theme or even a framework in the future, I might want to add features that make it easier to work with. Features such as action hooks or extra widget areas require extra planning.

THE SITE DESIGN

Next, I start thinking about the design, and more specifically the wireframe of my design. How you go about creating a design is unique to each individual. Some people build mockups in Photoshop, while others prefer to draw them on paper. I carry a Moleskine notebook with me (as you see in Figure 6-1) to sketch design ideas (and other ideas as well, for that matter). I then take them to Photoshop for a more accurate mock-up, or even go straight to creating the visual site elements, such as prominent graphics.

However you start, you need to figure out how you want your theme to look, and that means answering these questions:

- What general feeling do I want my theme to evoke: dark and heavy, light and bright, or maybe extremely experimental and abstract?
- Do I want visual flair and effects? If I do, how do I want these to look?
- Are there any ad spots, or other elements that I need to make room for?
- How will I present the content? Is it your typical list of posts or do I want large images to lead further into the site?

The last question is a big one, and if this was an in-depth book on how to actually design Web sites, it would be split up into a bunch of chapters. From a WordPress point of view, you may want to consider how you plan to code the content presentation you've opted for. You don't yet need the solution, you just want to know that you're capable of doing it. In that sense, start figuring out how to code your theme and set up your WordPress site in this design stage. Don't let it hamper you too much though: that's not the primary goal for designing mockups and wireframes.

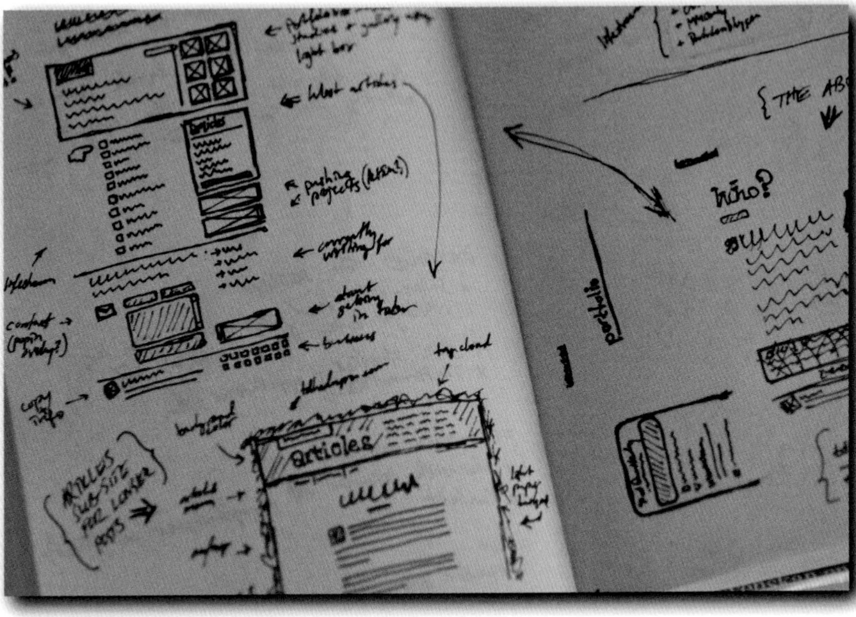

Figure 6-1: These scribbles can end up as many pretty Web sites in a browser near you

THE SITE MECHANICS

Finally, decide on the site mechanics: what categories and Pages you want, how you'll use and display posts, and things like that. It matters because you might want to create Page templates and various archive views to make the site behave the way you want. So figure out how to achieve the look and feel you decided upon. The following questions can help you work through this stage:

- How do I plan to use the front page?
- What will I use posts for, and how do I want to display them? In some projects, a post may be just a news item, in others it could be something entirely different.
- How do I want to display my posts in archive view?
- Do I need to use custom fields with my posts? How will I do this technically, and how can I integrate it into my theme?
- Will I use tags to further sort my content? Do I need some custom solution for this?
- How do I want to use Pages? What parts of my site should be driven by Pages, if any?
- Do I need Page templates for some part of my site?
- Will I use image galleries and other attachments in any way that needs my attention?

- Will I have other content types than posts and Pages (such as text widgets)? How will these work?
- Are there any plugins I need, and do I need to worry about them in my theme? (See Chapter 11 for details about plugins.)
- Will this be a stand-alone theme, or should I add a child theme and base it on another theme? (I discuss child themes in Chapter 4.)

Depending on the kind of site that you're building, you may need to ask yourself more questions. The answers to these critical questions tell you what template files you need to create, and how many custom elements you need to build.

Now you are set to create your theme files. The clearer the picture of your new theme, the easier it will be to make it all come together in the end. Do take notes and make diagrams and sketches that you can refer to when you suddenly can't remember how you chose to lay out your site. The more details the better; when it comes to creating a theme, structure is your friend.

YOUR OWN THEME FRAMEWORK

You can save a lot of time if you stick to a theme framework you know, whether you've developed it yourself (for use on future projects), or learned it from someone else's work. That means you don't have to redo the whole structure from scratch every time you start with a new site.

You can read more about theme frameworks in general in Chapter 4.

THE PURPOSE OF A FRAMEWORK

The sole purpose of any theme framework is to save time. Whether you use it as a parent for your child themes or just as a code base to build upon, the goal is the same. Why reinvent the wheel? No need, of course. And there's absolutely no need to create the same basic WordPress theme over and over again.

When building or choosing a theme framework, this is the sole notion you should focus on. It doesn't matter how good it looks if it doesn't fit your needs when you want to build new stuff later. Don't be lured off-track with bells and whistles. Your theme framework needs to be easy to build upon, to alter, and to work with. That's it.

It is way too easy to start adding stuff and brushing it up, and then release it to the wild. Then suddenly you realize that your framework became a regular theme. Every theme is a potential framework, but it usually means that there will be more things to override, to remove, and to alter than there should be for a framework. That doesn't help when you want to save time launching your next site. So stick to the purpose of your theme framework.

SHOULD YOU BUILD A THEME FRAMEWORK?

For those of you with time and patience, as well as the will to work, rework, and then rework it again, I definitely recommend creating your own theme framework. It is quite fun, and the fact that you know it inside out is a great benefit.

That's the good part, because it means you'll have no trouble working with it. You know the framework; you built it, after all, and that makes it a breeze to work with.

But, the bad part is that while your own framework may be easy to work with, it just may not be as great as the ones that you find online. Creating a brilliant framework takes time, and you won't get it right the first time, no matter how good your ideas are. Plus, it is constant work, adding new features and fine-tuning the theme to be an even better framework. Chances are, it'll just reach the good-enough stage, and then you'll wrestle with it every time you use it as a structure for a site.

If you lack the time to devote yourself to this, then creating a framework is probably not for you. Better to find a great theme online, learn it, and let its author keep it up to date for you.

RELEASING THEMES TO THE PUBLIC

So you plan to release your theme to the WordPress community? Good for you, and great for the community. It's always nice when someone gives back.

When releasing you're a theme you need to make sure that it works, meets the WordPress requirements, and has all the necessary template files. Also, document the code in a decent fashion as that makes it easier for the users to dig into it. Also, while you're at it, you may consider shipping a readme file that answers the basic questions, if you think it is necessary.

In short, make your theme as complete as possible, so that people can actually use it. After all, that's the whole idea with releasing the theme, right?

GETTING YOUR THEMES ON WORDPRESS.ORG

WordPress has well-documented rules for releasing a WordPress theme to the `wordpress.org` themes directory (see my theme in Figure 6-2). You need to license the theme under GPL, or a compatible license, and it needs to handle the default styles (for images, floats, and so on) in WordPress. You can download unit guidelines (at `http://codex.wordpress.org/Theme_Unit_Test`), which includes a database that you can import into your test blog to make sure that you style everything appropriately.

So, why would you want to host your theme on `wordpress.org` when you can share it on your own Web site, and perhaps even benefit from the traffic? Well, the main reason is that WordPress itself connects to the `wordpress.org` themes directory, so your users can install their themes directly from within the admin panel (as displayed in Figure 6-3), and update them, just like with plugins. This is very user friendly.

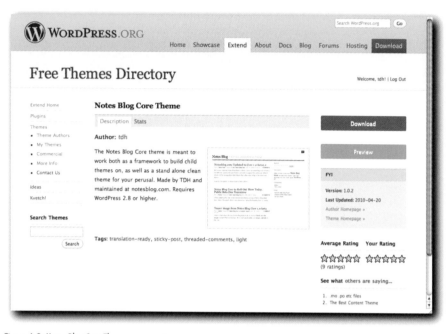

Figure 6-2: Notes Blog Core Theme on `wordpress.org`

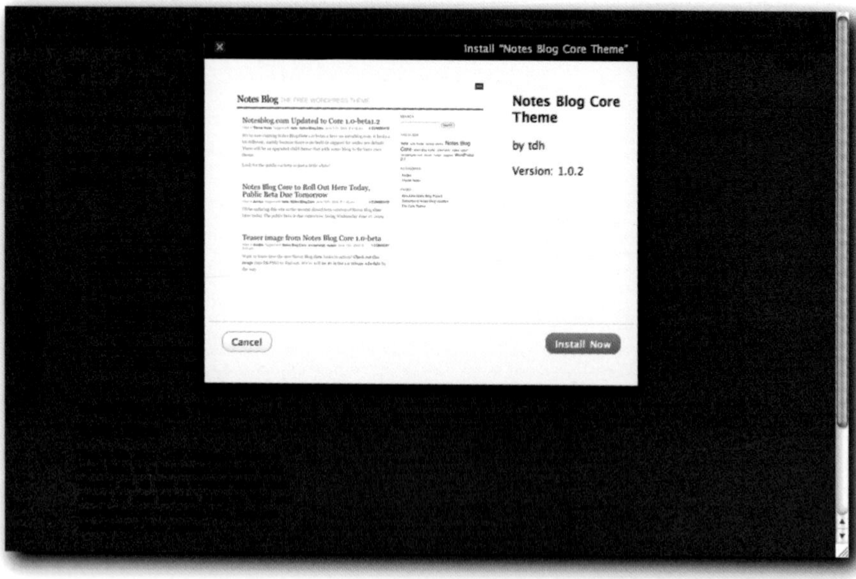

Figure 6-3: Notes Blog Core Theme from your WordPress admin panel

There's another benefit as well, and that's credibility. That your theme is in the official WordPress themes directory means that potential users can rest a bit easier as all themes in the directory are individually approved. So it is unlikely that you have installed malicious code by accident, which, unfortunately, can occur. Do not be afraid to download themes from sites other than `wordpress.org`. Just keep an eye out, and if things sound or look weird, then pay extra attention to the code in the theme files.

PICKING THE RIGHT LICENSE

If you intend to release your theme on `wordpress.org` it has to be licensed under GPL, or a compatible license. Otherwise, you're not welcome in the themes directory, and you'll have to offer your theme elsewhere.

Commercial themes also exist that are licensed under GPL, and you can even see them in the `wordpress.org` themes directory, which showcases some of the more popular ones (Figure 6-4 shows where you can access a commercial theme). They have the license in common, as well as professional support solutions for their users.

Figure 6-4: Commercially Supported GPL Themes on `wordpress.org`

You can pick whatever license you want for your theme, whether you intend to release it for free or sell it in some fashion. How you sell it is up to you; I wouldn't presume to know the ideal business model for such an endeavor. I would, however, recommend sticking to a GPL-compatible license.

LOCALIZATION

In Chapter 1, I touched briefly upon localization. By wrapping text strings in certain types of code, you can localize a theme. Thus, your theme could be available in several languages without you altering the theme files. This is a good idea overall, but it becomes even better when you intend to release a theme to the wild. While English is a widely used language, not all will want to use it for their site. If you have prepared your theme for localization, then anyone can localize the strings and change the language. Remember, the language of the install dictates what language your theme will be in, should WordPress support it. You can have a fully localized theme, but if you haven't set the correct language codes in wp-config. php during the install, then WordPress won't know to try and use a language file (Figure 6-5 shows a footer in English, and Figure 6-6 shows the same footer translated to Swedish).

Just to recap, within PHP, anything within the parentheses of __() or _e() is a localized string. First you pass the string that should be localized, and then you set the locale, like so:

```
<?php _e('That\'s it - back to the top of page!', 'notesblog');?>
```

The text That\'s it - back to the top of page! is my translatable text, and notesblog is the locale. The latter is set in my theme's functions.php (in this case the theme is Notes Blog):

```
// Localization support, fetches languages files from /lang/ folder
load_theme_textdomain( 'notesblog', TEMPLATEPATH . '/lang' );
```

You can read up on load_theme_textdomain() in the Codex at http://codex. wordpress.org/Function_Reference/load_theme_textdomain.

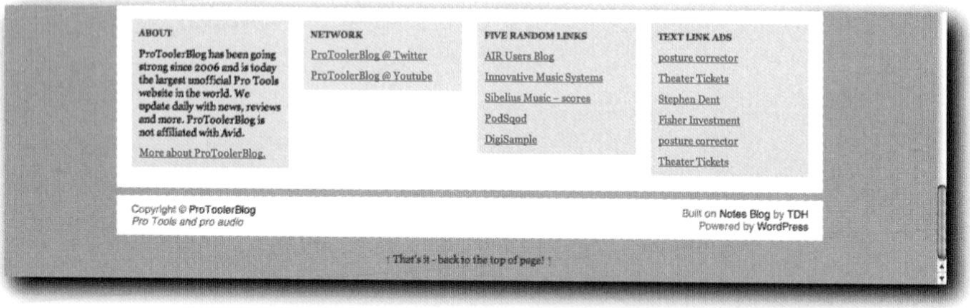

Figure 6-5: The footer on ProToolerBlog.com runs the Notes Blog theme in English

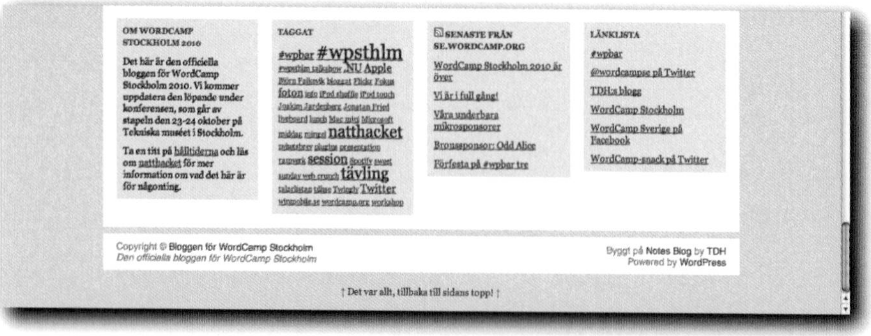

Figure 6-6: WordCamp Stockholm translates the Notes Blog theme footer to Swedish, thanks to a language file

So why did I use _e() in the string? Well, I wanted to echo the text, which is what it does. You probably noticed the backslash before the apostrophe in That's. I want to make sure that the first parameter (the text I want to translate) won't get interrupted prematurely. Another way to solve that problem is to use quotation marks instead of apostrophes:

```php
<?php _e("That's it - back to the top of page!", "notesblog");?>
```

Note the difference? No backslash is needed because an apostrophe won't break the parameter.

When adding __() and _e() to your theme you can have software like Poedit (free and multiplatform, available at http://www.poedit.net), that creates language files for you. The .po file (the working file that you ship with your theme) makes it easy for translators to create their own translations, whereas .mo files are actual translations. As you create these files, you may want to include them with your theme files. Name them just like WordPress names its language files, such as sv_SE for Sweden or de_DE for Germany (see the full list at http://codex.wordpress.org/WordPress_in_Your_Language).

Localization isn't a must; your theme won't be barred from the wordpress.org theme directory without it, but it is a good thing to include. Read more about how it works on the Codex page about translating WordPress. You'll also find links to other tools for working with language files at http://codex.wordpress.org/Translating_WordPress.

THE CHECKLISTS

So, you're building your very own theme? Make sure that you refer to these checklists as they will make your life easier. Perhaps not right now, as you're working on the code and pulling your hair out thanks to Web browser inconsistencies. But later you'll appreciate your decision to do everything right.

THE THEME CHECKLIST

You need to review this checklist if you intend to release your theme into the wild and want to host it at the wordpress.org themes directory (which you should if you want to offer those sweet upgrade notifications via the WordPress admin). You don't have to release your theme via wordpress.org; how you deliver it to the world is your own choice. But check the rules when submitting your theme, as they may change.

- Themes have to be fully GPL licensed, along with all images, stylesheets, and so on.
- Themes cannot include "WordPress" or "WP" in their names.
- Likewise, themes should not include markup-related language terms in their names, such as CSS3 or HTML5.
- Themes need the following template files:
    - style.css
    - index.php

- comments.php
- screenshot.png (which has to be a reasonable representation of how the theme looks)
- Themes can't have any PHP errors or similar.
- Themes can't have any JavaScript errors.
- Themes need a valid HTML declaration (valid DOCTYPE) with the correct content type, XFN and character set. For details, see `http://codex.wordpress.org/Theme_Review#Code_Quality`.
- Themes need to output the site's title in the `title` tag, using the `bloginfo()` template tag.
- Themes need to support widgets.
- Themes need to automatically generate feeds; `add_theme_support()` in functions.php helps with that if you have any problems.
- Themes should support comments.
- Themes should also support menus, post thumbnails, custom headers, and custom backgrounds, if they are suitable.
- Themes should support custom CSS for the Visual editor (with the `add_editor_style()` template tag).
- Themes need to have the following template hooks and tags:
  - `wp_head()` before closing the `head` tag.
  - `body_class()` inside the `body` tag.
  - `$content_width` in functions.php (defining the default content width).
  - `post_class()` in the post `div` tag.
  - `wp_link_pages()` for pagination on Pages.
  - Proper comment navigation for multiple pages of comments.
  - Navigational links between posts/Pages using `posts_nav_link()`, or `previous_posts_link()` and `next_posts_link()`.
  - `wp_footer()` just before the closing `body` tag.
- If there is a header.php file, it is called using `get_header()`.
- If there is a footer.php file, it is called using `get_footer()`.
- If there is a sidebar.php file, it is be called using `get_sidebar()`.
- If there is a comments.php file, it is called using `comments_template()`.
- The following template filenames are not allowed:
  - page-X.php
  - category-X.php
  - tag-X.php
  - taxonomy-X.php
- Search forms are called with `get_search_form()`.

- Login forms are called with `wp_login_form()`.
- Inclusion of custom template files/parts are done with `get_template_part()`, if possible.
- The following classes are required in the stylesheet:
  - `alignright`, `.alignleft`, and `.aligncenter` for alignments
  - `wp-caption`, `.wp-caption-text`, and `.gallery-caption` for attachment captions
- The following classes are recommended in the stylesheet:
  - `sticky` for sticky posts
  - `bypostauthor` for styling author comments
- Theme links in style.css need to point to an appropriate site and page for the theme.
- Credit links need to point to relevant sites for the theme, such as the theme author or theme home page.

And finally, the theme needs to pass the Theme Unit test. Download the test database and read more about that here: `http://codex.wordpress.org/Theme_Unit_Test`.

THE THEME FRAMEWORK CHECKLIST

If you intend to build a theme to use as a theme framework, whether it is for public release or just for your own private use, consider the following guidelines. Nothing here is required.

- Comment your code; that makes it easier for everyone to find their way.
- Avoid hardcoded links, use `bloginfo()`, and similar tags.
- Put the loop.php template file to good use, and include a unique loop.php file for every template file (such as `get_template_part('loop', 'author')` for the author archives) for easy overwriting in a child theme.
- Make sure that the elements in the design are easy to get to with CSS.
- Be as general as possible in your code: The fewer template files that you need in the child theme, the better.
- Provide general fallback files; this makes it easier to create specialized template files for parts of the new site that you're building.
- Keep the code simple; don't add too many features. Bare minimum is better; that way the child theme won't have to unregister so many functions and null out features.
- Keep the design clean and bare; dress it up when you're building your actual site instead!
- Stay away from ugly hacks and poorly written code! Remember, you're supposed to build upon this framework.
- Make sure that your theme framework validates. After all, you're building on it and it is better to have something sound to begin with, right?

THE CHILD THEME CHECKLIST

If you're building a child theme, observe the following guidelines, especially if you're releasing the child theme in any way.

- Document closely so that you know what you're overwriting.
- Solve as many issues in style.css as you can.
- Try to use loop.php template files, rather than create a ton of parent files overwriting the theme.
- Remember that the child theme's functions.php is loaded before the parent theme's file. You can control the latter's features this way.
- Add screenshot.png files for child themes, as well; don't forget that.
- Make sure that your site validates, even after activating your child theme.

WRAPPING IT UP

By now you have all the know-how not only to build your own WordPress theme, but to get yourself a theme framework to base future works on. Enough's enough, though. Next, you dig into practical examples and build some niche sites, putting your knowledge to good use.

7

A SEMI-STATIC THEME

THE EASE OF use that WordPress offers means that the platform is more often used as a traditional (yet modern) CMS. WordPress works perfectly well in this context, whether you intend to build a big newspaper site, or just a corporate or product site. The development team understands this. After all, the default tagline isn't "Just another WordPress blog" anymore, but "Just another WordPress site," which is closer to the truth in most cases. After all, blogs are often not really blogs as we tend to think of them, but Web sites with a bloggish format. Then again, wasn't that the case all along?

In this chapter, you use WordPress to build a simple, yet easily modifiable, semi-static Web site, which means that some of the content is meant to be somewhat static whereas other parts mimic the traditional news section. You can use this theme for a corporate site, a political campaign, or just about any project where your focus is on static content. If you like the format, you could also use it as a blog or news site, but that is not the focus.

So, let's get started!

WORDPRESS AND SEMI-STATIC WEB SITES

Before we begin, I want to clarify semi-static here. You'll be building a theme meant for (but not limited to) sites consisting mostly of Pages. These Pages could contain a corporate bio, contact information, a list of services, or something like that. When you update static content (Pages), you overwrite the old content and replace it with new information, or add it onto the same Page. Compare that to adding a news story to a news category or blog post to a blog for that matter. This is how you'll build this site, but let's not get ahead of ourselves.

OUR FICTIONAL SEMI-STATIC WEB SITE

The idea here is to build a site for a fictional company. You'll build a theme that can be used for that, and make sure that it is flexible and easy to modify with child theming should it be needed.

WEB SITE REQUIREMENTS

Here are the site requirements:

- On the front page, you need the following:
  - A large image that captures the company spirit.
  - A short paragraph or two about the company, and links for added reading.
  - The latest updates from the press section, along with the company's latest blog posts and tweets.
- A few content Pages about the company and its services, which you can add or remove in the WordPress admin panel without altering the theme.
- A press section.
- A blog section.
- Contact information with a contact form.

For this semi-static site, you focus on Pages, which can have sub-pages, as well as Page templates to customize the section. In this example, you manage both the press section updates and blog posts using categories, but an alternative would be to use a custom post type for the press section. The contact form is a plugin, and you change the permalink structure for category archives with another plugin. Other than that, you have no need for additional plugins.

Moving on, you manage the menus with the Custom Menus feature, so that the client can update the site on their own. You use the Custom Header feature, as well.

Figure 7-1 shows the preliminary sketch, made on plain old paper, since that's the way I usually work.

While I make something out of this simple sketch, you can read on about how you should make categories and Pages work together. When you're done, I should be ready to Photoshop this baby so that we can build it . . .

Figure 7-1: Sketch from my Moleskine notebook

MAKING CATEGORIES AND PAGES WORK IN HARMONY

Categories and Pages are completely different entities on a Web site. The former is in fact an archive page for posts, and the latter is a static Page with content. Category posts are updated whenever a new post is added to the category; Pages are updated when you actually alter them.

Structure-wise, categories and Pages sit on the same level, sort of. Your Pages get a permalink directly under the WordPress install root, so `yoursite.com/my-page-slug/` is the permalink for Pages. Categories on the other hand, sit under a default category label in the URL, so that permalink is `yoursite.com/category/my-category-slug/`.

Why is this important? Well, you want a decent URL structure in every site you build. When building a semi-static site, this becomes even more important.

FIXING THE CATEGORY URLS

First, get rid of that pesky category addition. You can change it to something else in the WordPress admin panel under the Settings section in Permalinks, shown in Figure 7-2. Here you can also change the default tag labeling for tag archives.

In some cases, it'll be enough to change the category labeling to something else, especially if you just have a news section. You do that under the Optional heading on the Permalinks Settings screen. Just change it to "news" instead of the default category, which would mean

151

that you'd get more appropriate URLs like `yoursite.com/news/my-category-slug/`. If you have company or product related news in their own categories, you get pretty nice looking URLs such as `yoursite.com/news/my-product/` and so on. Makes sense. You should remember that whatever you change the category slug to will be used for all categories, so be careful what you pick here. Going with "news" will only make sense if you set up a permalink structure that displays the category slug and then the post slug, and if you only have post content that would fit under "news."

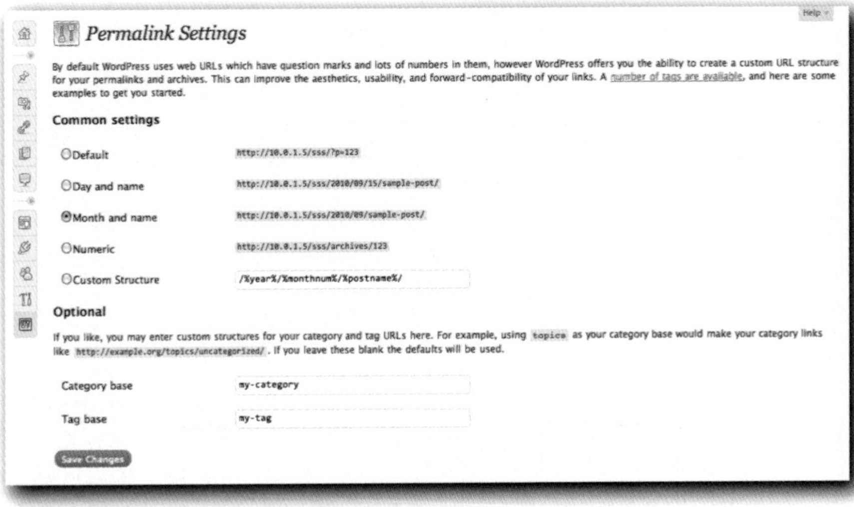

Figure 7-2: The now probably fairly well-known Permalinks Settings screen

However, sometimes you just want to get rid of the category labeling insertion altogether. In the example site that is the case, because you'll use categories for both the press section and the blog part of the site to separate posts. Having URLs like `yoursite.com/category/press/` and `yoursite.com/category/blog/` will look bad when compared to a contact page, for example, which would be at `yoursite.com/contact/` as Pages won't get any default labeling.

Luckily there is an absolutely lovely plugin that solves this problem, called WP No Category Base (get it at `http://wordpress.org/extend/plugins/wp-no-category-base/`). Just install and activate it, and all default category labeling is gone. Suddenly you can have `yoursite.com/press/` and `yoursite.com/blog/`, which you need for this project. This saves you the trouble of having to write a custom page template for each category, and makes it easier on the end user to add sections like these — all they have to do is add another category.

WHY IS THIS IMPORTANT?

It is all about appearances. Having a nice looking URL structure makes sense for the visitor; one look at the URL shows where he is on the site. Again, sometimes you want to insert the category label into the URL, but more often than not, it is a bad idea. In the semi-static site, you want both the press and blog sections to be top-level alternatives, and it would look weird if they sat further down in the URL structure than other top level items, which will be Pages.

A sound and clear URL structure is part of a site. You shouldn't forget about that, especially not when you're mixing Pages and categories in this matter.

THE SEMI-STATIC THEME LAYOUT

Welcome back! I've created a basic Photoshop mock-up of the simple sketch that you see in Figure 7-1 (but any graphics program would work). Now, you won't recreate this pixel by pixel. It is still a simple mock-up and while you'll pull some elements from it, you need to remember that you do not have an actual client here. Your semi-static corporate Web site can be for any fictional client that you may have. If this were the real deal, a number of wireframes, mock-ups, and so on would go back and forth with the client, along with meetings and whatnot to establish the needs.

So, Figure 7-3 shows what the site will sort of look like when it is done.

Figure 7-3: Photoshop front page mock-up

I've added a dummy logo and also a dummy header image. The logo will be hardcoded into the theme (which usually is OK), but the header image won't be because the company may want to switch this from time to time.

I did a quick mock-up of how a single view, both for Pages and posts, would look as well (see Figure 7-4). Real simple, sticking to the same site structure so to speak, as you can tell.

Figure 7-4: Single-post view mock-up in Photoshop

WHAT IS WHAT IN THE MOCK-UPS?

Perhaps a few clarifications are in order. Take a look at the front page design first, shown in Figure 7-5.

At the top of Figure 7-5 is the header area, where the menu is a Custom Menu area so that the client can create, edit, and drop Pages there.

The right column is the sidebar that uses sidebar.php. The widget areas make it is easy for the client to throw in more functionality. The text at the top is only shown on the front page and goes with the header image. The text widget is something the user may want to edit from time to time, just as with the header image.

The content on the front page is actually a Page, so WordPress displays any content put into this Page here, and the client can include whatever content they'd like. You'll create a Page template for the front page to make it behave the way we want. Outside of the editable area is the Custom Header.

Figure 7-5: Front page schematics

Moving on, the footer (not in the figure, mind you) starts with another menu because it may be nice to be able to navigate from down there. To the right is a widget area meant for dropping a Twitter widget in, and to the left is another widget area for short and quick contact information. Below that is hardcoded copyright text, credit links, and stuff like that.

That's basically it. The single-post view, shown in Figure 7-6, is similar, but take a quick look at it as well.

Pretty self-explanatory, right? We get into the fancy stuff, such as what is shown in the sidebar, in a little while.

Figure 7-6: Single-post view schematics

THE NECESSARY TEMPLATES

So here are the template files that you use, and how you use them:

- style.css contains all the necessary CSS styles, as well as the theme header.
- index.php act is a fallback because it is mandatory, and will work well enough for things like search, 404, and so on.
- pagetemplate-front.php is our Page template for the front page.
- sidebar.php contains all the necessary code for the sidebar. We could've gone with several sidebars here, but there really is no need.
- archive controls both the Press and the Blog categories.
- single.php controls all posts in the Press or Blog categories in single view.
- page.php controls all Pages in single view.
- header.php for our header needs.
- footer.php for our footer needs.
- functions.php supports all the features that we need, as well as for widget area declarations.

That's it. Let's build it!

BUILDING THE SEMI-STATIC SITE

This is where it gets interesting for real. You will build the theme from scratch, but because you already know most of these things, let's pick up the pace a bit. From now on, I won't describe every little template tag in detail, but I'll add plenty of comments in the code. You probably already know how commenting works, but in case you don't, here's a primer.

```html
<!-- This is a comment in HTML -->
```

```css
/* This is a comment in CSS */
```

```php
<?php
        // This is a comment in PHP
?>
```

Another quick recap might be in order, and that is localization. Everything in PHP that sits within __(' and ') are strings that can be localized through language files. It works like this:

```php
__( 'Top Menu', 'simple-static' )
```

The default output is "Top Menu," and the textdomain, defined in functions.php (we'll do that in a little bit) that the translation belongs to is "simple-static." Always put the string first, and the textdomain later so that WordPress knows where the string belongs.

Right, so let's get started.

THE FUNDAMENTALS: STYLE.CSS AND FUNCTIONS.PHP

Start out by creating the style.css file where you add the theme declaration. You will fill it with CSS stuff later on, but you can start here.

```css
/*
Theme Name: Simple Semi-Static Site
Theme URI: http://tdh.me/wordpress/simple-static/
Description: A theme meant for simple static websites, hence the name.
Version: 1.0
Tags: light, two-columns, right-sidebar, fixed-width, threaded-comments, sticky-
  post, translation-ready
Author: Thord Daniel Hedengren
Author URI: http://tdh.me/

        This theme was originally created for use in the book
        Smashing WordPress Themes, written by yours truly.

        Read more about my books at http://tdh.me/books/

*/
```

With that out of the way, let's move on to functions.php. You need support for custom menus, custom headers, and also custom backgrounds, because it would be pretty cool to change the body background of the site. You also need a couple widget areas. This is the necessary code, commented inline for your viewing pleasure.

```php
<?php
        // We need a textdomain for localization support,
        // with language files in the /lang folder
        load_theme_textdomain( 'simple-static', TEMPLATEPATH . '/lang' );

        // This is the default content width, 600 px
        if ( ! isset( $content_width ) )
                $content_width = 600;

        // Adding theme support for post thumbnails
        add_theme_support( 'post-thumbnails' );

        // Adding theme support for custom backgrounds
        add_custom_background();

        // Telling WordPress to use editor-style.css for the visual editor
        add_editor_style();

        // Adding feed links to header
        add_theme_support( 'automatic-feed-links' );

        // CUSTOM HEADER
        // -------------
        // Adding theme support for custom headers
        add_custom_image_header( '', 'simple-static_admin_header_style' );

        // Remove header text and null the text color
        define( 'NO_HEADER_TEXT', true );
        define( 'HEADER_TEXTCOLOR', '' );

        // Default header image, using 'stylesheet_directory' so that
        // child themes will work
        define( 'HEADER_IMAGE', get_bloginfo('stylesheet_directory') . '/img/
default-header.jpg' );

        // Header width and height, 920x200 px
        define( 'HEADER_IMAGE_WIDTH', 920 );
        define( 'HEADER_IMAGE_HEIGHT', 200 );

        // Adding post thumbnail support (same size as custom header images)
        set_post_thumbnail_size( HEADER_IMAGE_WIDTH, HEADER_IMAGE_HEIGHT, true );

        // MENU AREA
        // ---------
        // Adding and defining the Menu area found in the header.php file
```

```
        register_nav_menus( array(
                'top-menu' => __( 'Top Menu', 'simple-static' ),
                'bottom-menu' => __( 'Bottom Menu', 'simple-static' )
        ) );


        // WIDGET AREAS
        // ------------
        // Widget area used on the front page, on top of the header image
        register_sidebar( array(
                'name' => __( 'Header Text Blurb', 'simple-static' ),
                'id' => 'header-text-blurb',
                'description' => __( 'The blurb on top of the custom header.',
'simple-static' ),
                'before_widget' => '<div id="header-blurb"">',
                'after_widget' => '</div>',
                'before_title' => '<h3 class="widget-title">',
                'after_title' => '</h3>',
        ) );


        // Right column widget area on front page (default output on items)
        register_sidebar( array(
                'name' => __( 'Front Page Right Column', 'simple-static' ),
                'id' => 'front-page-right-column',
                'description' => __( 'The right column on the front page.', 'simple-
static' ),
        ) );


        // Right column widget area on the News/Press category
        register_sidebar( array(
                'name' => __( 'News and Press Right Column', 'simple-static' ),
                'id' => 'news-press-right-column',
                'description' => __( 'The right column on News/Press categories.',
'simple-static' ),
                'before_widget' => '<li id="%1$s" class="widget news %2$s">',
                'after_widget' => '</li>',
                'before_title' => '<h2 class="widgettitle">',
                'after_title' => '</h2>',
        ) );


        // Right column widget area on the Blog section
        register_sidebar( array(
                'name' => __( 'Blog Right Column', 'simple-static' ),
                'id' => 'blog-right-column',
                'description' => __( 'The right column on the Blog section.',
'simple-static' ),
                'before_widget' => '<li id="%1$s" class="widget blog %2$s">',
                'after_widget' => '</li>',
                'before_title' => '<h2 class="widgettitle">',
                'after_title' => '</h2>',
        ) );
```

```php
        // Right column widget area on Pages
        register_sidebar( array(
                'name' => __( 'Pages Column', 'simple-static' ),
                'id' => 'pages-right-column',
                'description' => __( 'The right column on Pages.', 'simple-static'
),
                'before_widget' => '<li id="%1$s" class="widget pages %2$s">',
                'after_widget' => '</li>',
                'before_title' => '<h2 class="widgettitle">',
                'after_title' => '</h2>',
        ) );

        // Left column in the footer
        register_sidebar( array(
                'name' => __( 'Footer Left Side', 'simple-static' ),
                'id' => 'footer-left-side',
                'description' => __( 'The left hand side of the footer.', 'simple-
static' ),
                'before_widget' => '<li id="%1$s" class="widget footer %2$s">',
                'after_widget' => '</li>',
                'before_title' => '<h2 class="widgettitle">',
                'after_title' => '</h2>',
        ) );

        // Right column in the footer
        register_sidebar( array(
                'name' => __( 'Footer Right Column', 'simple-static' ),
                'id' => 'footer-right-column',
                'description' => __( 'The right hand column in the footer.', 'sim-
ple-static' ),
                'before_widget' => '<li id="%1$s" class="widget footer %2$s">',
                'after_widget' => '</li>',
                'before_title' => '<h2 class="widgettitle">',
                'after_title' => '</h2>',
        ) );

        // Right column fallback widget area
        register_sidebar( array(
                'name' => __( 'Right Column Fallback', 'simple-static' ),
                'id' => 'right-column-fallback',
                'description' => __( 'The right column fallback area for those
non-posts and pages.', 'simple-static' ),
                'before_widget' => '<li id="%1$s" class="widget %2$s">',
                'after_widget' => '</li>',
                'before_title' => '<h2 class="widgettitle">',
                'after_title' => '</h2>',
        ) );
?>
```

That's actually the only thing you need in functions.php. You've added the theme support for all those cool features, included the content width and all the widget areas. Splendid!

THEME FILES FOR OUR SHELL (HEADER, FOOTER, AND INDEX)

Moving on, it's time to create the header.php, index.php, and footer.php template files, as well as a loop.php file for your loop needs. These are straightforward enough, but planning ahead is key. First, let's figure out how to build this site. This is the structure:

```
body
        div#site
                div#wrap
                        div#header
                        div#plate
                                div.top-menu
                                div#custom-header
                                div#content
                                div#sidebar-container
                                div#footer
                                        div.bottom-menu
                                        div.footer-left
                                        div.footer-right
                                        div#footer-bottom
```

You'll notice that `div#menu` is present twice. This is correct, but the two instances won't behave exactly the same way. Luckily you can control that with a class so that'll work well enough.

Next you'll glance through the necessary file, keeping sidebar.php and the loop templates for a little later.

Header.php

Start with header.php then, commented inline:

```php
<!DOCTYPE html>
<html <?php language_attributes(); ?>>
<head>
<meta charset="<?php bloginfo( 'charset' ); ?>" />
<title><?php
        // Changing the title for various sections on the site
        if ( is_home () ) {
            bloginfo('name');
        } elseif ( is_category() || is_tag() ) {
            single_cat_title(); echo ' &bull; ' ; bloginfo('name');
        } elseif ( is_single() || is_page() ) {
            single_post_title();
        } else {
            wp_title('',true);
        }
?></title>
<link rel="profile" href="http://gmpg.org/xfn/11" />
<link rel="stylesheet" type="text/css" media="all" href="<?php bloginfo( 'style-
```

```
  sheet_url' ); ?>" />
<link rel="pingback" href="<?php bloginfo( 'pingback_url' ); ?>" />
<?php wp_head(); ?>
</head>

<body <?php body_class(); ?>>
        <div id="site">
        <div id="wrap">
                <div id="header">
                <?php
                        // Checking if it is the front page in which case we'll use
    a h1
                        if ( is_front_page() ) { ?>
                        <h1 id="logo">
                                <a href="<?php bloginfo('url'); ?>" title="<?php
    bloginfo('title'); ?>">
                                        <?php
                                                // Getting the site title
                                                bloginfo('title');
                                        ?>
                                        </a>
                        </h1>
                        <?php }
                        // If it isn't the front page this is what we'll use
                        else { ?>
                        <div id="logo">
                                <a href="<?php bloginfo('url'); ?>" title="<?php
    bloginfo('title'); ?>">
                                        <?php
                                                // Getting the site title
                                                bloginfo('title');
                                        ?>
                                        </a>
                        </div>
                        <?php } ?>
                        <div class="search">
                                <?php
                                        // The default search form
                                        get_search_form();
                                ?>
                        </div>
                </div>
                <div id="plate">
                        <?php
                                // Checking if there's anything in Top Menu
                                if ( has_nav_menu( 'top-menu' ) ) {

                                        // If there is, adds the Top Menu area
                                        wp_nav_menu( array(
                                                'menu' => 'Top Menu',
                                                'container' => 'div',
```

```php
                                        'container_class' => 'top-menu',
                                        'theme_location' => 'top-menu',
                        ));
                }
        ?>
        <div id="custom-header">
        <?php
                // Header code from Twenty Ten
                // Check if this is a post or page, if it has a thumb-
nail, and if it's a big one
                if ( is_singular() &&
                        has_post_thumbnail( $post->ID ) &&
                        ( /* $src, $width, $height */ $image =
wp_get_attachment_image_src( get_post_thumbnail_id( $post->ID ), 'post-thumbnail' )
) &&
                        $image[1] >= HEADER_IMAGE_WIDTH ) :
                // Houston, we have a new header image!
                echo get_the_post_thumbnail( $post->ID, 'post-
thumbnail' );
                else : ?>
                        <?php
                        // The Front Page Header Text widget
area
                        // Empty by default
                                if ( !function_exists('dynamic_side-
bar') || !dynamic_sidebar('front-page-header-text-blurb') ) : endif;
                        ?>
                        <img src="<?php header_image(); ?>" width="<?php
echo HEADER_IMAGE_WIDTH; ?>" height="<?php echo HEADER_IMAGE_HEIGHT; ?>" alt="" />
                <?php endif; ?>
        </div>
```

You'll recognize most of the code in here, but some things might need clarification. The part within the `title` tag, which is the title of the Web page you're on at the moment, is a simple `if/else` check against conditional tags, checking if you're on the front page, and then doing one thing on a category page, and doing something else, and so on. You've got the same thing going on down in the `div#header` where you show the logo in two different ways, depending on where on the site you are. Or rather, if you're on the front page you display the logo within h1 tags, but on all other parts of the site, the logo sits in `div#logo` instead. The reason for this is simple semantics: The actual Web site title is only on the front page, including the logo, the most important thing to tell search engines. On every other page, the Page or post title is the thing search engines need to know.

After `div#header` you've got `div#plate`, which is the `div` containing the whole site. At the very top of it is a menu, which obviously is managed with the Menus feature in WordPress.

```php
<?php
    // Checking if there's anything in Top Menu
    if ( has_nav_menu( 'top-menu' ) ) {
```

163

```
                    // If there is, adds the Top Menu area
                wp_nav_menu( array(
                        'menu' => 'Top Menu',
                        'container' => 'div',
                        'container_class' => 'top-menu',
                        'theme_location' => 'top-menu',
                ));
        }
?>
```

Here you check if the Menu called "Top Menu," called via the 'top-menu' parameter in has_nav_menu(), has anything. If it does, you output the menu with wp_nav_menu(), otherwise not.

Finally, you'll find the Custom Header image part below the menu, in div#custom-header. The code is in part nicked from the Twenty Ten theme, with some alterations.

```
<div id="custom-header">
<?php
    // Header code from Twenty Ten
    // Check if this is a post or page, if it has a thumbnail,
    // and if it's a big one
    if ( is_singular() &&
                    has_post_thumbnail( $post->ID ) &&
                    ( /* $src, $width, $height */ $image = wp_get_attachment_image_
    src( get_post_thumbnail_id( $post->ID ), 'post-thumbnail' ) ) &&
                    $image[1] >= HEADER_IMAGE_WIDTH ) :
            // Houston, we have a new header image!
            echo get_the_post_thumbnail( $post->ID, 'post-thumbnail' );
    else : ?>
            <?php
                    // The Front Page Header Text widget area
                    // Empty by default
                    if ( !function_exists('dynamic_sidebar') || !dynamic_
    sidebar('front-page-header-text-blurb') ) : endif;
            ?>
            <img src="<?php header_image(); ?>" width="<?php echo HEADER_IMAGE_
    WIDTH; ?>" height="<?php echo HEADER_IMAGE_HEIGHT; ?>" alt="" />
<?php endif; ?>
</div>
```

First you check to see if you're on a single post or Page, in which case you'll check for a featured image. That's right, if you set a featured image on any post or Page that is used instead of the custom image. Fancy huh? Yeah, not really, but it might come in handy if you want to illustrate something a bit more visual, especially on product Pages, or whatever.

If there is no featured image, you first output a widget area, which contains the Header Text Blurb. This displays only on the Custom Header images that you've uploaded from within the admin panel, which is shown in Figure 7-7.

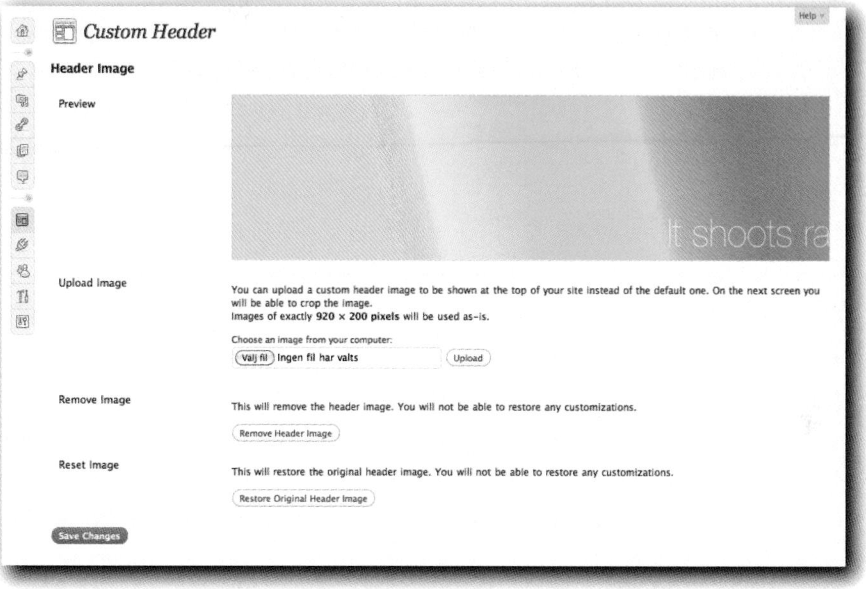

Figure 7-7: Custom Header images screen in WordPress admin panel

Under the widget declaration you'll find the image code that outputs the custom header.

```
<img src="<?php header_image(); ?>" width="<?php echo HEADER_IMAGE_WIDTH; ?>"
height="<?php echo HEADER_IMAGE_HEIGHT; ?>" alt="" />
```

Height and width is pulled from the functions.php file; I bet you recognize the HEADER_IMAGE_WIDTH and HEADER_IMAGE_HEIGHT, as well as the header_image() template tag in the img tag.

That's it for the header. When it ends you've got both div#site and div#wrap open, as well as div#plate, inside which the rest of the site will reside.

Index.php

You won't use index.php really, but the theme needs it as a fallback (and to be a valid theme). So here it is, as bare as it can be.

```
<?php get_header(); ?>

            <div id="content">
                    <?php get_template_part( 'loop', 'index' ); ?>
            </div>

<?php get_sidebar(); ?>
<?php get_footer(); ?>
```

Not much to talk about here: you fetch the header and then call the loop with `get_tem-`
`plate_part()`. You'll remember that this template tag first looks for loop-X.php where X is
the second (optional) parameter passed; in this case index so it is looking for loop-index.php.
It won't find it, so it'll revert to loop.php instead, which exists and we get to in a little bit. The
purpose for this is to let child themers get to the loop in index.php by including a loop-index.
php template file with the loop they want.

Finally, index.php is wrapped up with a sidebar and footer inclusion.

Footer.php

The footer.php template file is pretty straightforward. The first thing that happens in
`div#footer` is a menu check much like the one in header.php. If there's a header, you output
it. You can reach it by applying a Custom Menu to the Bottom Menu area in the admin panel
(see Figure 7-8).

Figure 7-8: The clean and simple footer

```
<div id="footer">
        <?php
                // Checking if there's anything in
Bottom Menu
                if ( has_nav_menu( 'bottom-menu' ) ) {
                        // If there is, adds the Bottom Menu
area
                        wp_nav_menu( array(
                                'menu' => 'Bottom Menu',
                                'container' => 'div',
                                'container_class' =>
'bottom-menu',
                                'theme_location' =>
'bottom-menu',
                        ));
                }
        ?>
        <div class="footer-left">
                <ul>
                <?php
                        // The Footer Left Side widget area
```

```
                                                dynamic_sidebar('footer-left-side');
                        ?>
                                <li class="widget widget-area-
empty">You should drop a widget here, mate!</li>
                        <?php endif; ?>
                        </ul>
                </div>
                <div class="footer-right">
                        <ul>
                        <?php
                                // The Footer Right Side widget area

dynamic_sidebar('footer-right-side');
                        ?>
                                <li class="widget widget-area-
empty">You should drop a widget here too, buddy!</li>
                        <?php endif; ?>
                        </ul>
                </div>
                <div id="footer-bottom">
                        <p><?php bloginfo('title'); ?> is proudly
powered by <a href="http://wordpress.org" title="WordPress">WordPress</a></p>
                </div>
        </div>

        </div> <!-- ends #plate -->
    </div> <!-- ends #wrap -->
    </div> <!-- ends #site -->

<?php wp_footer(); ?>
</body>
</html>
```

You've got two widget areas at the bottom of the page, a larger column to the right (`div.footer-left`) and a smaller one to the right (`div.footer-right`). Both output text that tells you to add widgets to the area should you not have done so already.

Finally, `div#footer-bottom` contains some basic information, and then you close your `div#site`, `div#wrap`, and `div#plate div` tags. Below that is the `wp_footer()` template tag that wraps up WordPress.

That's the primary shell, but I left out sidebar.php, as well as the loop templates. Let's take a look at those, shall we?

THE VARIOUS SIDEBARS

You're sticking with one sidebar.php file, although it would be possible to use several. The code separates the various sidebar views with conditional tags. For example, you can use this code to check if it is the front page and, if it is, output the appropriate widget area:

```
        // We want to show the right sidebar for the right area
// Checking to see if it is the front page
if ( is_front_page() ) {
    // The Front Page Right Column widget area
    dynamic_sidebar('front-page-right-column'); // -- Check ends
}
```

You've got three other sidebar views to take into account: one for the press section, which shows the latest press updates and a similar one for the blog section, which sticks to blog posts. Finally, there's the one for all the static Pages, which most likely contains a mixture of this. You show the correct sidebar using conditional tags, and every one of them contains their own widget area, so that it'll be easy for the client to drop things in it, like polls for the blog section, or whatever.

Let's take it from the top. The first thing you want is to check if you're on a single post or Page view, in which case, you output some post meta information or a Page menu, respectively.

```
// Single posts and Pages needs some meta data, but NOT the front page
if ( is_singular() &! is_front_page() ) { ?>
    <li id="postmeta" class="widget">
            <h2><?php echo __('Information', 'simple-static'); ?></h2>
            <?php
            // This is for Pages only
            if ( is_page() ) { ?>
                    <p><?php echo __('Page created ', 'simple-static'); ?><?php
  the_date(); ?> <?php echo __('by', 'simple-static'); ?> <?php the_author(); ?></p>
                    <?php
                        // Pages should have a page menu
                        wp_list_pages();
                    ?>
            <?php }
            // This is for posts only
            if ( is_single() ) { ?>
                    <p><span class="meta-category"><?php the_category(' &bull;
'); ?> &bull; </span><?php echo __('Written on ', 'simple-static'); ?><?php the_
date(); ?> @ <?php the_time(); ?> <?php echo __('by', 'simple-static'); ?> <?php
the_author(); ?></p>
                    <p><?php the_tags(); ?></p>
            <?php } ?>
    </li>
```

With is_singular() you can get to both single posts and single Pages. The &! tells WordPress that it not applies to something, in this case is_front_page(). Since the front page is meant to be a Page, this would be true otherwise, so you need to remove that.

After this little code snippet, you have all your widget area checks.

```
// Checking to see if it is the front page
if ( is_front_page() ) {
```

```php
        // The Front Page Right Column widget area
    dynamic_sidebar('front-page-right-column'); // -- Check ends
}
// Checking to see if it is related to the News category
// This widget area is empty by default
elseif ( is_category('news') || in_category('news') ) {
        // The News and Press Right Column widget area
    dynamic_sidebar('news-right-column'); // -- Check ends
}
// Checking to see if it is related to the Blog category
// This widget area is empty by default
elseif ( is_category('blog') || in_category('blog') ) {
        // The Blog Right Column widget area
    dynamic_sidebar('blog-right-column'); // -- Check ends
}
// Checking to see if it is a Page
// This widget area is empty by default
elseif ( is_page() ) {
        // The Pages Right Column widget area
    dynamic_sidebar('pages-right-column'); // -- Check ends
}
else {
        // Fallback widget area for everything else
        // This widget area is empty by default
    dynamic_sidebar('right-column-fallback'); // -- Check ends
}
```

Conditional tags in action!

That's it, then? Not quite. Although you could have used plugins to do something similar, this example uses two extra loops to fetch the latest posts from the News and Blog categories, respectively. Let's look at the first loop:

```php
<?php
    // Let's get the latest News posts with a loop
    $news_query = new WP_Query(array(
            'category_name' => 'news',
            'posts_per_page' => 5)
    ); ?>
    <?php
            // Any posts? Yay, let's loop 'em!
            if ($news_query->have_posts()) { ?>
            <?php while ($news_query->have_posts()) : $news_query->the_post(); ?>
                    <li class="latest-box-story">
                            <h4><a href="<?php the_permalink(); ?>"><?php the_
    title(); ?></a></h4>
                            <?php the_excerpt(); ?>
                    </li>
            <?php endwhile; // Loop ends ?>
    <?php } ?>
```

The first part gives you a new loop in $news_query so that you won't risk clashing with other loops on the site. Pass some data, the category name (with category_name) and the number of posts you want to fetch (5, with posts_per_page) to WP_Query and store that in $news_category so you have something to play with. You might recognize the parameters in WP_Query; they're the same as query_posts().

After that it gets easy. If there are any posts in $news_query, you loop them (five times since, that's what you stored in it) and for each post, output the title and excerpt within an li tag. When you've done that, you're done.

You want a box with the five latest news posts on the front page, on the News category page, and on posts in the News category, so put a conditional check for those things before running the loop. That way you won't get the news posts box in the wrong places.

```php
<?php
    // Showing latest News box on front page and News category
    if ( is_front_page() || is_category('news') || in_category('news') ) { ?>
        <li class="latest-box widget">
                <h3>News & Press</h3>
                <ul>
                <?php
                    // Let's get the latest News posts with a loop
                    $news_query = new WP_Query(array(
                            'category_name' => 'news',
                            'posts_per_page' => 5)
                    ); ?>
                <?php
                        // Any posts? Yay, let's loop 'em!
                        if ($news_query->have_posts()) { ?>
                        <?php while ($news_query->have_posts()) : $news_
query->the_post(); ?>
                                <li class="latest-box-story">
                                        <h4><a href="<?php the_permalink();
?>"><?php the_title(); ?></a></h4>
                                        <?php the_excerpt(); ?>
                                </li>
                        <?php endwhile; // Loop ends ?>
                    <?php } ?>
                </ul>
        </li>
    <?php }
?>
```

Now you do the same with the Blog category, that contains all your blog posts. However, this category is only shown on the front page (just like the News category) and on the Blog category and posts within it. You'll recognize the code . . .

```php
<?php
    // Showing latest Blog posts on front page and Blog category
```

```php
    if ( is_front_page() || is_category('blog') || in_category('blog') ) { ?>
        <li class="latest-box widget">
                <h3>Latest blog posts</h3>
                <ul>
                <?php
                    // Let's get the latest News posts with a loop
                    $news_query = new WP_Query(array(
                            'category_name' => 'blog',
                            'posts_per_page' => 5)
                    ); ?>
                <?php
                        // Any posts? Yay, let's loop 'em!
                        if ($news_query->have_posts()) { ?>
                        <?php while ($news_query->have_posts()) : $news_
query->the_post(); ?>
                                <li class="latest-box-story">
                                        <h4><a href="<?php the_permalink();
?>"><?php the_title(); ?></a></h4>
                                        <?php the_excerpt(); ?>
                                </li>
                        <?php endwhile; // Loop ends ?>
                <?php } ?>
                </ul>
        </li>
    <?php }
?>
```

That's it! Here's the full sidebar code, commented inline.

```php
<div id="sidebar-container">
        <ul id="sidebar">
        <?php
                // Single posts and Pages needs some meta data,
                // but NOT the front page
                if ( is_singular() &! is_front_page() ) { ?>
                        <li id="postmeta" class="widget">
                                <h2><?php echo __('Information', 'simple-static');
?></h2>
                                <?php
                                // This is for Pages only
                                if ( is_page() ) { ?>
                                        <p><?php echo __('Page created ', 'simple-
static'); ?><?php the_date(); ?> <?php echo __('by', 'simple-static'); ?> <?php
the_author(); ?></p>
                                        <?php
                                                // Pages should have a page menu
                                                wp_list_pages();
                                        ?>
                                <?php }
                                // This is for posts only
                                if ( is_single() ) { ?>
```

```
                                    <p><span class="meta-category"><?php
the_category(' &bull; '); ?> &bull; </span><?php echo __('Written on ', 'simple-
static'); ?><?php the_date(); ?> @ <?php the_time(); ?> <?php echo __('by', 'sim-
ple-static'); ?> <?php the_author(); ?></p>
                                    <p><?php the_tags(); ?></p>
                        <?php } ?>
                </li>
        <?php }
        // We want to show the right sidebar for the right area
        // Checking to see if it is the front page
        if ( is_front_page() ) {
                // The Front Page Right Column widget area
                dynamic_sidebar('front-page-right-column'); // -- Check ends
        }
        // Checking to see if it is related to the News category
        // This widget area is empty by default
        elseif ( is_category('news') || in_category('news') ) {
                // The News and Press Right Column widget area
                dynamic_sidebar('news-right-column'); // -- Check ends
        }
        // Checking to see if it is related to the Blog category
        // This widget area is empty by default
        elseif ( is_category('blog') || in_category('blog') ) {
                // The Blog Right Column widget area
                dynamic_sidebar('blog-right-column'); // -- Check ends
        }
        // Checking to see if it is a Page
        // This widget area is empty by default
        elseif ( is_page() ) {
                // The Pages Right Column widget area
                dynamic_sidebar('pages-right-column'); // -- Check ends
        }
        else {
                // Fallback widget area for everything else
                // This widget area is empty by default
                dynamic_sidebar('right-column-fallback'); // -- Check ends
        }
        ?>

        <?php
                // Showing latest News box on front page and
                // News category
                if ( is_front_page() || is_category('news') || in_
category('news') ) { ?>
                        <li class="latest-box widget">
                                <h3>News & Press</h3>
                                <ul>
                                <?php
                                    // Let's get the latest News posts with
a loop
                                        $news_query = new WP_Query(array(
```

```php
                                        'category_name' => 'news',
                                        'posts_per_page' => 5)
                        ); ?>
                    <?php
                        // Any posts? Yay, let's loop!
                        if ($news_query->have_posts()) {
?>
                        <?php while ($news_query->have_
posts()) : $news_query->the_post(); ?>
                                <li
class="latest-box-story">
                                    <h4><a
href="<?php the_permalink(); ?>"><?php the_title(); ?></a></h4>
                                    <?php the_
excerpt(); ?>
                                </li>
                        <?php endwhile; // Loop ends ?>
                    <?php } ?>
                </ul>
            </li>
        <?php }
    ?>

        <?php
            // Showing latest Blog posts on front page and
            // Blog category
            if ( is_front_page() || is_category('blog') || in_
category('blog') ) { ?>
                <li class="latest-box widget">
                    <h3>Latest blog posts</h3>
                    <ul>
                    <?php
                        // Let's get the latest News posts
                        // with a loop
                        $news_query = new WP_Query(array(
                                'category_name' => 'blog',
                                'posts_per_page' => 5)
                        ); ?>
                    <?php
                        // Any posts? Yay, let's loop!
if ($news_query->have_posts()) { ?>
                        <?php while ($news_query->have_
posts()) : $news_query->the_post(); ?>
                                <li
class="latest-box-story">
                                    <h4><a
href="<?php the_permalink(); ?>"><?php the_title(); ?></a></h4>
                                    <?php the_
excerpt(); ?>
                                </li>
                        <?php endwhile; // Loop ends ?>
```

```
                                                <?php } ?>
                                        </ul>
                                </li>
                        <?php }
                ?>

                </ul>
        </div>
```

THE LOOP TEMPLATE

You will keep most of your loops in the loop.php template. All `get_template_part()` calls, which are used to include the loop (much like `get_sidebar()` is used to include the sidebar.php template file, for example), are pointing to a specific loop template file for each template respectively. In other words, the index.php template points to loop-index.php, whereas page.php points to loop-page.php, and so on. Whenever the specific loop template file is missing, WordPress will try loop.php, and that's what you've got. You're doing it this way to make it easy to pinpoint specific template file loops in child themes.

So, what about loop.php then, and what do you need in it to make the theme work? The first thing you have is the 404 error message for when a page isn't found.

```php
<?php
        // No posts to show, the famous 404 error message
        if ( ! have_posts() ) :
?>
        <div id="post-0" class="post error404 not-found">
                <h1 class="entry-title"><?php __( 'Page Not Found', 'semi-static' );
 ?></h1>
                <div class="entry-content">
                        <p><?php
                                // Error message output (localized)
                                __( 'There is nothing here, besides this page which
 will tell you no more than that.
                                Why not try and search for whatever it was
 you were looking for?', 'semi-static' );
                        ?></p>
                        <?php get_search_form(); ?>
                </div>
        </div>
<?php endif; ?>
```

Basically this is a localized error message, and then the search form. Simple enough, right? The actual loop isn't much more complicated:

```php
        // The default loop
        while ( have_posts() ) : the_post();
```

```php
                // If it's an archive or search result
                if ( is_home() || is_archive() || is_search() ) :
                ?>
                <div id="post-<?php the_ID(); ?>" <?php post_class(); ?>>
                        <h2 class="entry-title"><a href="<?php the_permalink(); ?>"
title="<?php echo __('Permalink to ', 'simple-static'); the_title(); ?>"
rel="bookmark"><?php the_title(); ?></a></h2>

                        <div class="entry entry-excerpt">
                                <?php the_excerpt(); ?>
                        </div>

                <?php // Everything else
                else : ?>

                        <div id="post-<?php the_ID(); ?>" <?php post_class(); ?>>
                                <h1 class="entry-title"><?php the_title(); ?></h1>
                                <div class="entry entry-content">
                                        <?php the_content(); ?>
                                        <?php wp_link_pages( array( 'before' =>
'<div class="page-link">' . __( 'Pages:', 'semi-static' ), 'after' => '</div>' ) );
?>
                                </div>
                                <?php // Let's check to see if the comments are open
                                if (comments_open()) { ?>
                                <div class="entry-meta">
                                        <span class="comments-link">
                                                <?php echo __('There are', 'simple-
static'); ?> <?php comments_popup_link( __( 'no comments - pitch in!', 'semi-
static' ), __( '1 comment', 'semi-static' ), __( '% comments', 'semi-static' ) ); ?>
                                        </span>
                                        <?php edit_post_link( __( 'Edit', 'semi-
static' ), '<span class="meta-sep">|</span> <span class="edit-link">', '</span>' );
?>
                                </div>
                                <?php } ?>

                <?php endif; ?>

                </div>

                <?php
                                                // If the comments are open we'll
need the comments
                                // template
                                                if (comments_open()) {
                                comments_template( '', true );
                                                }
                ?>

<?php endwhile; ?>
```

First start the loop (with `while` and the whole `have_posts()` thing), then check to see if you're on either the home page (should you display posts on the front page), on an archive (categories, tags, and other taxonomies fall in here), or if it's a search result. If true, you get a simple post listing displaying the linked post title and the excerpt.

If you're not in any of those sections, you move on to, well, everything else. In this case, that's just singular posts. So your title is in an `h1` tag, unlinked, and you output the full content with `the_content()` and so on. This is basically how a post looks.

This little part is important to know.

```php
<?php
    // If the comments are open we'll need the comments template
    if (comments_open()) {
        comments_template( '', true );
    }
?>
```

It checks to see if comments are open, and if they are, it outputs the comments template. This is nice because if your comments are closed, you won't have to look at the "Sorry, comments are closed" message, as it won't even be called.

Here's the complete loop.php template:

```php
<?php
        // No posts to show, the famous 404 error message
        if ( ! have_posts() ) :
?>
        <div id="post-0" class="post error404 not-found">
                <h1 class="entry-title"><?php __( 'Page Not Found', 'semi-static' );
    ?></h1>
                <div class="entry-content">
                        <p><?php
                                // Error message output (localized)
                                __( 'There is nothing here, besides this page which
    will tell you no more than that.                        Why not
    try and search for whatever it was you were looking for?', 'semi-static' );
                        ?></p>
                        <?php get_search_form(); ?>
                </div>
        </div>
<?php endif; ?>

<?php
        // The default loop
        while ( have_posts() ) : the_post();

                // If it's an archive or search result
                if ( is_home() || is_archive() || is_search() ) :
```

```php
                ?>
                <div id="post-<?php the_ID(); ?>" <?php post_class(); ?>>
                    <h2 class="entry-title"><a href="<?php the_permalink(); ?>"
title="<?php echo __('Permalink to ', 'simple-static'); the_title(); ?>"
rel="bookmark"><?php the_title(); ?></a></h2>

                    <div class="entry entry-excerpt">
                        <?php the_excerpt(); ?>
                    </div>

            <?php // Everything else
            else : ?>

                    <div id="post-<?php the_ID(); ?>" <?php post_class(); ?>>
                        <h1 class="entry-title"><?php the_title(); ?></h1>
                        <div class="entry entry-content">
                            <?php the_content(); ?>
                            <?php wp_link_pages( array( 'before' =>
'<div class="page-link">' . __( 'Pages:', 'semi-static' ), 'after' => '</div>' ) );
?>
                        </div>
                        <?php // Let's check to see if the comments are open
                        if (comments_open()) { ?>
                        <div class="entry-meta">
                            <span class="comments-link">
                                <?php echo __('There are', 'simple-
static'); ?> <?php comments_popup_link( __( 'no comments - pitch in!', 'semi-
static' ), __( '1 comment', 'semi-static' ), __( '% comments', 'semi-static' ) );
?>
                            </span>
                            <?php edit_post_link( __( 'Edit', 'semi-
static' ), '<span class="meta-sep">|</span> <span class="edit-link">', '</span>' );
?>
                        </div>
                        <?php } ?>

            <?php endif; ?>

            </div>

            <?php
                                        // If the comments are open we'll
    need the
                    // comments template
                                        if (comments_open()) {
                        comments_template( '', true );
                                        }
            ?>

<?php endwhile; ?>
```

THE FRONT PAGE TEMPLATE

This theme is built to have a static Page as the front page. You want to keep that free of the Page title and stuff, so for this Page template, which you can call `pagetemplate-frontpage.php`, you don't want to keep the loop in a separate file. Here's the whole thing.

```php
<?php
/*
Template Name: Front Page
*/
?>

<?php get_header(); ?>

                        <div id="content">
                        <?php
                                // The front page loop
                                while ( have_posts() ) : the_post(); ?>

                                        <div id="post-<?php the_ID(); ?>" <?php
                                            post_class(); ?>>
                                            <div class="entry entry-content">
                                                    <?php the_content(); ?>
                                            </div>
                                        </div>

                        <?php endwhile; ?>
                        </div>

<?php get_sidebar(); ?>
<?php get_footer(); ?>
```

To use it, just create a Page (called "Welcome" or something similar) in the WordPress admin panel and then apply the template called Frontpage to it. Then go to Settings and click Reading to see the Page displayed in Figure 7-9. Select your Page as the front page on your site from the drop-down menu.

The Frontpage template, shown in Figure 7-10, is displayed.

Now your newly created Page, with the Frontpage template, will be the first thing that greets your visitors. Swell.

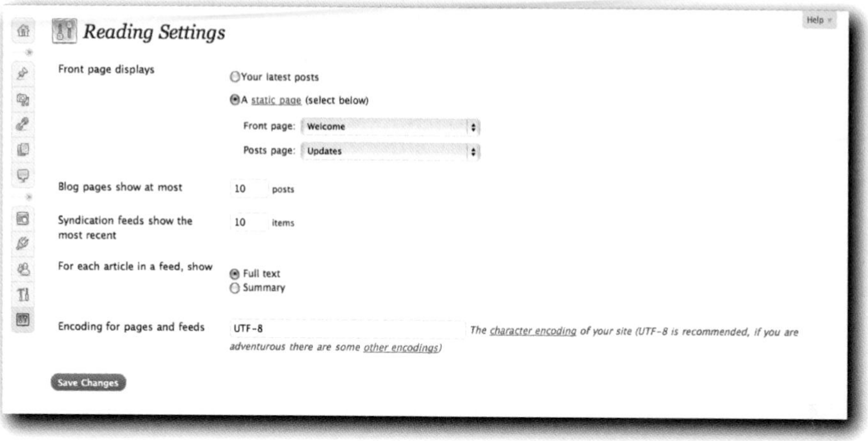

Figure 7-9: Under Settings, click Reading to select your Front page

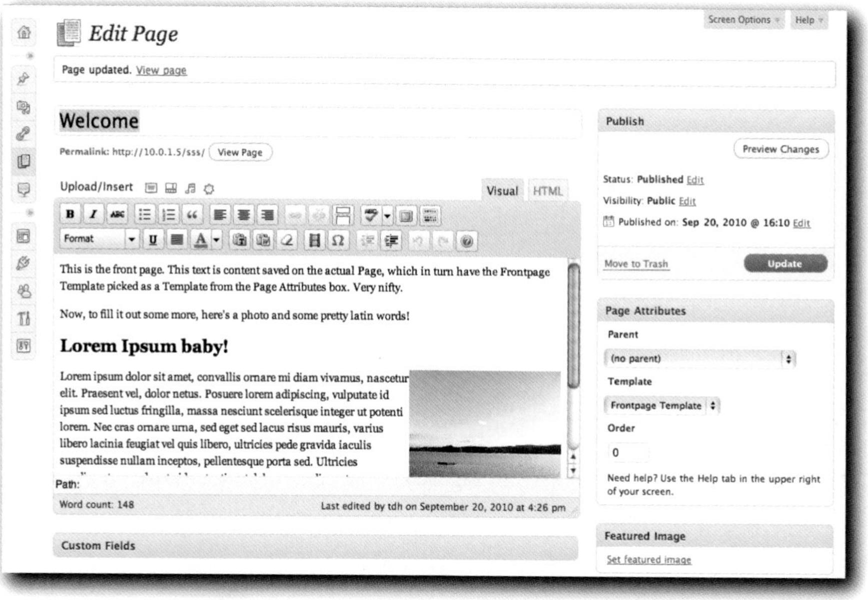

Figure 7-10: Editing the front page using the Front Page template

NEWS AND BLOG TEMPLATES

The press and blog sections are both categories. You could have used different category templates to manage these (category-press.php and category-blog.php for example), but instead you're using a general archive.php template instead, since that's a fallback for them both and also works with other taxonomies (both tags and custom stuff).

Start by taking a look at the archive.php template file:

```php
<?php get_header(); ?>

            <div id="content">
                    <h1 id="taxonomy-title">
                        <?php
                            echo __('<span>Browsing</span> ',
    'simple-static');

                                if ( is_category() ) {
                                    single_cat_title();
                                } elseif ( is_tag() ) {
                                    single_tag_title();
                                }
                        ?>
                    </h1>

                    <?php get_template_part( 'loop', 'archive' ); ?>
            </div>

<?php get_sidebar(); ?>
<?php get_footer(); ?>
```

The contents of the `h1#archive-title` is a simple conditional check to see if you're on a category or tag archive, and outputting the category or tag respectively depending on the result.

The fact that you're relying on archive.php for these things makes it really easy to overwrite, even if you need more fine-grained control than just editing the loop for archive.php (you'll reach that on loop-archive.php, as you've probably seen already). There are several layers of category and tag templates that takes precedence over archive.php, so you can overwrite it that way without much hassle.

WAIT, WHAT ABOUT THE STYLESHEET?

Oh yeah, you need some styling as well. This is a pretty straightforward design, there's nothing particularly complicated in here either.

A few things are worth mentioning though, and that is the classes for styling the top right text widget on the front page. Look for `div#header-blurb` in the code. Other than that, this is pretty straightforward. So I'll let the code speak for itself; it is commented as well.

If you want, you could style these two categories differently, maybe making the news section feel a bit more "official" than the blog section, but that's just some CSS wizardry, so we'll leave that for now. In case you're curious as to how to do that, check out the CSS classes that `post_class()` *outputs for every* `div.post`. *You'll find classes for categories, tags, and so on in there, letting you get to the content easily enough.*

```
/*
Theme Name: Simple Static Site
Theme URI: http://tdh.me/wordpress/simple-static/
Description: A theme meant for simple static websites, hence the name.
Version: 1.0
Tags: light, two-columns, right-sidebar, fixed-width, threaded-comments, transla-
   tion-ready, custom-header, custom-background, custom-menu, editor-style
Author: Thord Daniel Hedengren
Author URI: http://tdh.me/


        This theme was originally created for use in the book
        Smashing WordPress Themes, written by yours truly.


        Read more about my books at http://tdh.me/books/

*/


/* RESET
   ----- */

body, h1, h2, h3, h4, h5, h6, p, form, img, ul, ol,
table, tbody, thead, tr, td
        {
        margin: 0;
        padding: 0;
        border: 0;
        vertical-align: baseline;
        }



/* LAYOUT
   ------ */

#site {
        width: 100%;
}

#wrap {
        width: 960px; /* The full site width */
        margin: 40px auto;
}

#header {
        width: 100%;
        float: left;
}
        h1#logo, div#logo {
                width: 620px;
                float: left;
        }
```

```
div.search {
        width: 320px;
        float: right;
        text-align: right;
}
div#header-blurb { /* The text blurb on the front page header */
        position: absolute;
        width: 260px;
        margin-left: 620px;
        background: url(img/white-50.png);
}
        div#header-blurb p {
                padding: 20px;
        }


#plate {
        width: 100%;
        float: left;
        background: #fff; /* This is the actual site background */
}

div.top-menu {
        width: 100%;
        float:left;
        background: #d5cba7;
}
        div.top-menu ul {}
                div.top-menu ul li {
                        float: left;
                        list-style: none;
                        padding: 15px 0;
                }

#custom-header {
        float: left;
        padding: 20px;
        }

#content {
        width: 620px; /* Active content width is 600 px due to left margin */
        float: left;
}
        div.post, div.page, h1#archive-title {
                padding-left: 20px; /* The left margin */
                margin-bottom: 30px;
        }
        div.entry-content, div.entry-meta {
                margin-bottom: 24px;
        }
        div.entry-meta {
                padding: 20px;
```

```css
        background: #f6f5ef;
        border: 1px solid #f3ecd2;
        border-width: 1px 0; /* Only top and bottom */
}

/* Comments style */
h3#comments {
        margin-bottom: 10px;
        padding-bottom: 10px;
        border-bottom: 1px solid #888;
}
h3#comments, div.navigation, ol.commentlist, div#respond {
        margin-left: 20px; /* Getting the left column right */
}
ol.commentlist {
        margin-bottom: 20px;
}
        li.comment {
                list-style: none;
                margin-top: 10px;
        }
        li.depth-1 {
                padding-bottom: 10px;
                border-bottom: 1px solid #888; /* Bottom border on top
                                                level comments */
        }
                div.comment-author {}
                        div.comment-author img.avatar {
                                float:left;
                                margin-right: 10px;
                        }
                div.comment-meta, div.comment-body p {
                        margin-bottom: 10px; /* Adding some space */
                }
                ul.children {
                        margin-left: 20px; /* Left margin for replies in
                                                threaded comments */
                }
                div.reply { /* Reply link in threaded comments */
                        padding-top: 5px;
                        text-align: right;
                        border-top: 1px solid #bfbfbf;
                }
div#respond {} /* The reply to comments box */
        form#commentform {
                margin-top: 10px;
                padding: 20px 20px 10px 20px; /* We only need 10px
                                                bottom */
                background: #f6f5ef;
        }
                form#commentform p {
```

```
                                        margin-bottom: 10px;
                                }
                                form#commentform input {
                                        margin-right: 10px;
                                        padding: 3px; /* Some space in input fields */
                                        width: 200px;
                                }
                                textarea#comment {
                                        width: 540px;
                                        padding: 10px;
                                }

        #sidebar-container {
                width: 320px; /* Active sidebar width is 300 px due to right margin */
                float: right;
        }

                ul#sidebar {
                        padding-right: 20px; /* The right margin */
                }
                        ul#sidebar li {
                                list-style: none;
                        }
                        li.widget {
                                margin-bottom: 20px;
                        }
                        li#postmeta {}
                                li#postmeta h2 {
                                        margin-bottom: 4px;
                                }
                                li.pagenav {
                                        background: #f6f5ef;
                                        padding: 10px;
                                        margin-bottom: 20px;
                                        font-weight: bold;
                                }
                                        li.pagenav ul {
                                                margin-top: 5px;
                                        }
                                                li.pagenav ul li.page_item {
                                                        margin-top: 5px;
                                                        border-width: 0 0 1px 0;
                                                }
                                                li.pagenav ul li.current_page_item {}
                        li.latest-box {
                                padding: 20px;
                                background: #f6f5ef;
                        }
                                li.latest-box-story {
                                        margin-top: 10px;
                                }
```

```
#footer {
        width: 100%;
        float: left;
        padding: 20px 0;
}
        div.bottom-menu {
                float: left;
                padding: 10px 20px;
        }
                div.bottom-menu ul {
                        width: 920px; /* Full width 960 px -40px padding
                                          from div.bottom-menu */
                        float: left;
                        padding: 10px 0;
                        border: 1px solid #d5cba7;
                        border-width: 1px 0;
                }
                        div.bottom-menu ul li {
                                float: left;
                                padding: 0 5px;
                                list-style: none;
                        }

        div.footer-left {
                width: 620px; /* Active width is 600 px due to left margin */
                float: left;
        }
                div.footer-left ul {
                        padding-left: 20px;
                }
                        div.footer-left ul li {
                                list-style: none;
                        }

        div.footer-right {
                width: 320px; /* Active width is 300 px due to right margin */
                float: right;
        }
                div.footer-right ul {
                        padding-right: 20px;
                }
                        div.footer-right ul li {
                                list-style: none;
                        }

        #footer-bottom {
                width: 100%;
                float:left;
        }
                #footer-bottom p {
                        padding: 20px 20px 0 20px;
```

```
        }


/* LINKS
   ----- */

#logo a {
      color: #000;
      text-decoration: none;
}

div.top-menu ul li.menu-item a {
      padding: 15px 20px;
      color: #2d2d2d;
      border: 1px solid #f3ecd2;
      border-width: 0 1px 0 0;
      text-decoration: none;
      font-weight: bold;
}
      div.top-menu ul li.menu-item a:hover {
            color: #fff;
            background: #985;
      }

div.entry a, h2.entry-title a {
      color: #630;
      text-decoration: none;
}
      div.entry a:hover, h2.entry-title a:hover {
            color: #a80;
            text-decoration: underline;
      }

div.entry-meta a, ul#sidebar a, div#footer a, li.comment a {
      color: #222;
      text-decoration: none;
}
      div.entry-meta a:hover, ul#sidebar a:hover, div#footer a:hover, li.comment
  a:hover {
            color: #000;
            text-decoration: underline;
      }

span.meta-category a {
      color: #887b4c !important;
      text-transform: uppercase;
      font-weight: bold;
}
```

```css
/* TYPOGRAPHY
   ---------- */

#header, div.top-menu, div.bottom-menu, #sidebar,
div.comment-author, div.comment-meta, div.reply,
h1, h2, h3, h4, h5, h6 {
        font-family: Helvetica, Arial, sans-serif;
}

h1#logo, div#logo, div.entry p, #footer-bottom,
input, textarea, div#header-blurb p {
        font-family: „Adobe Garamond Pro", Garamond, Georgia, „Times New Roman",
  serif;
}

h1#logo, div#logo {
        font-weight: normal;
        font-size: 48px;
        font-variant: small-caps;
}

div#header-blurb p {
        font-style: italic;
        line-height: 24px;
}

div.entry p {
        font-size: 16px;
        line-height: 24px;
        margin-bottom: 16px;
}

div.comment-body p, div.entry-meta, li.menu-item, h2.widgettitle,
li.latest-box-story h4, input, textarea {
        font-size: 14px;
}

li.menu-item {
        line-height: 14px;
        text-transform: uppercase;
}

div.search, ul#sidebar li, div.reply,
div.comment-author, div.comment-meta {
        font-size: 12px;
}

li.widget {
        color: #666;
}
```

187

```
li.widget p {
    margin-bottom: 8px;
    line-height: 18px;
}

h1.entry-title, h1#archive-title {
        font-size: 36px;
        line-height: 36px;
}
        h1.entry-title {
                margin-bottom: 24px;
        }
        h1#archive-title {
                margin-bottom: 36px;
        }
                h1#archive-title span {
                        font-weight: normal;
                        color: #666;
                }

h2.entry-title {
        font-size: 24px;
        line-height: 24px;
        margin-bottom: 6px;
}

div.entry h2 {
        margin: 48px 0 12px 0;
}

h2.widgettitle, li.pagenav {
        text-transform: uppercase;
        margin-bottom: 8px;
}

li.latest-box h3 {
        text-transform: uppercase;
        color: #887b4c;
}

li.latest-box-story p {
        margin: 4px 0 0 0;
        color: #666;
        line-height: 12px;
}

li.pagenav ul { /* Fix for Pages lacking proper h2 */
        text-transform: none;
        margin-bottom: 0;
        font-weight: normal;
```

```
}

span.meta-category {
        color: #666;
}

div.comment-author, div.comment-meta {
        line-height: 16px;
}

li.widget-area-empty {
        color: red;
}

input {
        font-style: italic;
}


/* WORDPRESS STYLES
   ---------------- */

img.alignleft {
        float:left;
        margin: 0 15px 15px 0;
}

img.alignright {
        float:right;
        margin: 0 0 15px 15px;
}

.wp-caption {
        padding: 10px 7px;
        border: 1px solid #bfbfbf;
        font-size: 12px;
        color: #888;
        font-style: italic;
        text-align:center;
}

p.wp-caption-text {
        margin:10px 0 0 0 !important;
        padding:0;
        line-height: 14px !important;
}

div.gallery {
        margin-bottom: 14px;
}
```

```
dl.gallery-item {}
    dt.gallery-icon {}
        img.attachment-thumbnail {
            border:0;
        }
    dd.gallery-caption {
        margin-top: 8px;
        font-size: 12px;
        color: #888;
        font-style: italic;
    }
}
```

There's another stylesheet as well, the one for the Visual editor in the admin panel. It is called editor-style.css and is really simple, just passing the basic fonts and colors to the editor for the common tags, like this.

```
/*
Theme Name: Simple-Static
*/


/*
        Visual editor styles (for TinyMCE)
*/

html .mceContentBody {
        max-width:620px;
}


p, ul, ol, blockquote {
        font-family: "Adobe Garamond Pro", Garamond, Georgia, "Times New Roman",
   serif;
        font-size: 16px;
        line-height: 24px;
}


h1, h2, h3, h4, h5, h6 {
        font-family: Helvetica, Arial, sans-serif;
}


body, input, textarea {
        font-size: 14px;
        line-height: 18px;
}


p {
        margin-bottom: 16px;
}


ul {
```

```
        margin: 0 0 16px 24px;
}

ol {
        margin: 0 0 16px 24px;
}

ul ul, ol ol, ul ol, ol ul {
        margin-bottom:0;
}

cite, em, i {
        font-style: italic;
        border: none;
}

blockquote {
        font-style: italic;
        padding: 0 24px;
}

abbr, acronym {
        border-bottom: 1px dotted #666;
        cursor: help;
}

a:link, a:visited {
        color:#630;
}

a:active, a:hover {
        color: #a80;
}

h1 {
        margin: 48px 0 24px 0;
        font-size: 36px;
        line-height: 36px;
}

h2 {
        margin: 48px 0 12px 0;
        font-size: 24px;
        line-height: 24px;
}

img {
        margin: 0;
        max-width: 620px;
}
```

```
.alignleft, img.alignleft {
        display: inline;
        float: left;
        margin: 0 15px 15px 0;
}

.alignright, img.alignright {
        display: inline;
        float: right;
        margin: 0 0 15px 105px;
}

.aligncenter, img.aligncenter {
        clear: both;
        display: block;
        margin-left: auto;
        margin-right: auto;
}

.wp-caption {
        padding: 10px 7px;
        border: 1px solid #bfbfbf;
        font-size: 12px;
        color: #888;
        font-style: italic;
        text-align:center;
}

.wp-caption img {
        margin: 5px;
}

p.wp-caption-text {
        margin: 10px 0 0 0;
        padding: 0;
        line-height: 14px;
}
```

Defining the commonly used elements like this will make your Visual editor feel a lot more like your site, as you'll see in Figure 7-11.

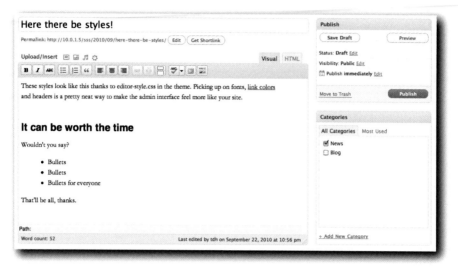

Figure 7-11: Editing the front page using the Visual editor

AND WE'RE DONE!

There you go; one theme suitable for many semi-static sites, as shown in Figure 7-12. Your fictional company got their Web site, shown in Figure 7-13, and they were mighty happy with it and how easy it is to update.

193

Figure 7-12: A static front page in need of some TLC

Figure 7-13: Reading a single, dummy news post

GET THE SEMI-STATIC THEME FOR FREE

My semi-static Web site theme is available for free under the GPL license, obviously. If you don't want to copy and paste the code, you can always get the theme yourself and use it as is; or hack it any way you'd like. The theme is called Semi-Static and you can get links and whatnot from `http://tdh.me/wordpress/semi-static`.

And yes, Semi-Static is hosted on `wordpress.org`, but the link is not available at the time of publication. Just visit the previously mentioned semi-static link for everything you need.

The Semi-Static described and discussed in this book was version 1.0. Be aware that when you download the theme, things might have changed slightly as you read this chapter.

BUILDING CHILD THEMES ON SEMI-STATIC SITES

I would've done an awfully poor job if Semi-Static wasn't ready for child theming, and so it is. All themes can act as a parent theme obviously, but they can be better or less suited to do so, and I've been aiming for the latter. That's why the `get_template_part()` that calls for the loop always points to a specific loop file, to make it easier for you to overwrite a specific functionality. If you need a different kind of sidebar, that's easily added in a child theme as well, as is just about any template file you'd want to treat differently. Because the menus are managed with the custom Menus feature, you can easily extend Semi-Static without altering too many files, which makes it easy to customize using a child theme. Not to mention the obvious alterations, such as fonts and colors.

WRAPPING IT UP

As this chapter has surely shown, WordPress works perfectly well for powering traditional Web sites. Sure, there are a few things you need to keep in mind, such as category links and whatnot, but what CMS doesn't need for you to actually plan how the site should be built and working? Yeah, that's what I thought. . .

Next up is something a bit flashier. You'll create a theme meant primarily for displaying media content. That's right; text will have to take a step back as we put the attachments in focus.

8

A MEDIA THEME

IN THIS CHAPTER, I show you how to build a theme that focuses on images rather than text. This site could be a portfolio that shows off your photos, videos, or art, or any site that relies heavily on images and their descriptions. An image may speak a thousand words, but when it comes to WordPress that phrase simply means you need to think a bit differently about layout and design. You have to consider other issues and concerns as well, such as how to show image information, image titles, and so on when browsing a media-focused site.

In the following sections, I show you how to build a portfolio theme.

BUILDING SITES FOR IMAGES AND VIDEO

Text isn't always the primary type of content on the site you're building. You may also want to showcase your photographs or videos. You can use just about any theme for this, of course, but if you want to display a large, pretty image (see Figure 8-1), the ideal column width for text just won't do.

In short, sometimes you're not building for text, you're building for attachments.

Attachments are the kinds of files you typically add to your post and often these files are images. The main template file for displaying attachments, when they're not just sitting in a post, is attachment.php.

Figure 8-1: This is what you're after, a display focused on image content

PLANNING YOUR PORTFOLIO SITE

The theme I build in this chapter has a simple layout that I designed primarily for showcasing images and video. I want some text to go with every media file that I show, so I still keep it pretty simple; but I also offer links to larger versions without the text.

Figure 8-2 shows the simple sketch I made in my notebook for this portfolio site.

SITE LAYOUT

If you can tell from my rough sketch, the site layout is pretty straightforward. You're looking at a single view post here, not the front page. The design features a simple header with a menu, the main content (an image from a gallery) is the focus, and some text on the right-hand side (along with meta data, and stuff like that). Below the image is the option to go to the previous or next image in the gallery, and underneath it all are widget areas.

This design is 960 pixels wide, which means that it can work with text in the main content area as well because it is 640 pixels wide. If you use an appropriate font size, this layout can work well enough. With a single click, I give visitors a larger view of the images, using the full width of the design. I have designed a front page as well, but it is not as important at this time. The image content is key here, so that's what you should focus on.

I did a Photoshop mock-up for the project in Chapter 7. That's not all that important in this case because the primary element is media content, which in this case means photos. I'll tackle the minor stuff as I go along.

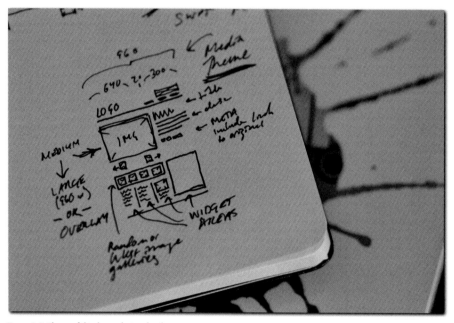

Figure 8-2: The portfolio theme design sketch

MAKING EVERYTHING FIT TOGETHER

You use the WordPress media manager to upload attachments by clicking the Add an Image icon in your post screen (in action in Figure 8-3). These attachments are usually images, but they needn't be. In the case of this theme, I focus on images, but several different MIME types are supported. As mentioned earlier, the template file for showing attachments in single view is attachment.php. If you need more fine-grained control, you can rely on more in-depth categories, such as image.php and video.php.

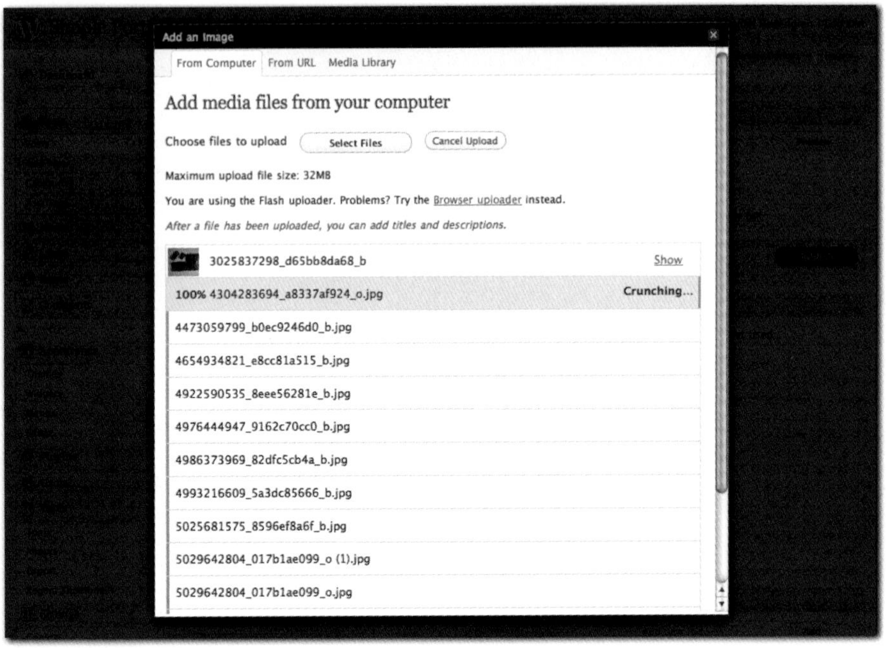

Figure 8-3: Uploading some media files

AN IMAGE GALLERY

Although it's great that you can control single view when it comes to attachments, images usually reside within posts. So when building a portfolio site like this one, I have to decide how to display the content. Because I need gallery support, that sort of decides it for me: The images need to be in posts. In this case, I create a category named Portfolio; but it could just as well have been a custom post type if I needed to keep them entirely separate from the rest of the site.

So, each gallery will be a post in the Portfolio category. Right, glad we got that out of the way.

THE CONTENT FLOW

Next, I need to figure out how the site will actually work. My front page will list the latest galleries from the portfolio, which translates to the latest posts in the Portfolio category. The front page also needs some descriptive text about the site, and stuff like that, but I'll not worry about that for now.

Clicking a link for a portfolio gallery leads to the post with the gallery. This consists of a gallery (using the [gallery] shortcode, which I'm sure you're familiar with) and some descriptive text using excerpt and content when needed. You can manage this with the single.php template file.

Clicking an image in the gallery opens the image view, which is the image.php template file. This is what you saw in the simple design sketch in Figure 8-2. When I click the image from the gallery post, I open the default view, which shows the medium-size image at 640 pixels wide. The content to the right is fetched from the image title and description. There will also be links for viewing the original version of the image. At the bottom, I have thumbnails for browsing the gallery.

What else? Well, I'll have the necessary template files for Pages and widget areas in the footer. The header will use the Menus feature for easy management.

BUILDING THE MEDIA SITE

It is time to build the portfolio theme. First, create the style.css file with the following theme header, declaring everything necessary, which in this case means the theme name, tags, and so on.

```
/*
Theme Name: Simple Pfolio
Theme URI: http://tdh.me/wordpress/simple-pfolio/
Description: A theme meant for simple portfolio sites, hence the name.
Version: 1.0
Tags: light, two-columns, right-sidebar, fixed-width, threaded-comments, transla-
  tion-ready, custom-menu, editor-style
Author: Thord Daniel Hedengren
Author URI: http://tdh.me/

    This theme was originally created for use in the book
    Smashing WordPress Themes, written by yours truly.

    Read more about my books at http://tdh.me/books/

*/
```

As you can see I've named this theme Simple Pfolio. I'll return to the stylesheet later.

THE FUNCTIONS.PHP FILE

Let's start with the functions.php file. This theme needs it for the custom menu feature, as well as for several widget areas. Four of these widget areas are in the footer; one is on the right-hand side everywhere except on the front page or on a page belonging to the Portfolio category, which has its own right-side widget area. The final widget areas are for the front page.

Portfolio posts don't use the right column for widgets.

Here is the functions.php file, properly commented.

```php
<?php
    // We need a textdomain for localization support,
    // with language files in the /lang folder
    load_theme_textdomain( 'simple-pfolio', TEMPLATEPATH . '/lang' );
```

```php
        // This is the default content width, 640 px
        if ( ! isset( $content_width ) )
               $content_width = 640;

        // Adding theme support for post thumbnails
        add_theme_support( 'post-thumbnails' );

        // Telling WordPress to use editor-style.css for the visual editor
        add_editor_style();

        // Adding feed links to header
        add_theme_support( 'automatic-feed-links' );

        // MENU AREA
        // ---------
        // Adding and defining the Menu area found in the header.php file
        register_nav_menus( array(
               'top-menu' => __( 'Top Menu', 'simple-pfolio' ),
        ) );

        // WIDGET AREAS
        // ------------
        // Right column widget area
        register_sidebar( array(
               'name' => __( 'Default Right Column', 'simple-pfolio' ),
               'id' => 'default-right-column',
               'description' => __( 'The right column on pages outside the Portfolio.',
'simple-pfolio' ),
        ) );

        // Right column widget area on the Portfolio category
        register_sidebar( array(
               'name' => __( 'Portfolio Right Column', 'simple-pfolio' ),
               'id' => 'portfolio-right-column',
               'description' => __( 'The right column on the Portfolio category.',
'simple-pfolio' ),
               'before_widget' => '<li id="%1$s" class="widget news %2$s">',
               'after_widget' => '</li>',
               'before_title' => '<h2 class="widgettitle">',
               'after_title' => '</h2>',
        ) );

        // Right column widget area on the front page
        register_sidebar( array(
               'name' => __( 'Front Page Right Column', 'simple-pfolio' ),
               'id' => 'frontpage-right-column',
               'description' => __( 'The right column on the front page.', 'simple-
pfolio' ),
               'before_widget' => '<li id="%1$s" class="widget news %2$s">',
               'after_widget' => '</li>',
               'before_title' => '<h2 class="widgettitle">',
```

```
                'after_title' => '</h2>',
        ) );


        // Left column in the footer
        register_sidebar( array(
                'name' => __( 'Footer Left Side', 'simple-pfolio' ),
                'id' => 'footer-left-side',
                'description' => __( 'The left hand side of the footer.', 'simple-
pfolio' ),
                'before_widget' => '<li id="%1$s" class="widget footer %2$s">',
                'after_widget' => '</li>',
                'before_title' => '<h2 class="widgettitle">',
                'after_title' => '</h2>',
        ) );


        // Middle column in the footer
        register_sidebar( array(
                'name' => __( 'Footer Middle Column', 'simple-pfolio' ),
                'id' => 'footer-middle-column',
                'description' => __( 'The middle column in the footer.', 'simple-pfolio'
),
                'before_widget' => '<li id="%1$s" class="widget footer %2$s">',
                'after_widget' => '</li>',
                'before_title' => '<h2 class="widgettitle">',
                'after_title' => '</h2>',
        ) );


        // Right column in the footer
        register_sidebar( array(
                'name' => __( 'Footer Right Column', 'simple-pfolio' ),
                'id' => 'footer-right-column',
                'description' => __( 'The right hand column in the footer.', 'simple-
pfolio' ),
                'before_widget' => '<li id="%1$s" class="widget footer %2$s">',
                'after_widget' => '</li>',
                'before_title' => '<h2 class="widgettitle">',
                'after_title' => '</h2>',
        ) );


        // Far right column in the footer
        register_sidebar( array(
                'name' => __( 'Footer Far Right Column', 'simple-pfolio' ),
                'id' => 'footer-far-right-column',
                'description' => __( 'The far right column in the footer.', 'simple-
pfolio' ),
                'before_widget' => '<li id="%1$s" class="widget %2$s">',
                'after_widget' => '</li>',
                'before_title' => '<h2 class="widgettitle">',
                'after_title' => '</h2>',
        ) );
```

```
        // Front page widget area
        register_sidebar( array(
                'name' => __( 'Front Page Welcome Area', 'simple-pfolio' ),
                'id' => 'home-welcome',
                'description' => __( 'The welcome area in the content column on the
    front page.', 'simple-pfolio' ),
                'before_widget' => '<div id="%1$s" class="widget-home %2$s">',
                'after_widget' => '</div>',
                'before_title' => '<h2 class="widgettitle">',
                'after_title' => '</h2>',
        ) );
    ?>
```

You'll recognize most of this code from Chapter 7. I've used textdomain for localization, this time called simple-pfolio. I'm adding theme support for featured images (that is, post-thumbnails), a stylesheet for the Visual editor, and so on. If you don't remember what these things are, jump back to Chapter 7 and read up.

SETTING UP THE BASIC SHELL

As always, I want to kick off the site with header.php, containing every opening `div` needed for the page, and wrap it up in footer.php. This is a two-column page (which breaks up into four columns in the footer), so it is pretty straightforward. I've got the necessary wrapping div's, a `div#content` column to the left, and a sidebar column to the right.

Let's start by looking at header.php.

```
<!DOCTYPE html>
<html <?php language_attributes(); ?>>
<head>
<meta charset="<?php bloginfo( 'charset' ); ?>" />
<title><?php
    // Changing the title for various sections on the site
    if ( is_home () ) {
        bloginfo('name');
    } elseif ( is_category() || is_tag() ) {
        single_cat_title(); echo ' &bull; ' ; bloginfo('name');
    } elseif ( is_single() || is_page() ) {
        single_post_title();
    } else {
        wp_title('',true);
    }
?></title>
<link rel="profile" href="http://gmpg.org/xfn/11" />
<link rel="stylesheet" type="text/css" media="all" href="<?php bloginfo( 'style-
    sheet_url' ); ?>" />
<link rel="pingback" href="<?php bloginfo( 'pingback_url' ); ?>" />
<?php wp_head(); ?>
</head>
```

```php
<body <?php body_class(); ?>>
    <div id="site">
    <div id="wrap">
        <div id="header">
        <?php
            // Checking if it is the front page in which case we'll use an h1
            if ( is_front_page() ) { ?>
            <h1 id="logo">
                <a href="<?php bloginfo('url'); ?>" title="<?php
bloginfo('title'); ?>">
                    <?php
                        // Getting the site title
                        bloginfo('title');
                    ?>
                </a>
            </h1>
            <?php }
            // If it isn't the front page this is what we'll use
            else { ?>
            <div id="logo">
                <a href="<?php bloginfo('url'); ?>" title="<?php
bloginfo('title'); ?>">
                    <?php
                        // Getting the site title
                        bloginfo('title');
                    ?>
                </a>
            </div>
            <?php } ?>
            <div class="search">
                <?php
                    // The default search form
                    get_search_form();
                ?>
                <?php
                    // Checking if there's anything in Top Menu
                    if ( has_nav_menu( 'top-menu' ) ) {

                        // If there is, adds the Top Menu area
                        wp_nav_menu( array(
                            'menu' => 'Top Menu',
                            'container' => 'div',
                            'container_class' => 'top-menu',
                            'theme_location' => 'top-menu',
                        ));
                    }
                ?>
            </div>
        </div>
        <div id="plate">
```

You may recognize a lot of the code from the semi-static theme example in Chapter 7. The custom header isn't there, as I won't be using that, and I moved the custom menu up to the right, under the search form. Other than that, the theme is basically the same and ends by opening up the div#plate tag for the actual site. While Simple Pfolio won't have support for custom backgrounds at the moment, it may be nice to be able to add it later, right?

I'll get to the footer later in this section, as it contains some nice things. For now, I want to review the site structure before moving on:

```
[div#site]
    [div#wrap]
        [div#header]
        [div#plate]
            [div#content]
            [div#sidebar-container]
            [div#footer-widgets]
        [div#footer]
```

The index.php template is simple enough when put into context here. After all, it only featured the div#content contents, which is a call to the loop.php template tag — or loop-index.php really, because we want to make this theme as child themeable as possible. The Simple Pfolio only features one loop template, just as Simple Static did.

```php
<?php get_header(); ?>

        <div id="content">
            <?php get_template_part( 'loop', 'index' ); ?>
        </div>

<?php get_sidebar(); ?>
<?php get_footer(); ?>
```

With that, let's get down to business.

SINGLE POSTS AND ATTACHMENTS

My galleries reside in posts, which in turn lead to a single image view. In other words, I use single.php to display the content properly. After all, there is content, and there is content on a site like this. I check the category to see if it is a Portfolio post. If it is, I use the full width, as it is supposed to contain a gallery. If it's not a Portfolio post, I use the default sidebar to the right of the content.

```php
<?php get_header(); ?>

            <div id="content" class="<?php portfoliocheck(); ?>">
                <?php get_template_part( 'loop', 'single' ); ?>
            </div>
```

```php
<?php
    // Check whether this is NOT the Portfolio category
    if ( !in_category('portfolio') ) {
        get_sidebar();
    }
?>
<?php get_footer(); ?>
```

You no doubt noticed the `portfoliocheck()` tag. This isn't a standard WordPress template tag but a function I added to functions.php to check whether I'm on a post belonging to the Portfolio category. Following is the function code, added at the end of functions.php.

```php
// PORTFOLIO CATEGORY CHECK
// Function to be used with div#content
function portfoliocheck() {
    // Check whether this is NOT the Portfolio category
    // If it is NOT, echo column
    if ( !in_category('portfolio') ) {
        echo 'column';
    }
    // If it is the Portfolio category, echo widecolumn
    else {
        echo 'widecolumn';
    }
}
```

The function echoes either `column` or `widecolumn` depending on whether the post belongs to the Portfolio category or not. By sticking this code in a function (in functions.php) and using that in single.php, I keep the latter cleaner. You could also swap `portfoliocheck()` in single.php for the contents on the function in functions.php, but it wouldn't look as good.

Back to single.php then. Besides the check to see what class `div#content` should get, you also need to take the sidebar into account. If there's no sidebar, which there isn't on Portfolio posts thanks to the check in single.php, you obviously want to use the full width, hence the `widecolumn` class. If there is a sidebar, you need to take that into account and use the `column` class. I set the width in style.css, which I revisit later.

```css
.column {
    width: 640px; /* Active content width 640 px */
}

.widecolumn {
    width: 960px; /* Full width 960 px */
}
```

So how do these checks work? Take a look at the sidebar code. Because I don't want a sidebar on Portfolio posts, I check to confirm that I'm not on a Portfolio post, in which case I call `get_sidebar()`. That's what the exclamation mark means in front of the `in_category()` conditional tag, as PHP savvy people already know.

Now, my single-post template outputs a sidebar on every single-post view, other than posts belonging to the Portfolio category. I can style this and make it pretty later; for now, I want to move on to the image.php (rather than the more general attachment.php) template. This is what opens (see Gallery Settings in Figure 8-4) when you click an image pointing to an attachment page (something you control on a per-image basis in the media manager). Thus, this is the actual image view (Figure 8-5 displays my Portfolio post).

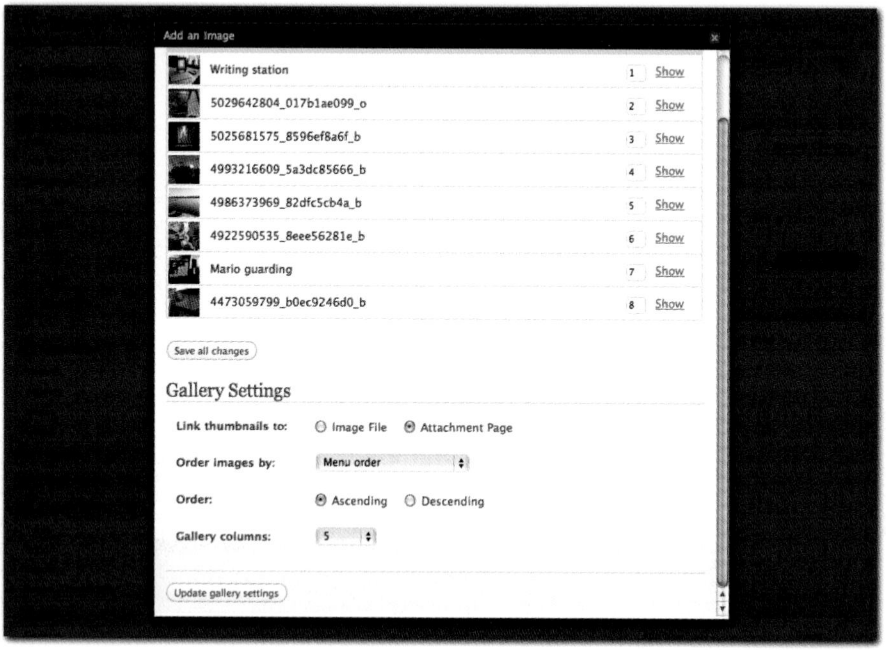

Figure 8-4: Inserting a gallery from the media manager, via the Edit Post screen

My image.php template file is simple enough. All I need is the loop (otherwise, I don't get the image description, which incidentally doesn't have to reside within it), a code snippet that outputs the actual attachment (the image) the way I want, the obvious calls to the header and the footer, as well as the sidebar I want to use.

Before you take a look at the following code, remember that I haven't added the thumbnail browsing yet. I get to that a little later in this chapter.

Figure 8-5: That big image is a gallery inserted into a post on the Edit Post screen

```php
<?php get_header(); ?>

                <div id="content">

        <?php
                // Loop it
                if (have_posts ()) : while ( have_posts() ) : the_post(); ?>

                <div class="medium-image">
                        <?php echo wp_get_attachment_image( $post->ID,
    $size='medium', false); ?>
                </div>

        <?php
                // End the loop
                endwhile; endif; ?>

                </div>

<?php get_sidebar('attachment'); ?>
<?php get_footer(); ?>
```

The loop is familiar by now, but the part about outputting the image might not be. I'm using
`wp_get_attachment_image()`, which needs to get the correct ID with the `$post->ID`
parameter. The `$image='medium'` is obviously the image size for this particular image call.
I'm using the medium-size image, which I've set to 640 pixels width under Settings, Media in

the WordPress admin panel (see Figure 8-6). In the preceding code, the last parameter, set to false, actually defaults to false and decides whether the MIME type (image in this case, which could be video, audio, and so on) icon should be shown. That's a no on the icon here.

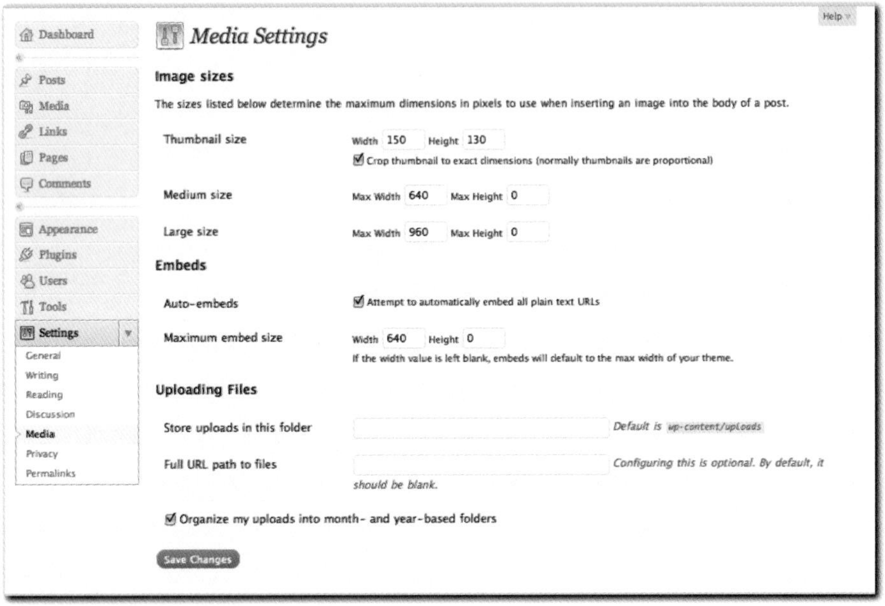

Figure 8-6: Media Settings screen; note the Medium size setting

I hope you recognize the `get_sidebar('attachment')` code. This means that the sidebar I'm calling is sidebar-attachment.php, and not the regular sidebar.php template. I'll get to that next.

THE ATTACHMENT SIDEBAR

This sidebar is meant to work on all kinds of attachments, not just images. I have some conditional tags to sort that out. You use this sidebar whenever you're viewing an attachment, which most often means you clicked an image from a gallery within a post.

```
<div id="sidebar-container">
      <ul id="sidebar">
            <li id="postmeta" class="widget">
                  <p>
                        <!-- Link back to original post -->
                        &larr; <a href="<?php echo get_permalink( $post->post_parent
); ?>">
                        <?php echo get_the_title( $post->post_parent ); ?>
                        </a>
                  </p>
            <h1>
                  <?php
```

```php
                // Title of the attachment
                the_title();
        ?>
    </h1>
    <p class="meta-attachment">
            <!-- Metadata -->
            <?php the_date(); ?>
            <?php echo __('by', 'simple-pfolio'); ?>
            <?php the_author(); ?>
            <?php edit_post_link(); ?>
    </p>

    <?php
            // Outputs the attachment Caption if available
            if ( !empty( $post->post_excerpt ) ) {
                    echo '<h2>';
                    the_excerpt();
                    echo '</h2>';
            }
    ?>

    <?php
            // Outputs the attachment Description if available
            if ( !empty( $post->post_excerpt ) ) {
                    echo '<div class="entry-attachment">';
                    the_content();
                    echo '</div>';
            }
    ?>

      <?php
                // If it is an image, output data
                // Thanks Twenty Ten
            if ( wp_attachment_is_image() ) {
                    $metadata = wp_get_attachment_metadata();
                    echo '<p>';
                    printf( __( 'The full sized image is %s pixels',
'simple-pfolio'),
                            sprintf( '<a href="%1$s" title="%2$s">%3$s &times;
%4$s</a>',
                                    wp_get_attachment_url(),
                                    esc_attr( __('Link to full-size image',
'simple-pfolio') ),
                                    $metadata['width'],
                                    $metadata['height']
                            )
                    );
                    echo '</p>';
            }
        ?>
```

211

```
                </li>
        </ul>
</div>
```

If you look under the Link back to original post comment, you can see that I use `$post->post_parent` for the `get_permalink()` and `get_the_title()` tags. This is obviously to fetch the data from the parent post, which is the actual portfolio post to which this attachment belongs. Had I used the regular permalink and title tags, I'd get the data from the attachment post that I'm on, and that's not really the idea when linking back. Hence, I need to rely on the slightly more flexible `get_permalink()` and `get_the_title()`. Neither of these output the results by default, so I need to output them with PHP, hence the echo.

Moving on, I've shown a great example of why `get_the_title()` is needed because the h1 heading uses `the_title()` to output the title of the attachment.

The tags outputting the meta data for the attachment are simple enough, `the_author()`, `the_date()`, and a PHP snippet for localization purposes — you've seen it all before.

The two snippets for outputting the attachment caption and description, managed with `the_excerpt()` and `the_content()`, respectively, need a bit more explaining. First, take a look at where I actually put the caption and description in the WordPress panel shown in Figure 8-7.

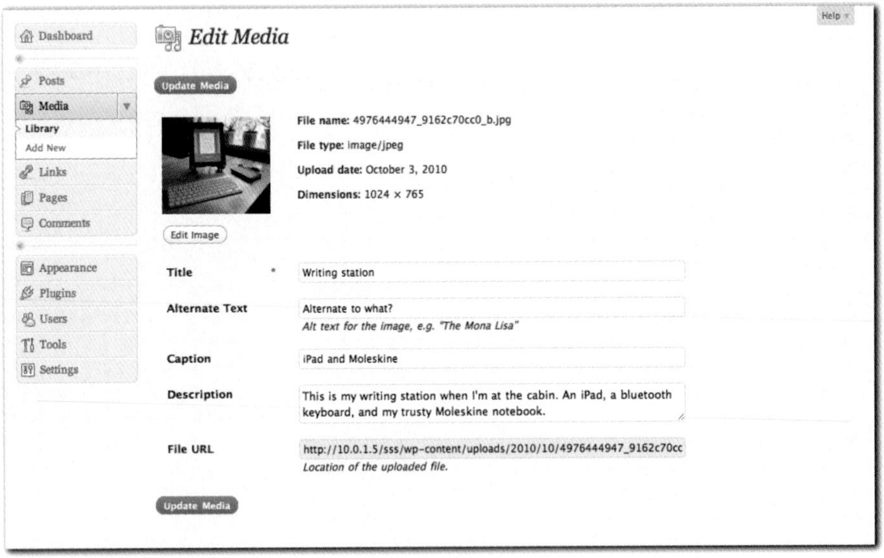

Figure 8-7: Use this Edit Media screen to revise text after uploading the image

You probably recognize this screen from when you upload images. The same workflow is used if you upload images by using the Media Library screen with the Add New option, but not as a popover overlaying your Edit Post screen, but as a standalone page.

Let's focus on the code that outputs these things in our sidebar — attachment.php template.

```php
<?php
    // Outputs the attachment Caption if available
    if ( !empty( $post->post_excerpt ) ) {
        echo '<h2>';
        the_excerpt();
        echo '</h2>';
    }
?>
```

```php
<?php
    // Outputs the attachment Description if available
    if ( !empty( $post->post_content ) ) {
        echo '<div class="entry-attachment">';
        the_content();
        echo '</div>';
    }
?>
```

The `if` clause checks whether the `post_excerpt` and `post_content`, respectively, are empty. If they are empty, nothing happens; but if they contain something, you get the echos and `the_excerpt()` and `the_content()`. Hence, the content shows up in your sidebar. I use `$post->post_excerpt` and `$post->post_content` to make this check. `$post` is the post that I'm viewing, which is the current attachment; compare that to the `$post->post_parent` above where I checked for where the attachment belonged, and the `$post->ID` where I pass the ID number of the post I'm on. Very handy, that `$post` thingy!

Aside from closing tags, the last thing I do in the sidebar-attachment.php template is output some extra information if I'm looking at an image. Again, because sidebar-attachment.php is meant to be used for all kinds of attachments and not just images (as is the case with the image.php template), I need to make a conditional check to ensure that I'm not outputting image-specific stuff on a non-image attachment.

```php
<?php
    // If it is an image, output data
    // Thanks Twenty Ten
    if ( wp_attachment_is_image() ) {
        $metadata = wp_get_attachment_metadata();
        echo '<p>';
        printf( __( 'The full sized image is %s pixels', 'simple-pfolio'),
            sprintf( '<a href="%1$s" title="%2$s">%3$s &times; %4$s</a>',
                wp_get_attachment_url(),
                esc_attr( __('Link to full-size image', 'simple-pfolio') ),
                $metadata['width'],
                $metadata['height']
            )
        );
        echo '</p>';
    }
?>
```

213

This code is in part borrowed from the Twenty Ten theme. I have a simple `if` check to see whether `wp_attachment_is_image()` returns true, in which case I move along with this code and output its result; otherwise, nothing happens. If it is true, I store the data from `wp_get_attachment_metadata()` in a function called `$metadata`. Then I output some stuff, using percentage placeholders to get the correct width and height in pixels from my stored away data.

The output gives us the following text (assuming you haven't localized it already): "The full sized image is 1024 × 765 pixels."

The `%s` in the `printf` line is a placeholder for the content in the `sprintf` line, which in turn uses its own percentage placeholder to fetch the data. That's what the `$metadata['width']` and `$metadata['height']` are there for. If that all sounds way over your head, don't worry. You just need to brush up a bit on your PHP, but that's not a big deal in this case, so just accept it and move on. For further reference, check out these pages in the PHP manual, for `printf` (`http://php.net/manual/en/function.printf.php`) and `sprintf` (`http://php.net/manual/en/function.sprintf.php`), respectively.

Now I've got a working image view page. All it needs is some styling, and the thumbnail browsing, of course, and I'm good to go. Well, almost. First, I'll take a quick jump to the front page, shown in Figure 8-8, and make that one pretty.

Figure 8-8: A crude image of the front page view

THE FRONT PAGE

You can build the front page for this theme in a number of ways. I'm going with home.php this time, which will show the latest posts from the Portfolio category. I also have a fully widgetized sidebar, as well as a widget area at the top of the content column into which I can drop an info box or whatever.

As with every page, you can add subtle changes using child themes; home.php uses a dedicated loop. This loop is actually present in the theme once, but it's easy to overwrite from a child theme. Start by looking at the home.php template.

```php
<?php get_header(); ?>

            <div id="content" class="column">
                <div class="widget-area-home">
                <?php
                    // The front page widget area
                    dynamic_sidebar('home-welcome'); ?>
                </div>

                <?php get_template_part( 'loop', 'home' ); ?>
            </div>

<?php get_sidebar(); ?>
<?php get_footer(); ?>
```

Pretty simple, right? I've got a widget area, which I define in functions.php, and a `get_template_part()` call to loop-home.php. I show you that loop in a little bit; first I want to revisit the home-welcome widget area declaration from functions.php (see Figure 8-9):

```php
// Front page Welcome area
register_sidebar( array(
    'name' => __( 'Front Page Welcome Area', 'simple-pfolio' ),
    'id' => 'home-welcome',
    'description' => __( 'The welcome area in the content column on the front
 page.', 'simple-pfolio' ),
    'before_widget' => '<div id="%1$s" class="widget-home %2$s">',
    'after_widget' => '</div>',
    'before_title' => '<h2 class="widgettitle">',
    'after_title' => '</h2>',
) );
```

This widget area isn't meant to be your traditional list of widgets. Rather, it is meant to display welcome text. At first, I contemplated creating an option page for it, but that felt too limiting for the end user. Hence, the simple widget solution, which you can use to host text, images, or whatever, really.

With that in mind, having `div`'s before and after the widget rather than the usual `li`'s makes a lot more sense, right? The widget is not meant to be a list of stuff after all, but a block with info text and possibly an image, depending on the end user's needs. Look for `before_widget` and `after_widget` in the widget declaration code from functions.php above.

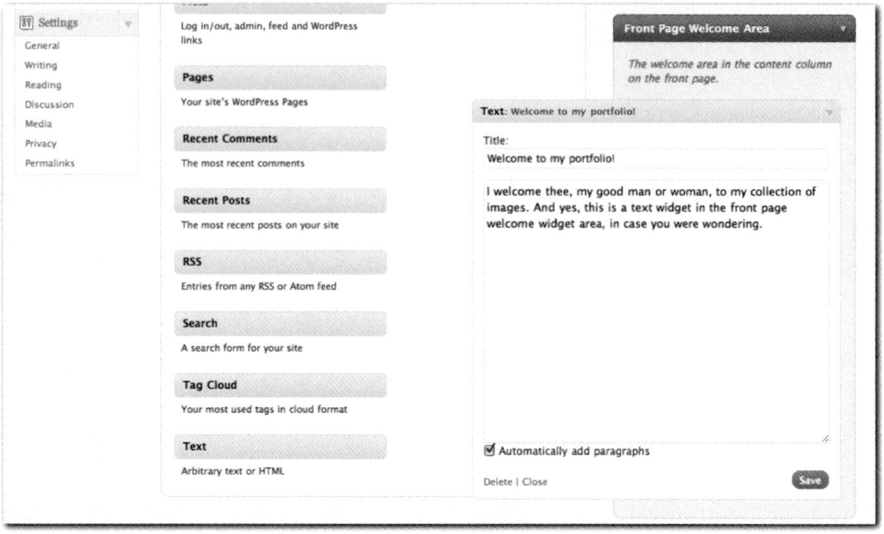

Figure 8-9: The welcome widget area found under Appearance → Widgets in WordPress admin panel

Now, move on to the actual front page loop. In home.php, we said that we'd use loop-home.php if present (otherwise revert to loop.php as usual), and for once we've got the file in our theme. Here's loop-home.php.

```php
<?php
    // The home loop
    if ( have_posts() ) : while ( have_posts() ) : the_post();
?>

            <div id="post-<?php the_ID(); ?>" <?php post_class(); ?>>
                <div class="entry-thumbnail">
                    <a href="<?php the_permalink(); ?>">
                    <?php
                        // Fetching a thumbnail from post attachments
                        // First some parameters for later
                        $args = array(
                            'numberposts' => 1,
                            'post_type' => 'attachment',
                            'status' => 'publish',
                            'post_mime_type' => 'image',
                            'post_parent' => $post->ID
                        );
                        $images =& get_children($args);
                        // Loop the attachments
                        foreach ( (array) $images as $attachment_id =>
$attachment ) {

                                // Output an attachment in thumbnail size
                                echo wp_get_attachment_image($attachment_id,
'thumbnail', ''); 

                        }
```

```
                              ?>
                          </a>
                  </div>
                  <div class="entry-content">
                      <h2 class="entry-title">
                          <a href="<?php the_permalink(); ?>" title="<?php
  the_title(); ?>" rel="bookmark"><?php the_title(); ?></a>
                      </h2>
                      <?php the_excerpt(); ?>
                  </div>
              </div>

<?php
     // Loop ends
     endwhile; endif;
?>

          <div class="navigation">
              <div class="nav-previous"><?php next_posts_link( __( '<span
  class="meta-nav">&larr;</span> Older entries', 'simple-pfolio' ) ); ?></div>
              <div class="nav-next"><?php previous_posts_link( __( 'Newer entries
  <span class="meta-nav">&rarr;</span>', 'simple-pfolio' ) ); ?></div>
          </div>
```

This code shows your basic loop at first; but then you need to do some fancy stuff to fetch a thumbnail from the post attachment, should it have one of those. In the following, I break that part out for clarity.

```
<?php
     // Fetching a thumbnail from post attachments
     // First some parameters for later
     $args = array(
         'numberposts' => 1,
         'post_type' => 'attachment',
         'status' => 'publish',
         'post_mime_type' => 'image',
         'post_parent' => $post->ID
     );
     $images =& get_children($args);
     // Loop the attachments
     foreach ( (array) $images as $attachment_id => $attachment ) {
         // Output an attachment in thumbnail size
         echo wp_get_attachment_image($attachment_id, 'thumbnail', '');
     }
?>
```

As the name implies, I'm storing my arguments in $args, which get_children() uses. This means that the strings stored in $args is used by get_children(), which in turn is used to fetch attachments (the "children," in this case). Then, I cram this into $images and loop the attachments with `foreach`. I end up with an echo of `wp_get_attachment_image()` in which the ID echoed sits in `$attachment_id` from my `foreach` loop. The `wp_get_attachment_image()` also decides which image version (thumbnail, medium, large, or original) to use; it uses the thumbnail in this case. And around this I've got a link to make sure that the image links to the post.

The rest of the code is pretty self-explanatory, just outputting the excerpt (using `the_excerpt()`) and the post title in suitable `div`'s so that I can style it properly later on. Obviously, I only get a thumbnail image from the posts that actually have an attachment. If you intend to mix text posts with image-based posts like this, you should probably style the two differently; you might even consider using conditional tags to get more control. In this case, I don't worry about that; after all, this is just a portfolio site. For now . . . .

Anyway, what we get is something crude and ugly, as shown in Figure 8-10, with some nonsense text thrown into the widget area for good measure.

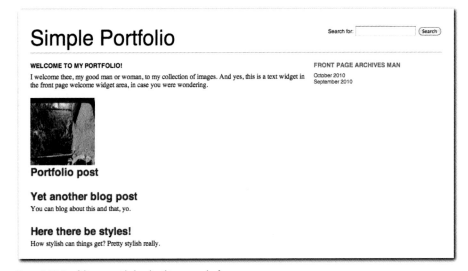

Figure 8-10: Portfolio posts with thumbnail image on the front page

Sweet. Next, I add thumbnail browsing to the image view as well.

THUMBNAIL BROWSING IN POSTS

So now I want to add thumbnails to the posts that have attachments. I want easy gallery browsing with the previous and next thumbnail beneath the image in single image view, which is when you've clicked through on an image from a gallery within a regular post. As you probably recall, a click on an image leads to an attachment page, and in this case the template file for that is image.php.

You would think that it would be just as easy to add next/previous image thumbnail browsing to the image.php template; but that's not the case. The only thing I need is previous_image_link() and next_image_link(), to which I'll also pass the thumbnail parameter to make sure we get the size we want.

This is what is added, below the actual image, just before div#content is closing, in .image.php:

```
<div class="navigation">
    <div class="nav-previous">
        <?php next_image_link( 'thumbnail' ); ?>
    </div>
    <div class="nav-next">
        <?php previous_image_link( 'thumbnail' ); ?>
    </div>
</div>
```

Our single image view is still in dire need of proper styling, but this little snippet at least adds the proper navigation. I did cheat a bit though (as I've done before with the stylesheet to make the working design make sense): I applied a float left and right, respectively, on the navigation links (see Figure 8-11).

Figure 8-11: Browse the gallery with the thumbnails below the main image

Here's the complete image.php template, with the thumbnail navigation added.

```
<?php get_header(); ?>

        <div id="content">

        <?php
```

```
                             // Loop it
                             if (have_posts ()) : while ( have_posts() ) : the_post();
                    ?>

                             <div class="medium-image">
                                 <?php
                                         // Outputs the image in medium size
                                         echo wp_get_attachment_image( $post->ID,
         $size='medium', false);
                                 ?>
                             </div>

                         <?php
                                 // End the loop
                                 endwhile; endif;
                         ?>

                             <div class="navigation">
                                 <div class="nav-previous">
                                         <?php next_image_link( 'thumbnail' ); ?>
                                 </div>
                                 <div class="nav-next">
                                         <?php previous_image_link( 'thumbnail' ); ?>
                                 </div>
                             </div>

                         </div>

<?php get_sidebar('attachment'); ?>
<?php get_footer(); ?>
```

I think it's about time to make this baby look good, don't you? So next I tackle the stylesheet!

TAKING CARE OF THE FOOTER

The footer is an important part of this theme as you may recall from the sketch in Figure 8-2. It consists of four columns: three small ones sharing 640 pixels, and one larger one to the right of them that offers you 300 pixels to play with. Above the three small columns, I have a box with the latest updates from the Portfolio category, each featured with a thumbnail. That's the only part of the actual footer content that is not a widget area; the rest are, as you'll remember, from functions.php. Following is the code that controls them, from functions.php, of course:

```
// Left column in the footer
register_sidebar( array(
    'name' => __( 'Footer Left Side', 'simple-pfolio' ),
    'id' => 'footer-left-side',
    'description' => __( 'The left hand side of the footer.', 'simple-pfolio' ),
    'before_widget' => '<li id="%1$s" class="widget footer %2$s">',
    'after_widget' => '</li>',
    'before_title' => '<h2 class="widgettitle">',
```

```
            'after_title' => '</h2>',
    ) );


    // Middle column in the footer
    register_sidebar( array(
        'name' => __( 'Footer Middle Column', 'simple-pfolio' ),
        'id' => 'footer-middle-column',
        'description' => __( 'The middle column in the footer.', 'simple-pfolio' ),
        'before_widget' => '<li id="%1$s" class="widget footer %2$s">',
        'after_widget' => '</li>',
        'before_title' => '<h2 class="widgettitle">',
        'after_title' => '</h2>',
    ) );


    // Right column in the footer
    register_sidebar( array(
        'name' => __( 'Footer Right Column', 'simple-pfolio' ),
        'id' => 'footer-right-column',
        'description' => __( 'The right hand column in the footer.', 'simple-pfolio' ),
        'before_widget' => '<li id="%1$s" class="widget footer %2$s">',
        'after_widget' => '</li>',
        'before_title' => '<h2 class="widgettitle">',
        'after_title' => '</h2>',
    ) );


    // Far right column in the footer
    register_sidebar( array(
        'name' => __( 'Footer Far Right Column', 'simple-pfolio' ),
        'id' => 'footer-far-right-column',
        'description' => __( 'The far right column in the footer.', 'simple-pfolio' ),
        'before_widget' => '<li id="%1$s" class="widget %2$s">',
        'after_widget' => '</li>',
        'before_title' => '<h2 class="widgettitle">',
        'after_title' => '</h2>',
    ) );
```

Without further ado, take a look at the footer.php template.

```
<div id="footer">
    <div class="footer-left">
        <div id="footer-thumbs">
            <ul>
                <li>thumbs go here</li>
            </ul>
        </div>
        <div class="footer-column left">
            <ul class="footer-widget-area">
            <?php
                // The Footer Left Side widget area
                dynamic_sidebar('footer-left-column');
            ?>
```

```
                                        <li class="widget widget-area-empty">
                                                Left widget column - drop a widget
                                                here!
                                        </li>
                                <?php endif; ?>
                                </ul>
                        </div>
                        <div class="footer-column-middle left">
                                <ul class="footer-widget-area
footer-widget-area-middle">
                                <?php
                                        // The Footer Left Side widget area
dynamic_sidebar('footer-middle-column');
                                ?>
                                        <li class="widget widget-area-empty">
                                                Middle widget column - drop a widget
                                                here!
                                        </li>
                                <?php endif; ?>
                                </ul>
                        </div>
                        <div class="footer-column right">
                                <ul class="footer-widget-area">
                                <?php
                                        // The Footer Left Side widget area
dynamic_sidebar('footer-right-column');
                                ?>
                                        <li class="widget widget-area-empty">
                                                Right widget column - drop a widget
                                                here!
                                        </li>
                                <?php endif; ?>
                                </ul>
                        </div>
                </div>
                <div class="footer-right">
                        <ul>
                        <?php
                                // The Footer Right Side widget area
dynamic_sidebar('footer-right-side');
                        ?>
                                <li class="widget widget-area-empty">
                                        Far right widget column - drop a widget
                                        here!
                                </li>
                        <?php endif; ?>
                        </ul>
                </div>
                <div id="footer-bottom">
                        <p><?php bloginfo('title'); ?> is proudly powered by
<a href="http://wordpress.org" title="WordPress">WordPress</a></p>
```

```
            </div>
        </div>

        </div> <!-- ends #plate -->
    </div> <!-- ends #wrap -->
    </div> <!-- ends #site -->

<?php wp_footer(); ?>
</body>
</html>
```

You can see I've got a div#footer where most of the action is. It is split into div. footer-left (which is 640 pixels) and div.footer-right (which is 300 pixels). The div.footer-left element starts with a full width div#footer-thumbs, for now just featuring placeholder text for where the thumbs of the latest Portfolio updates will go (we get to that in a little while). Then the footer goes on with two div.footer-column tags and a div.footer-column-middle for fixing the width issue (it is hard to divide 640 pixels by 3, so the middle column is 240 pixels wide, the other two just 200 pixels). These are the three small widget columns.

In div.footer-right, you find the far right footer widget area. Below all this is div#footer-bottom, which just contains some text. You can then close the div's from the header.php template. I wrap up WordPress with the wp_footer() template tag and close the HTML starting tags. Figure 8-12 shows how the footer looks at this point.

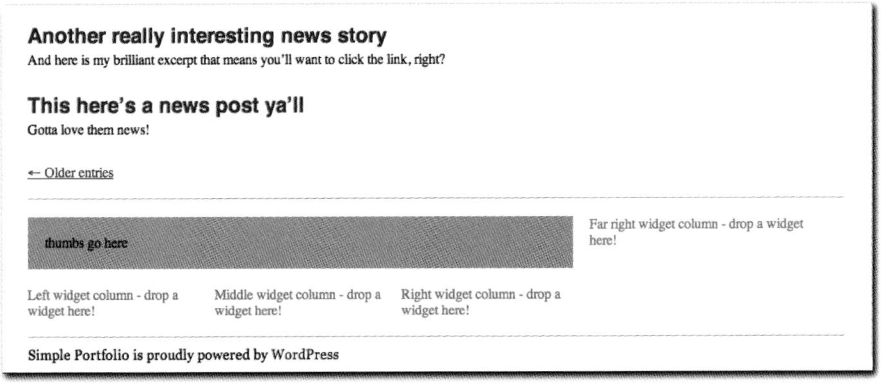

Another really interesting news story
And here is my brilliant excerpt that means you'll want to click the link, right?

This here's a news post ya'll
Gotta love them news!

← Older entries

thumbs go here

Far right widget column - drop a widget here!

Left widget column - drop a widget here!   Middle widget column - drop a widget here!   Right widget column - drop a widget here!

Simple Portfolio is proudly powered by WordPress

Figure 8-12: The footer with widget areas, no thumb block though

With this markup, it's a breeze to style the footer area thus far. The three footer columns need a bit of thought to make them align properly, but we'll manage.

Now, I need to get those thumbs in. For clarity's sake, this is the part I'll focus on:

```
<div id="footer-thumbs">
    <ul>
        <li>thumbs go here</li>
```

```
        </ul>
</div>
```

I want a box here showing the four latest posts from the Portfolio gallery, each one represented by a thumbnail. The box is 640 pixels wide, but I want it to be spacious so I'll give it a 20-pixel padding, meaning that there are only 600 pixels to work with. Four thumbnails mean that I have 150 pixels for each. Some spacing is necessary within each thumbnail element so that they don't sit too tightly (see Figure 8-13).

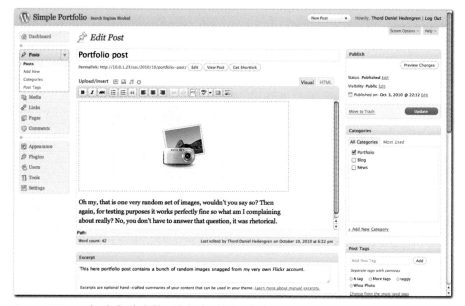

Figure 8-13: Here is what the box looks like with the thumbnails in the footer

I'll start with the actual code to get the four latest posts from the Portfolio gallery. But first, the loop is needed, without thumbnails.

```
<div id="footer-thumbs">
    <ul>
    <?php
        // Store 4 posts from Portfolio in $lastposts
        // then loop it with foreach
        $lastposts = get_posts('numberposts=4&category_name=portfolio');
        foreach($lastposts as $post) :
            setup_postdata($post); // Gives us post access
    ?>
        <li class="footer-thumb-post">
            <a href="<?php the_permalink(); ?>" id="post-<?php the_ID(); ?>">
                <?php the_title();?>
            </a>
```

```
            </li>
    <?php
            // Stop loop
            endforeach; ?>
    </ul>
</div>
```

I'm using `get_posts()` with the appropriate variables (the number of posts and what category to fetch them for) to store the query in `$lastposts` and then loop it with `foreach`. Easy, huh? But what is `setup_postdata()` and why do I need it? Well, you can't get to some post content using `get_posts()` without using `setup_postdata()`. Otherwise, you have to hit up the specific part in the database to get things like the post ID or `the_content()`, for that matter. So I use `setup_postdata()` because I want to pull an attachment (the thumbnail, remember?) for our post list.

Finally, we've got the output. In the preceding code, it is the title linked within an `li`, and ending the `foreach` loop with `endforeach`.

So how do you get the thumbnails in there? You just borrow some code from the loop-home. php template!

```
<a href="<?php the_permalink(); ?>">
<?php
    // Fetching a thumbnail from post attachments
    // First some parameters for later
    $args = array(
        'numberposts' => 1,
        'post_type' => 'attachment',
        'status' => 'publish',
        'post_mime_type' => 'image',
        'post_parent' => $post->ID
    );
    $images =& get_children($args);
    // Loop the attachments
    foreach ( (array) $images as $attachment_id => $attachment ) {
        // Output an attachment in thumbnail size
        echo wp_get_attachment_image($attachment_id, 'thumbnail', '');
    }
?>
</a>
```

If you don't remember what this code does, go back and revisit the front page section earlier in this chapter, especially the part about the loop-home.php template where it is described in detail.

This code gives us the output shown in Figure 8-14, which is a thumbnail linked to its post.

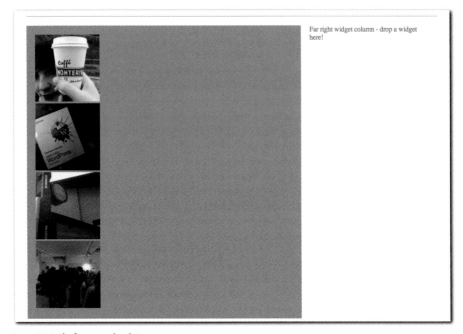

Figure 8-14: The footer got thumbs!

This is enough to style this baby, but you have one more thing to consider — the thumbnail size. These are the wrong size, although they adhere to the WordPress default of 150 × 150 pixel thumbnails. Not so pretty, are they? The proper way to solve this dilemma is to set up the thumbnail size from the start. (Of course, then I wouldn't have the opportunity to show you how to fix it here.) The key to the problem is `wp_get_attachment_image()`, which contains all the settings for the pulled attachment. Among other things, I'm telling it to fetch the thumbnail version of the image. Now, I could just as well define the size of the image here, and WordPress will scale the nearest available image accordingly. Instead of passing `'thumb-nail'` as the size, I pass an array with the sizes I want, like this:

```
wp_get_attachment_image($attachment_id, array(X,Y), '');
```

The X and Y in the array are the width and height, in pixels, that you want to use for the output of the image.

In this case, I want to make the box spacious and nice. First, I alter the `wp_get_attach-ment_image()` code to scale the image to 130 × 130 pixels, which gives me this complete footer.php template:

```
<div id="footer">
    <div class="footer-left">
        <div id="footer-thumbs">
            <ul>
            <?php
                // Store 4 posts from Portfolio in
```

```php
                                        // $lastposts then loop with foreach
                                        $lastposts =
get_posts('numberposts=4&category_name=portfolio');
                                        foreach($lastposts as $post) :
                                            setup_postdata($post); // Gives us post
                                                                      access
                              ?>
                        <li class="footer-thumb-post">
                            <a href="<?php the_permalink(); ?>">
                            <?php
                                // Fetching a thumbnail from
                                    post attachments
                                // First some parameters for
                                    later
                                $args = array(
                                    'numberposts' => 1,
                                    'post_type' => 'attachment',
                                    'status' => 'publish',
                                    'post_mime_type' => 'image',
                                    'post_parent' => $post->ID
                                );
                                $images =& get_children($args);
                                // Loop the attachments
                                foreach ( (array) $images as
$attachment_id => $attachment ) {

                                    // Output an attachment in
                                        thumbnail size
                                    echo wp_get_attachment_
image($attachment_id, array(130,130), '');
                                }
                            ?>
                            </a>
                        </li>
                    <?php
                        // Stop loop
                        endforeach; ?>
                    </ul>
                </div>
                <div class="footer-column left">
                    <ul class="footer-widget-area">
                    <?php
                        // The Footer Left Side widget area
dynamic_sidebar('footer-left-column');
                    ?>
                        <li class="widget widget-area-empty">
                            Left widget column - drop a widget
                            here!
                        </li>
                    <?php endif; ?>
                    </ul>
                </div>
```

```php
                            <div class="footer-column-middle left">
                                    <ul class="footer-widget-area
footer-widget-area-middle">
                                        <?php
                                            // The Footer Left Side widget area
dynamic_sidebar('footer-middle-column');
                                        ?>
                                            <li class="widget widget-area-empty">
                                                Middle widget column - drop a widget
                                                here!
                                            </li>
                                        <?php endif; ?>
                                        </ul>
                            </div>
                            <div class="footer-column right">
                                    <ul class="footer-widget-area">
                                        <?php
                                            // The Footer Left Side widget area
dynamic_sidebar('footer-right-column');
                                        ?>
                                            <li class="widget widget-area-empty">
                                                Right widget column - drop a widget
                                                here!
                                            </li>
                                        <?php endif; ?>
                                        </ul>
                            </div>
                    </div>
                    <div class="footer-right">
                            <ul>
                            <?php
                                    // The Footer Right Side widget area
dynamic_sidebar('footer-right-side');
                            ?>
                                    <li class="widget widget-area-empty">
                                        Far right widget column - drop a widget
                                        here!
                                    </li>
                            <?php endif; ?>
                            </ul>
                    </div>
                    <div id="footer-bottom">
                            <p><?php bloginfo('title'); ?> is proudly powered by
<a href="http://wordpress.org" title="WordPress">WordPress</a></p>
                    </div>
            </div>

        </div> <!-- ends #plate -->
```

```
    </div> <!-- ends #wrap -->
    </div> <!-- ends #site -->

<?php wp_footer(); ?>
</body>
</html>
```

Then I add the following CSS to my stylesheet (style.css obviously), just to make sure everything floats okay:

```
div#footer-thumbs {
    width: 100%;
    float:left;
    margin-bottom: 20px;
    background: #9e9e9e;
}
    div#footer-thumbs ul {
        float:left;
        padding: 10px; /* 10px padding gives us 620px width */
    }
        div#footer-thumbs ul li {
            float: left;
            width: 155px; /* Width per thumbnail li block */
            list-style: none;
        }
            div#footer-thumbs ul li img {
                padding: 10px; /* Add more space between images */
            }
```

I style this a bit more shortly; for now, I just want the thumbnails to float in a nice manner and align properly. Note that I'm using 10 pixels of padding for the containing `ul` element, but I want 20 pixels between images and the box borders, as well as between the images. That's why we add another 10 pixels to the `img` element within the `li`, that way it'll seem as if there's more room than there is. Figure 8-15 shows what we have right now.

Figure 8-15: Thumbs aligned and floating well in the footer

ADDING A BIT OF STYLE

I haven't gone through every little part of the theme, but most of the important stuff is in here. The rest is more or less similar, or borrowing from previous themes. So in an effort not to repeat everything, I'm moving on to styling the site.

Right now, my theme looks like Figures 8-16 through 8-20, which includes front page views, a Portfolio post, a sample Page, and a typical blog post. You'll notice some elements from the semi-static site I built in Chapter 7. The similarities are obviously due to the fact that I borrowed my own code from Chapter 7. Usually when you design a new theme, you want to keep it clean and not have too much old garbage lying around. But during the development process, it can be helpful to have something in the stylesheet so that you can see what happens and what works.

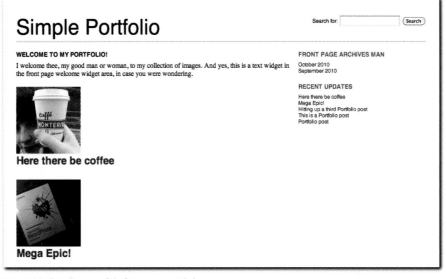

Figure 8-16: The upper part of the front page, unstyled

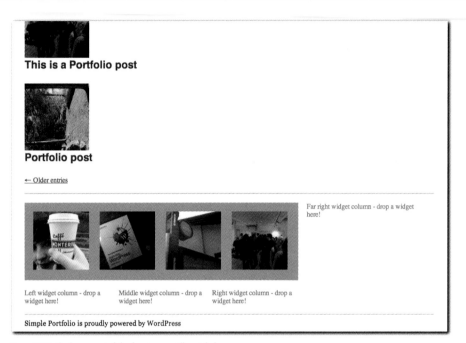

Figure 8-17: The lower part of the front page, still unstyled

Figure 8-18: A Portfolio post in need of some styling

Figure 8-19: The ever present About page at an early state

Figure 8-20: A typical blog post

Next, I make it pretty, starting with the front page. I want to style the welcome widget properly to make it useful as a welcome block. I make it ready for text widgets, but it can obviously house anything. Below the welcome widget I list the latest updates, with the thumbnail floating left and with the title and the excerpt to the right. The typography got an update, as well as the links, which lacked proper styling before. I went with a somewhat controversial block on hover style. This changes the background color of the link to the same color as the link — black in this case — making it impossible to read when you hover. That made sense to me because there are no colors in this design, just black and white and gray.

While I was at it, I spiced up the header a bit. Now I have a background color behind the search form floating to the right, and the menu below is a bit styled as well. The sidebar also got some style, with simple headings and every link listing ending up on a background plate. Text widgets can still contain scripts or whatever. I'm demonstrating that with the default Twitter widget in Figure 8-21.

Figure 8-21: A slightly more styled front page

All single posts, as well as Pages, need some TLC. This was actually not so hard, especially since I borrowed the comments code from the Simple Static theme. Styling comments can be a real bore, so the more often you can reuse code the better.

The Pages templates rely on the same loop as the single posts, so we're getting most of these things two for one. There are some things that won't show up on Pages (category and tags for one), and then there are the various sidebars as well, or right-column widget areas, as they like to be called. Figure 8-22 shows the revised About page.

Figure 8-22: The About page

You would think that a lot of code is involved in getting the galleries to look good, but most of it is pretty basic. This is, in fact, the only related code that you'll find in the theme's style.css, and that's including the image alignments for floating images to the left and right in posts.

```
img.alignleft {
       float:left;
       margin: 0 15px 15px 0;
}

img.alignright {
       float:right;
       margin: 0 0 15px 15px;
}

img.aligncenter {
       margin: 0 auto 16px auto;
}

img.attachment-thumbnail {
       padding: 10px;
       border: 1px solid #bfbfbf !important;
}

.wp-caption {
       padding: 10px 7px;
       border: 1px solid #bfbfbf;
       font-size: 12px;
       color: #888;
       font-style: italic;
       text-align:center;
}
```

```
p.wp-caption-text {
     margin: 10px 0 0 0;
     padding: 0;
     line-height: 14px;
}

div.gallery {
     margin-bottom: 14px;
}
     dl.gallery-item {}
          dt.gallery-icon {}
               img.attachment-thumbnail {
                    border:0;
               }
          dd.gallery-caption {
               margin-top: 8px;
               font-size: 12px;
               color: #888;
               font-style: italic;
          }
```

Simple stuff, I know, but this is all that is needed at this point. You could obviously trim this further if necessary. But this theme is supposed to keep things simple (as you'll see in Figures 8-23 through 8-25) — in part to ensure that it's easy to build upon, but also because a simple theme with less bling makes the images stand out better. And that's what it's all about, after all.

235

Figure 8-23: The Portfolio post revisted

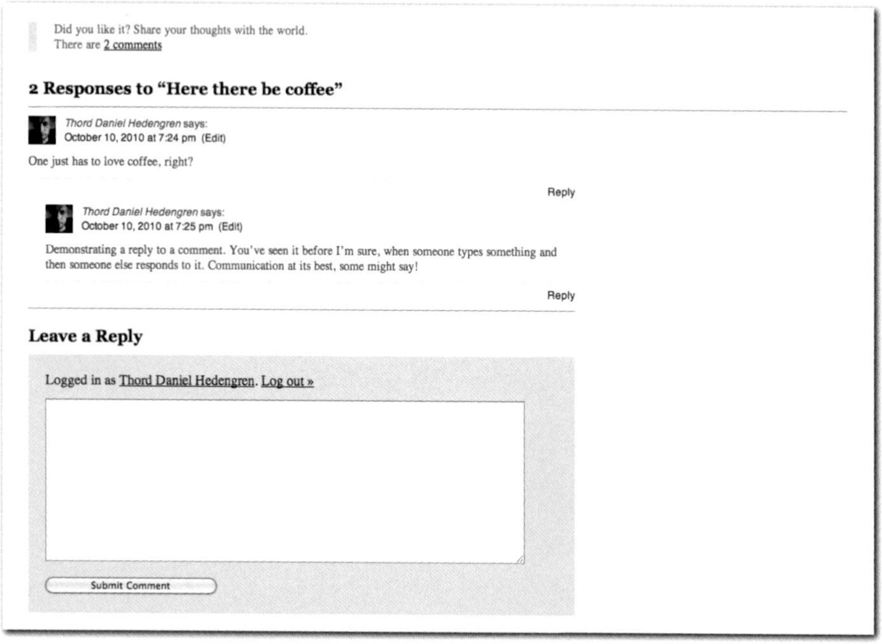

Did you like it? Share your thoughts with the world.
There are 2 comments

2 Responses to "Here there be coffee"

Thord Daniel Hedengren says:
October 10, 2010 at 7:24 pm (Edit)

One just has to love coffee, right?

Reply

Thord Daniel Hedengren says:
October 10, 2010 at 7:25 pm (Edit)

Demonstrating a reply to a comment. You've seen it before I'm sure, when someone types something and then someone else responds to it. Communication at its best, some might say!

Reply

Leave a Reply

Logged in as Thord Daniel Hedengren. Log out »

[   ]

Submit Comment

Figure 8-24: Comments are working

Simple Portfolio

Search for: [   ] Search

ABOUT   GET IN TOUCH   PORTFOLIO   FRONT PAGE

← Portfolio post

Writing station

October 3, 2010 by Thord Daniel Hedengren Edit This

iPad and Moleskine

This is my writing station when I'm at the cabin. An iPad, a bluetooth keyboard, and my trusty Moleskine notebook.

The full sized image is 1024 x 765 pixels

Figure 8-25: Image view got a slight brush-up as well

That's about it. You can find the full style.css file, commented where need be, at the companion Web site for this book. Otherwise, the best way to dig deeper and see what does what is to look at the theme files and what ID's and classes I have given the various elements. Or, you can use your favorite Web developer toolbar to inspect elements in the Web browser.

> Get the complete style.css file from this book's companion Web site at www.wiley.com/go/smashingwordpressthemes.

SPICING IT UP WITH PLUGINS

Generally speaking, I think it's best to do as much as possible within the theme, staying clear of taking the plugin shortcut. Most of the things you want to do can be accomplished in your theme. Theoretically, you can have a whole plugin residing in your functions.php file.

Plugins can add bloat, so beware of using more than you really need. Having a lot of plugins can make your site load unnecessarily slow.

When it comes to images and video, however, plugins can really add some functionality. JavaScript mavens may very well be able to duplicate all the cool features that plugins can add to your site, but images and video are one area in which I feel a shortcut is merited.

LIGHTBOXES

The lightbox effect (see Figure 8-26) is something of a Web phenomenon. You probably know it, even if it is not by name. Click an image and it opens on top of the site, not as a pop-up, but as an overlay, dimming out the background (but usually not quite all the way) and focusing on the image.

There are a ton of JavaScript scripts that can do this for you, and implementing them is fairly easy. Although you do have to remember to add some code to every linked thumbnail you want to open up in lightbox view. Plugins make that so much easier by adding the necessary data automatically when inserting images from the media browser within the WordPress admin panel, for example.

There aren't as many plugins as there are JavaScript solutions for your lightbox needs, but there are quite a few. You might want to search for lightbox in the WordPress plugin directory to determine your full set of options. Or, you can just pick a recommended one from the plugins chapter of this book.

Figure 8-26: A typical lightbox effect that overrides the image view page with an overlay

A FEW WORDS ABOUT GALLERY PLUGINS

There are plugins written to expand the gallery feature in WordPress — some even replace it. I'm all for extending WordPress when needed, and there is always room for improvement when it comes to media managing. But sidestepping the default media library isn't the solution. Some plugins do that, adding cool gallery functionality and a bunch of bling, which is great, pretty, and sometimes even amazingly easy to work with. Problem is, when that plugin suddenly breaks, or when WordPress changes and the plugin author can't keep up with the updates, you'll be hanging out to dry. This is obviously true for all plugins; changes within WordPress can make them obsolete or broken. But the problem is very visible when it comes to media.

If you're considering a gallery plugin, make sure that it just replaces or alters functionality and doesn't change how images are stored, where they are stored, and so on. You want to be able to go back to the default media manager at any time; otherwise, I strongly advise against the use of the plugin.

You have been warned. Now go pimp your site!

WRAPPING IT UP

There you have it, a theme focusing on your images rather than your text. Working with content other than text forces you to take a different approach to theme design, which is a good thing. You want to be able to tackle the type of content from the angle that fits the most. There are always angles; the question is how much these angles differ from one another. Two text-focused sites may be done differently, thereby having two different angles. But the angle for a site focused on images will more often than not be far enough off the two text-focused sites that you can't really compare them.

Remember what you're building for. The purpose of the site is the most important thing.

9

A MAGAZINE THEME

MAGAZINE-INSPIRED THEMES have become a sub-type of themes, alongside traditional blog themes, portfolios, and niche themes meant for other distinct kinds of Web sites. You know the type, with big blurbs to catch the reader, prominent ad spots, and a content flow that uses images and text to lure the reader into reading the piece.

In short, online magazines with a touch of blog are both a popular and modern style of Web sites. In this chapter, I build one of these.

PLANNING AN ONLINE MAGAZINE

In this chapter, I thought I'd try something different. I'll let you tag along as I create the Notes Mag theme, which is available for free at `http://notesblog.com/mag`.

The idea is to build an online magazine theme, with all the elements you need to roll out your own online magazine. I include content sliders, image position control in post listings, a grid-based layout, ad spots, and all the widget areas you could possibly need.

So, let's build the first version of Notes Mag 1.0 together!

THE NOTES MAG 1.0 THEME LAYOUT

The first thing I do is to bring out my trusty old (actually it's spanking new) Moleskine notebook. I've made a sketch of what I want to do, with some notes that you may not be able to discern (see my home page layout in Figure 9-1). If my handwriting is anything to go by, I was obviously a medical doctor in a past life. This is the front page, the one that greets readers every time they tap in the URL to a Web site based on the Notes Mag theme.

Figure 9-1: The front page sketch for Notes Mag

As you can see in the sketch, it is quite boxy here; but it won't be in reality. Proper whitespace keeps the elements apart, reverting to boxes only when necessary. I want a clean and sober design here that puts the content first.

An online magazine has some special needs, so I've also made sketches for both single-post views (and Page views, as you see Figure 9-2) and archives. I've opted for simpler content listings in the archives as those are more direct per topic than the front page. Future versions may offer the option of a content slider, or something similar to this, but for now that feels a bit redundant.

Figure 9-2: An archives page sketch for Notes Mag

As for single-post (see Figure 9-3) and Page view, content is foremost. Clean, simple, and straightforward is what I'm going for here.

DYNAMIC ELEMENTS FOR NOTES MAG

Most of the dynamic stuff in this theme I manage using widget areas. In fact, depending on how you use these areas, you can do things quite differently from my simple sketches. For example, the recent post and comment boxes in the lower part of the front page will obviously be widget areas. But you can easily add whatever content works best for you, such as a forum that you want to promote or links that you want to share. There are a ton of possibilities; you just have to be sure that the items are widgetized so you can drop them wherever you want.

Some of the elements in this theme force me to use custom fields and action hooks. Action hooks make it is easy to extend the theme with added functionality.

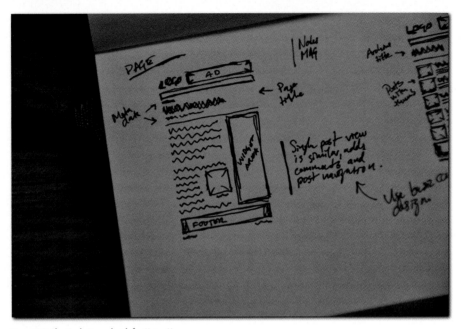

Figure 9-3: The single Page sketch for Notes Mag

BUILDING THE MAGAZINE SITE

Starting off, let's set up the basic shell for the theme. What I want when I'm done is a (some-what) working structure of a site. The grid will be in place, content will be output (but look awful), and boxes will align the way they should.

What I won't have is working functionality for the cooler parts of the site. That means no widget areas, no action hooks, or anything like that. I get to that stuff in the next phase, later in this chapter.

THE BASIC SITE STRUCTURE

I've decided to make Notes Mag 960 pixels wide. This is a fairly common width, is easy to work with column-wise, and offers a nice grid. If you want to take a shortcut, you can visit `http://960.gs` for a bunch of downloadables for 960-pixel grids. I'm not relying on any of that for this one, though.

One important thing here is to give the end user the option to have a completed site, with a background color (or image) behind it. That means there will be elements (`div`'s, really) wider that 960 pixels here, where the actual site will adhere to the 960-pixel width.

This is the basic structure:

```
body
    div#site
```

```
div#top
    div#wrap
        div#wrap-inner
            div#header
            div#plate
                div#content
                div#sidebar-container
            div#footer
    div#footer-outside
```

The `div#site` uses the full width and is there only if I need it in the future. The whole thing really starts with `div#wrap`, which is what sets the full width and then centers it. The `div#wrap-inner` uses padding so that the active width is 960 pixels. This means that I can set a background color on `div#wrap`, hence getting a background on which the actual site sits, and have a different background for the body. I obviously enable custom backgrounds for this.

Moving on, `div#header` contains the header parts of the site: `div#plate` is the content (both left and right columns) and `div#footer` contains the footer. I've also added a `div#footer-outside` that sits outside the `div#wrap`. This could be useful for adding credits and whatnot; it'll be a widget area that defaults to that at least.

OK, so let's build this puppy!

STARTING WITH THE HEADER

I start with the header code. Remember, I'm just building the shell here, not adding any dynamic features. That means that the logo will be an h1 tag with the text logo in it, and I won't have any widget areas or working menus.

The one thing I do let into this one is the necessary code to output the proper title tags. I'm just swiping that from previous themes anyway, and it might help me test the theme out.

Here is header.php:

```php
<!DOCTYPE html>
<html <?php language_attributes(); ?>>
<head>
<meta charset="<?php bloginfo( 'charset' ); ?>" />
<title>
    <?php
        // Print the right title
        if (is_home () ) {
            bloginfo('name');
        } elseif (is_category() || is_tag()) {
            single_cat_title(); echo ' &bull; ' ; bloginfo('name');
        } elseif (is_single() || is_page()) {
            single_post_title(); } else { wp_title('',true);
        }
    ?>
```

```
</title>
<link rel="profile" href="http://gmpg.org/xfn/11" />
<link rel="stylesheet" type="text/css" media="all" href="<?php bloginfo( 'style-
  sheet_url' ); ?>" />
<link rel="pingback" href="<?php bloginfo( 'pingback_url' ); ?>" />
<?php
      // Kick off WordPress
      wp_head();
?>
</head>

<body <?php body_class(); ?>>

<div id="site">
      <div id="top">
            This area won't be seen unless there
            is something in the action hook that
            will power it!
      </div>
      <div id="wrap">
            <div id="wrap-inner">
                  <div id="header">
                        <div id="header-middle">
                              <div class="ad right">
                                    Here we'll have an ad!
                              </div>
                              <h1 id="site-header">
                                    <a href="<?php bloginfo('url'); ?>" title="<?php
  bloginfo('name'); ?>">
                                          LOGO GOES HERE
                                    </a>
                              </h1>
                        </div>
                        <div id="header-bottom">
                              MENU GOES HERE
                        </div>
                  </div>
            </div>
            <div id="plate">
```

Simple enough, right? The header.php template ends just after div#plate, so everything below it will, until I close it, be inside the box containing the left and right columns.

ENDING WITH THE FOOTER

It's a good idea to tackle the footer.php template right away, being sure to close everything I just did in the footer. In other words, I don't work with the actual content of the site, such as index.php and sidebar.php, among other things, until I've coded both the header and footer.

```
      </div><!--/#plate-->
            <div id="footer">
```

```
            This is the footer area!
        </div>
    </div><!--/#wrap-inner-->
</div><!--/#wrap-->
<div id="footer-outside">
        This is the footer that sits outside the site!
    </div>
</div><!--/#site-->

<?php wp_footer(); ?>
</body>
</html>
```

To make it a bit easier to piece everything together, I've added HTML comments after every closing div that relates to something I opened in another file. This is always a good idea, even in cases like this one when everything really starts in header.php and it would be easy enough to backtrack to it.

GETTING TO THE CONTENT

Now that I have a header and footer, I need to put something in between. I use index.php at this stage, but later on I'll obviously want to create more templates for delivering the content.

The index.php template is a lot simpler these days, thanks to the fact that you can put the loop in its own template:

```
<?php get_header(); ?>

        <div id="content" class="widecolumn">
            <?php
                // Look for loop-index.php, fallback to loop.php
                get_template_part( 'loop', 'index' );
            ?>
        </div>

<?php get_sidebar(); ?>
<?php get_footer(); ?>
```

Nothing fancy here either. I get the header with get_header(), include the loop with get_template_part() by first looking for loop-index.php; failing that, I default to loop.php. I then get the sidebar with get_sidebar() and wrap it up with the footer using get_footer(). You know all this by now, right?

Now I need a sidebar. This one is really easy at this stage:

```
<div id="sidebar-container">
    <ul id="sidebar" class="column">
        <li>
            This is the sidebar. It'll be fully widgetized of course.
```

```
            </li>
        </ul>
</div>
```

For this to work, even at this scale, I'll need a functional loop. That's why I create loop.php, which index.php obviously defaults to when there's no loop-index.php.

```php
<?php
    // When possible, display navigation at the top
    if ( $wp_query->max_num_pages > 1 ) : ?>
    <div id="nav-above" class="navigation">
        <div class="nav-previous">
            <?php next_posts_link( __( '<span class="meta-nav">&larr;</span>
    Older posts', 'notesmag' ) ); ?>
        </div>
        <div class="nav-next">
            <?php previous_posts_link( __( 'Newer posts <span class="meta-
    nav">&rarr;</span>', 'notesmag' ) ); ?>
        </div>
    </div>
<?php endif; ?>


<?php
    // 404 Page Not Found or empty archives etc.
    if ( !have_posts() ) : ?>
    <div id="post-0" class="post error404 not-found">
        <h1 class="entry-title">
            <?php _e( 'Not Found', 'notesmag' ); ?>
        </h1>
        <div class="entry-content">
            <p><?php _e( 'Sorry, there is nothing here. You might want to try
    and search for whatever it was you were looking for?', 'notesmag' ); ?></p>
            <?php get_search_form(); ?>
        </div>
    </div>
<?php endif; ?>


<?php
    // The basic loop
    while ( have_posts() ) : the_post(); ?>

    <div id="post-<?php the_ID(); ?>" <?php post_class(); ?>>
        <h2 class="entry-title">
            <a href="<?php the_permalink(); ?>" title="<?php the_title_
    attribute(); ?>" rel="bookmark">
                <?php the_title(); ?>
            </a>
        </h2>
        <div class="entry-meta">
            <?php the_category(', '); the_tags(' &bull; ', ', ', '' ); _e( '
    by ', 'notesmag' ); the_author_posts_link(); ?>
```

```php
        </div>

    <?php
        // For archives and search results, use the_excerpt()
        if ( is_archive() || is_search() ) : ?>
            <div class="entry-summary">
                <?php the_excerpt(); ?>
            </div>
    <?php
        // For everything else
        else : ?>
            <div class="entry-content">
                <?php
                    the_content();
                    wp_link_pages( array( 'before' => '<div class="page-
 link">' . __( 'Pages:', 'notesmag' ), 'after' => '</div>' ) );
?>
            </div>
    <?php endif; ?>
        <div clas="entry-meta-lower"
            <span class="comments-link">
                <?php comments_popup_link( __( 'Leave a comment', 'notesmag'
 ), __( '1 comment', 'notesmag' ), __( '% comments', 'notesmag' ) ); ?>
            </span>
            <?php edit_post_link( __( 'Edit', 'notesmag' ), '<span
class="meta-sep">|</span> <span class="edit-link">', '</span>' ); ?>
        </div>
    </div>

    <?php
// The comments template
comments_template( '', true );

// End the loop
    endwhile;
?>

<?php
    // When possible, display navigation at the top
    if ( $wp_query->max_num_pages > 1 ) : ?>
    <div id="nav-below" class="navigation">
        <div class="nav-previous">
            <?php next_posts_link( __( '<span class="meta-nav">&larr;</span>
 Older posts', 'notesmag' ) ); ?>
        </div>
        <div class="nav-next">
            <?php previous_posts_link( __( 'Newer posts <span class="meta-
nav">&rarr;</span>', 'notesmag' ) ); ?>
        </div>
    </div>
<?php endif; ?>
```

You'll recognize most of this loop from before, so refer to previous chapters if you find it a bit tricky to wade through. There's nothing fancy in it at all, just some navigational links at the top and bottom of the code should there be more pages for listings. On archives (be it date, category, or tags), I get `the_excerpt()`, and on single posts and Pages, I use `the_content()`. I use this loop as a basis when I build the site; it's a decent fallback.

CREATING THE STYLESHEET

The stylesheet is pretty straightforward. It starts with the theme declaration and then moves on to a simple CSS reset. Then I've got the layout section where everything gets its intended position and some margins so that it's a little easier to see what's what. I've also added a background color to the body tag so that I can see how the site sits on top of the background. This background color is temporary, obviously.

Other than that, it is pretty straightforward. I'm using CSS classes to set the column widths and to make sure there are classes for floating left or right from the start, despite that they are not being used at this stage.

Here's the full style.css at this point:

```css
/*
Theme Name: Notes Mag
Theme URI: http://notesblog.com/mag/
Description: The Notes Mag theme is an online magazine theme. <a href="http://tdh.
  me/">Made by TDH</a> and maintained at <a href="http://notesblog.com/">notesblog.
  com</a>. Requires WordPress 3.0 or higher.
Version: 1.0
Tags: light, two-columns, right-sidebar, fixed-width, threaded-comments, sticky-
  post, translation-ready, custom-header, custom-background, editor-style,
  custom-menu
Author: Thord Daniel Hedengren
Author URI: http://tdh.me/

      Get support and services for the Notes Blog Core Theme:
      http://notesblog.com

      Created and managed by Thord Daniel Hedengren:
      http://tdh.me

*/

/* =====
   RESET */

html, body, div, span, applet, object, iframe,
h1, h2, h3, h4, h5, h6, p, blockquote, pre,
abbr, acronym, address, big, cite, code,
del, dfn, em, font, img, ins, kbd, q, s, samp,
small, strike, strong, sub, sup, tt, var,
```

```
b, u, i, center,
dl, dt, dd, ol, ul, li,
fieldset, form, label, legend,
table, caption, tbody, tfoot, thead, tr, th, td {
      border: 0;
      margin: 0;
      padding: 0;
      vertical-align: baseline;
}

ol, ul {
      list-style: none;
}

table {
      border-collapse: collapse;
      border-spacing: 0;
}


/* ======
   LAYOUT */

.right, .alignright {
      float: right;
}

.left, .alignleft {
      float: right;
}

.column {
      width: 320px; /* One column */
}

.widecolumn {
      width: 640px; /* Two columns */
}

.fullcolumn {
      width: 960px; /* Three columns */
}

body {
      background-color: #efefef; /* Temporary background color */
}

div#site {
      width: 100%;
      float: left;
      padding-top: 20px;
```

```
    }

    div#top {
        width: 980px; /* Full site width */
        margin: 0 auto 20px auto; /* Center the site */
    }

    div#wrap {
        width: 980px; /* Full site width */
        margin: 0 auto; /* Center the site */
        overflow: hidden;
        background-color: #fff;
    }

    div#wrap-inner {
        float: left;
        padding: 10px; /* Site width 980-10-10=960 px */
    }

    div#header {
        width: 100%;
        margin-bottom: 20px;
    }
        div#header-top {}
        div#header-middle {}
            #site-title {
                float: left;
            }
        div#header-bottom {}

    div#plate {
        width: 100%;
        float: left;
    }

    div#content {
        float: left;
    }

    div#sidebar-container {
        float: right;
    }

    div#footer {
        width: 100%;
        float: left;
        margin-top: 20px;
    }
```

```
div#footer-outside {
    width: 960px;
    margin: 10px auto;
}
```

VIEWING THE THEME THUS FAR

Now I have a working theme (as you can see in Figure 9-4)! It's not pretty, but it does work as intended. Next up is adding some features, and then I get to make it look the way I want.

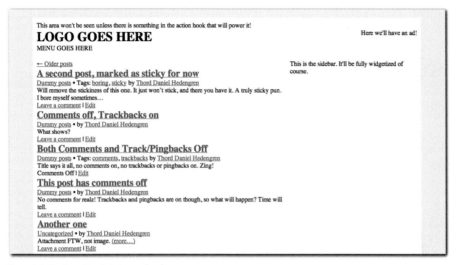

Figure 9-4: The Notes Mag 1.0 theme, thus far

ADDING FUNCTIONALITY

Now that I've got the skeleton theme working, I can add the necessary functionality. Because widgets make the WordPress world go 'round and 'round (not counting the loop, of course), I start with those. Widgets make up the bulk of the areas I need to add, so it's good to get them out of the way.

After adding widgets, I add the menu area, get the custom header (which is the logo) in there, along with support for custom backgrounds. Finally, I add four action hooks and wrap up with that.

STARTING WITH FUNCTIONS.PHP

All these nifty features start in functions.php. Without the necessary code there, they just won't work. I'll be jumping back and forth here, adding stuff to functions.php and then doing things with the other template files in the Notes Mag theme.

But before I get started, I want to get a basic functions.php up and running:

```php
<?php // Here we go!

// The default content width
if ( ! isset( $content_width ) )
    $content_width = 640;

// The visual editor will use editor-style.css
add_editor_style();

// Adding support for featured images
add_theme_support( 'post-thumbnails' );

// Add default posts and comments RSS feed links
add_theme_support( 'automatic-feed-links' );

// Localization support, fetches languages files from /lang/
load_theme_textdomain( 'notesmag', TEMPLATEPATH . '/lang' );

// Add custom background support
add_custom_background();

?>
```

Pretty basic stuff, adding the default width and all. The theme is localized, as I'm sure you've seen already (refer to Chapter 6), so the `load_theme_textdomain()` specifies where the files are (in the `/lang` folder within the theme folder) and what the textdomain is — "notes-mag." Then I add support for Visual editor styles, meaning that I can style it with editor-style. css. There are also RSS feed links added to the header and support for featured images. Finally, I add support for custom backgrounds. Because I've got `body_class()` in the body tag (see header.php in previous code snippet), that works out of the box.

That's the basic functions.php file for Notes Mag. Next, I add to it by enabling all the cool stuff.

ADDING WIDGET AREAS

When adding widget areas, you need to think ahead. At this point in the theme development process, I haven't yet created all our templates. Sometimes it is a better idea to do that first. But, in this case, I know what I want from this version of the theme, so I can plan ahead.

The front page has four widget areas that I use there and only there (as you can see in Figure 9-5). One on the top right just beside the featured content slider, underneath the menu, and one three columns below the tags divider. These are front page only widgets. I have two more widget areas here as well. The first one is meant for an ad (or similar) to the right of the logo in the header, and the second one is the footer. These two widget areas are global, and hence are the same all across the site.

Figure 9-5: The front page widget areas

Planning the widget areas

Now I need to create the following widget areas (as shown in Figure 9-6), not counting the one in the header or footer at this time:

- Front Page Top Right
- Front Page Column Left
- Front Page Column Middle
- Front Page Column Right

Problem is, it doesn't stop there. The archive pages also need widget areas, and some of them are for archive pages only.

Notes Mag obviously supports all types of archives, but when it comes to widgets only three are needed:

- Right Column Archive
- Right Column Category
- Right Column Tag

These are used for date based, category, and tag archives, respectively.

Figure 9-6: The archive templates widget areas

Moving on, I have the single-post view and single-Page view (see Figure 9-7). These aren't widget heavy because focus is on the content, but they both have widget areas in the right column, or sidebar in WordPress lingo, so I need another two for these two types of content.

This brings us the following widget areas.

- Post Right Column
- Page Right Column

That's a lot of widget areas, but it doesn't stop there. Random pages, like the 404 and search results all need some widget areas, and then there's the footer. All in all, I need these widget areas as well:

- Header
- Footer
- Right Column Fallback

Phew, quite a few. Now how about actually adding them to the theme?

Figure 9-7: Posts and Pages widget areas

Defining the widget areas

All these widget areas need to be defined in the functions.php file. This is easy enough; and since none of these areas is intended to do anything other than display a list, I won't have to fiddle so much with how I declare them. You'll recognize this code, which offers the widget declarations for all these areas.

```
// WIDGET AREAS ->
// Front Page Top Right widget area
register_sidebar( array(
    'name' => __( 'Front Page Top Right', 'notesmag' ),
    'id' => 'front-page-top-right',
    'description' => __( 'Widget area on the top right, visible on the front page
 only', 'notesmag' ),
    'before_widget' => '<li id="%1$s" class="widget-container %2$s">',
    'after_widget' => '</li>',
    'before_title' => '<h2 class="widget-title">',
    'after_title' => '</h2>',
) );
// Front Page Columns Left widget area
register_sidebar( array(
    'name' => __( 'Front Page Columns Left', 'notesmag' ),
    'id' => 'front-page-columns-left',
    'description' => __( 'The left column in the lower part of the front page.',
```

```php
    'notesmag' ),
        'before_widget' => '<li id="%1$s" class="widget-container %2$s">',
        'after_widget' => '</li>',
        'before_title' => '<h2 class="widget-title">',
        'after_title' => '</h2>',
) );
// Front Page Columns Middle widget area
register_sidebar( array(
        'name' => __( 'Front Page Columns Middle', 'notesmag' ),
        'id' => 'front-page-columns-middle',
        'description' => __( 'The middle column in the lower part of the front page.',
 'notesmag' ),
        'before_widget' => '<li id="%1$s" class="widget-container %2$s">',
        'after_widget' => '</li>',
        'before_title' => '<h2 class="widget-title">',
        'after_title' => '</h2>',
) );
// Front Page Columns Right widget area
register_sidebar( array(
        'name' => __( 'Front Page Columns Right', 'notesmag' ),
        'id' => 'front-page-columns-left',
        'description' => __( 'The right column in the lower part of the front page.',
 'notesmag' ),
        'before_widget' => '<li id="%1$s" class="widget-container %2$s">',
        'after_widget' => '</li>',
        'before_title' => '<h2 class="widget-title">',
        'after_title' => '</h2>',
) );
// Right Column Archive widget area
register_sidebar( array(
        'name' => __( 'Right Column Archive', 'notesmag' ),
        'id' => 'right-column-archive',
        'description' => __( 'The right column on date-based archive pages.', 'notesmag'
 ),
        'before_widget' => '<li id="%1$s" class="widget-container %2$s">',
        'after_widget' => '</li>',
        'before_title' => '<h2 class="widget-title">',
        'after_title' => '</h2>',
) );
// Right Column Category widget area
register_sidebar( array(
        'name' => __( 'Right Column Category', 'notesmag' ),
        'id' => 'right-column-category',
        'description' => __( 'The right column on category archive pages.', 'notesmag'
 ),
        'before_widget' => '<li id="%1$s" class="widget-container %2$s">',
        'after_widget' => '</li>',
        'before_title' => '<h2 class="widget-title">',
        'after_title' => '</h2>',
) );
// Right Column Tag widget area
```

```php
register_sidebar( array(
    'name' => __( 'Right Column Tag', 'notesmag' ),
    'id' => 'right-column-tag',
    'description' => __( 'The right column on tag archive pages.', 'notesmag' ),
    'before_widget' => '<li id="%1$s" class="widget-container %2$s">',
    'after_widget' => '</li>',
    'before_title' => '<h2 class="widget-title">',
    'after_title' => '</h2>',
) );
// Post Right Column widget area
register_sidebar( array(
    'name' => __( 'Post Right Column', 'notesmag' ),
    'id' => 'post-right-column',
    'description' => __( 'The right column on single posts.', 'notesmag' ),
    'before_widget' => '<li id="%1$s" class="widget-container %2$s">',
    'after_widget' => '</li>',
    'before_title' => '<h2 class="widget-title">',
    'after_title' => '</h2>',
) );
// Page Right Column widget area
register_sidebar( array(
    'name' => __( 'Page Right Column', 'notesmag' ),
    'id' => 'page-right-column',
    'description' => __( 'The right column on Pages.', 'notesmag' ),
    'before_widget' => '<li id="%1$s" class="widget-container %2$s">',
    'after_widget' => '</li>',
    'before_title' => '<h2 class="widget-title">',
    'after_title' => '</h2>',
) );
// Right Column Fallback widget area
register_sidebar( array(
    'name' => __( 'Right Column Fallback', 'notesmag' ),
    'id' => 'right-column-fallback',
    'description' => __( 'When all else fails, this widget area will be used for the
 right column.', 'notesmag' ),
    'before_widget' => '<li id="%1$s" class="widget-container %2$s">',
    'after_widget' => '</li>',
    'before_title' => '<h2 class="widget-title">',
    'after_title' => '</h2>',
) );
// Header widget area
register_sidebar( array(
    'name' => __( 'Header', 'notesmag' ),
    'id' => 'header',
    'description' => __( 'The widget area just beside the logo in the header.',
 'notesmag' ),
    'before_widget' => '<li id="%1$s" class="widget-container %2$s">',
    'after_widget' => '</li>',
    'before_title' => '<h2 class="widget-title">',
    'after_title' => '</h2>',
) );
```

```
// Footer widget area
register_sidebar( array(
    'name' => __( 'Footer', 'notesmag' ),
    'id' => 'footer',
    'description' => __( 'The footer widget area.', 'notesmag' ),
    'before_widget' => '<li id="%1$s" class="widget-container %2$s">',
    'after_widget' => '</li>',
    'before_title' => '<h2 class="widget-title">',
    'after_title' => '</h2>',
) );
// <-- ENDS
```

Now I've got some widget areas to play with. I can find them in the WordPress admin panel, but nothing shows up on my theme just yet. I'll add the Footer widget area in the footer.php template file right now, and then I'll sort out the right-column widget areas using a few conditional tags in sidebar.php.

First, here's the code to add the Footer widget area to the footer:

```
<?php
    // Adding the Footer widget area
    if ( !dynamic_sidebar('footer') ) : ?>
        <li class="widget">You need to add a widget in the Footer widget area,
        mate!</li>
    <?php endif;
?>
```

You recognize that, of course. This is what footer.php looks like right now:

```
</div><!--/#plate-->
<div id="footer">
    <ul>
    <?php
        // Adding the Footer widget area
        if ( !dynamic_sidebar('footer') ) : ?>
        <li class="widget">You need to add a widget in the Footer widget area,
        mate!</li>
        <?php endif;
    ?>
    </ul>
</div>               </div><!--/#wrap-inner-->
        </div><!--/#wrap-->
        <div id="footer-outside">
            This is the footer that sits outside the site!
        </div>
</div><!--/#site-->

<?php wp_footer(); ?>
</body>
</html>
```

I'm giving header.php the same treatment, adding the appropriate widget area code to it.

Sidebar.php is used as the right column. I use conditional tags to make sure I load the correct widget area. There are six possible right-column widget areas, all being used in different situations, so this shouldn't be too hard to figure out. You'll recognize the code, I'm sure:

```php
<?php
// Check whether this is a date based archive
    if ( is_date() || is_year() || is_month() || is_date() || is_time() ) {
                // It was! Adding the Right Column Archive widget area
                if ( !dynamic_sidebar('right-column-archive') ) : ?>
            <li class="widget">Add a widget in the Right Column Archive widget area,
            will you please?</li>
        <?php endif;
    }
// Check whether this is a category archive
    elseif ( is_category() ) {
                // It was! Adding the Right Column Category widget area
                if ( !dynamic_sidebar('right-column-category') ) : ?>
            <li class="widget">Add a widget in the Right Column Category widget
            area, will you please?</li>
        <?php endif;
    }
// Check whether this is a tag archive
    elseif ( is_category() ) {
                // It was! Adding the Right Column Tag widget area
                if ( !dynamic_sidebar('right-column-tag') ) : ?>
            <li class="widget">Add a widget in the Right Column Tag widget area,
            will you please?</li>
        <?php endif;
    }
// Check whether this is a single post
    elseif ( is_single() ) {
                // It was! Adding the Post Right Column widget area
                if ( !dynamic_sidebar('post-right-column') ) : ?>
            <li class="widget">Add a widget in the Post Right Column widget area,
            will you please?</li>
        <?php endif;
    }
// Check whether this is a Page
    elseif ( is_page() ) {
                // It was! Adding the Page Right Column widget area
                if ( !dynamic_sidebar('page-right-column') ) : ?>
            <li class="widget">Add a widget in the Page Right Column widget area,
            will you please?</li>
        <?php endif;
    }
// None of the above? Then I'll use the Right Column Fallback widget area
    else {
                // Adding the Right Column Fallback widget area
```

```
            if ( !dynamic_sidebar('right-column-fallback') ) : ?>
        <li class="widget">Add a widget in the Right Column Fallback widget
        area, will you please?</li>
    <?php endif;
  }
// We're done!
?>
```

This is just an `if else` clause going through a number of conditions. If you need to read up on what all these conditional tags do, such as `is_date()` or `is_category()`, refer to the Codex page at `http://codex.wordpress.org/Conditional_Tags`.

This is how sidebar.php looks in all its glory, right now:

```
<div id="sidebar-container" class="column">
  <ul id="sidebar">
        <?php
                // Check whether this is a date based archive
                if ( is_date() || is_year() || is_month() || is_date() || is_time()
        ) {
                        // It was! Adding the Right Column Archive widget area
                        if ( !dynamic_sidebar('right-column-archive') ) : ?>
                    <li class="widget">Add a widget in the Right Column Archive
                    widget area, will you please?</li>
                <?php endif;
        }

                // Check whether this is a category archive
                elseif ( is_category() ) {
                        // It was! Adding the Right Column Category widget area
                        if ( !dynamic_sidebar('right-column-category') ) : ?>
                    <li class="widget">Add a widget in the Right Column Category
                    widget area, will you please?</li>
                <?php endif;
        }

                // Check whether this is a tag archive
                elseif ( is_category() ) {
                        // It was! Adding the Right Column Tag widget area
                        if ( !dynamic_sidebar('right-column-tag') ) : ?>
                    <li class="widget">Add a widget in the Right Column Tag widget
                    area, will you please?</li>
                <?php endif;
        }

                // Check whether this is a single post
                elseif ( is_single() ) {
                        // It was! Adding the Post Right Column widget area
                        if ( !dynamic_sidebar('post-right-column') ) : ?>
                    <li class="widget">Add a widget in the Post Right Column widget
                    area, will you please?</li>
                <?php endif;
        }
```

```
                // Check whether this is a Page
                elseif ( is_page() ) {
                        // It was! Adding the Page Right Column widget area
                        if ( !dynamic_sidebar('page-right-column') ) : ?>
                    <li class="widget">Add a widget in the Page Right Column widget
                    area, will you please?</li>
                <?php endif;
        }

                // None of the above? Then we'll use the Right Column Fallback
                widget area
                else {
                        // Adding the Right Column Fallback widget area
                        if ( !dynamic_sidebar('right-column-fallback') ) : ?>
                    <li class="widget">Add a widget in the Right Column Fallback
                    widget area, will you please?</li>
                <?php endif;
                }
        // We're done!
        ?>
  </ul>
</div>
```

That's it for now; widget areas are in place. Let's move on.

PLANNING THE CUSTOM MENU

The menu is located just below the logo, in `div#header-bottom` within the `div#header` element, in header.php, of course. I am adding a custom menu here, not a regular widget area.

I have just one menu area in Notes Mag, but I still need to name it and add it to functions.php.

```
// Add the Top Navigation menu
register_nav_menus( array(
     'top-navigation' => __( 'Top Navigation', 'notesmag' ),
) );
```

Now I've got a menu area called Top Navigation (see Figure 9-8) where you can add menus using the Menus interface in the admin panel (under the Appearance settings, Menus option).

However, the menu won't show up anywhere until I put the necessary code in the theme. In this case, I'll add `wp_nav_menu()` to header.php, where my placeholder text for the menu resides. Because I only have one menu area defined (Top Navigation, remember?), I could just add the template tag and be done with it. But, who knows what the future may bring? That's why I pass the menu to `wp_nav_menu()`, as well, to make sure it'll work in the future. That the menu will, incidentally, default to listing Pages as `wp_nav_menu()` will do. I could alter that if I wanted to, which I don't.

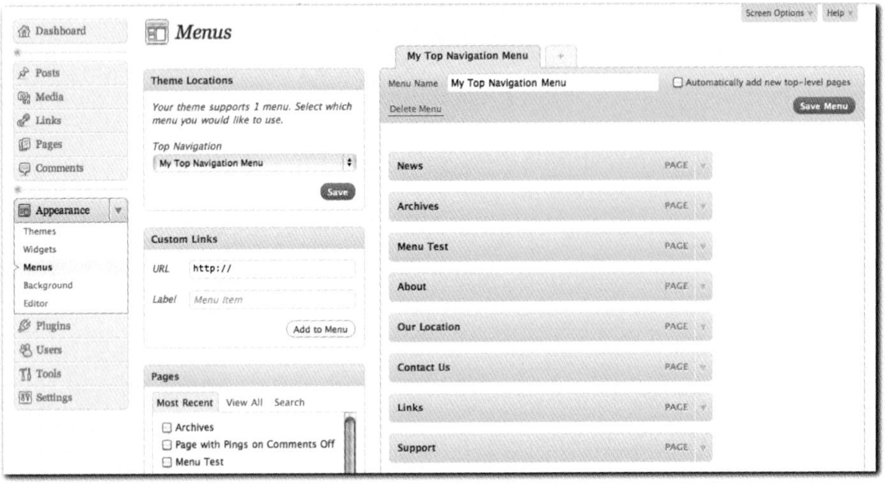

Figure 9-8: Working with Menus in the admin panel

```php
<?php wp_nav_menu('top-navigation'); ?>
```

Simple, huh? Here's the header.php template at this stage.

```php
<!DOCTYPE html>
<html <?php language_attributes(); ?>>
<head>
<meta charset="<?php bloginfo( 'charset' ); ?>" />
<title>
       <?php
              // Print the right title
              if (is_home () ) {
                     bloginfo('name');
              } elseif (is_category() || is_tag()) {
                     single_cat_title(); echo ' &bull; ' ; bloginfo('name');
              } elseif (is_single() || is_page()) {
                     single_post_title(); } else { wp_title('',true);
              }
       ?>
</title>
<link rel="profile" href="http://gmpg.org/xfn/11" />
<link rel="stylesheet" type="text/css" media="all" href="<?php bloginfo( 'style-
  sheet_url' ); ?>" />
<link rel="pingback" href="<?php bloginfo( 'pingback_url' ); ?>" />
<?php
       // Kick off WordPress
       wp_head();
?>
</head>
```

```php
<body <?php body_class(); ?>>

<div id="site">
    <div id="top">
        This area won't be seen unless there
        is something in the action hook that
        will power it!
    </div>
    <div id="wrap">
        <div id="wrap-inner">
            <div id="header">
                <div id="header-middle">
                    <div class="ad right">
                    <?php
                        // Adding the Header widget area, empty by
                        // default
                        if ( !function_exists('dynamic_sidebar') ||
    !dynamic_sidebar('Footer') ) : endif;
                    ?>
                    </div>
                    <h1 id="site-header">
                        <a href="<?php bloginfo('url'); ?>" title="<?php
    bloginfo('name'); ?>">
                            LOGO GOES HERE
                        </a>
                    </h1>
                </div>
                <div id="header-bottom">
                    <?php wp_nav_menu('top-navigation'); ?>
                </div>
            </div>
            <div id="plate">
```

One created and saved menu later, and we've got a working menu system! Nifty and neat.

ADDING OUR CUSTOM HEADER LOGO

It's about time I did something about that logo, wouldn't you say? I mean, this isn't exactly the prettiest thing on the block now, is it (see Figure 9-9)?

I use the custom header feature to manage the logo. That means that I have to register it in functions.php and also set a default logo or it will look weird. These logos are graphics, so I also want to turn off the option that adds text to the header.

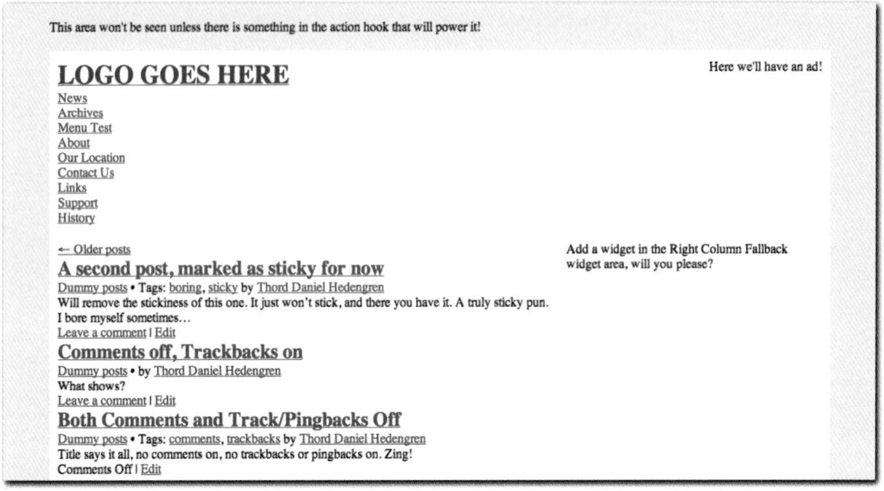

Figure 9-9: The logo looks awful, the rest is OK, right? No?

Here's the functions.php code:

```
// CUSTOM HEADER ->
// No header text please
define('NO_HEADER_TEXT', true );
// No text colors either, then
define('HEADER_TEXTCOLOR', '');
// The default header image, found in /img/header-default.gif
define('HEADER_IMAGE', get_bloginfo('stylesheet_directory') . '/img/header-default.
 gif');
// Width and height in pixels: 480x120 px
define('HEADER_IMAGE_WIDTH', 480);
define('HEADER_IMAGE_HEIGHT', 120);
// For our custom header admin needs
function notesmag_admin_header_style() {
        ?><style type="text/css">
          #headimg {
              width: <?php echo HEADER_IMAGE_WIDTH; ?>px;
              height: <?php echo HEADER_IMAGE_HEIGHT; ?>px;
              background: no-repeat;
          }
      </style><?php
}
// Add it to the hook for admin usage
add_custom_image_header('header_style', 'notesmag_admin_header_style');
// <- ENDS
```

One thing is worth noting here. The common use for a custom header is for background images. In this case, however, I use it to manage the actual logo (see Figure 9-10). That's why I've got the background: no-repeat; line for #heading ID, which is used for display in the admin settings screen.

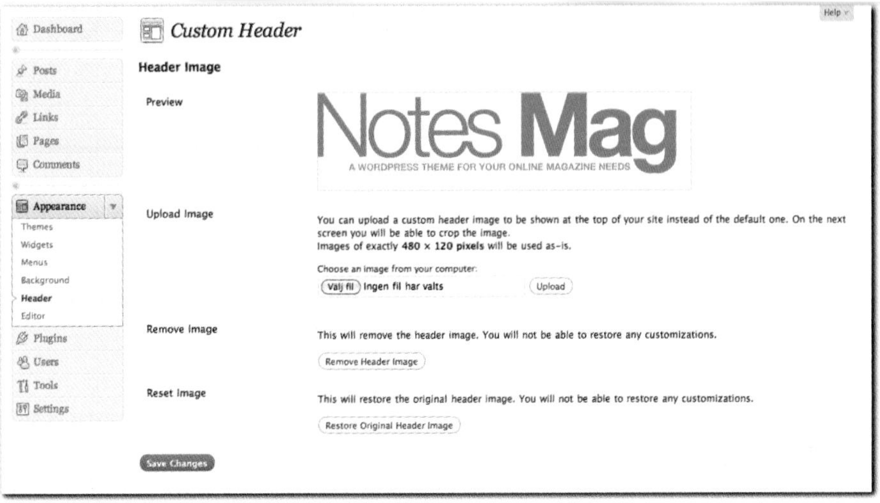

Figure 9-10: The custom header screen in the WordPress admin panel

After adding the preceding code to functions.php, I can add header images, logos in this case, from the Appearance settings, Custom Header screen in the admin panel. However, the header won't actually show up until I display it in header.php. The `header_image()` template tag outputs the URL to the header image, so I can just put that in an image tag.

```
<img src="<?php header_image(); ?>" alt="<?php bloginfo('name'); ?>" />
```

There you go; here's the full header.php file up to this point, with a working, clickable header:

```
<!DOCTYPE html>
<html <?php language_attributes(); ?>>
<head>
<meta charset="<?php bloginfo( 'charset' ); ?>" />
<title>
        <?php
                // Print the right title
                if (is_home () ) {
                    bloginfo('name');
                } elseif (is_category() || is_tag()) {
                    single_cat_title(); echo ' &bull; ' ; bloginfo('name');
                } elseif (is_single() || is_page()) {
                    single_post_title(); } else { wp_title('',true);
                }
        ?>
</title>
<link rel="profile" href="http://gmpg.org/xfn/11" />
<link rel="stylesheet" type="text/css" media="all" href="<?php bloginfo( 'style-
sheet_url' ); ?>" />
<link rel="pingback" href="<?php bloginfo( 'pingback_url' ); ?>" />
<?php
```

```
        // Kick off WordPress
        wp_head();
?>
</head>

<body <?php body_class(); ?>>

<div id="site">
    <div id="top">
        This area won't be seen unless there
        is something in the action hook that
        will power it!
    </div>
    <div id="wrap">
        <div id="wrap-inner">
            <div id="header">
                <div id="header-middle">
                    <div class="ad right">
                    <?php
                        // Adding the Header widget area,
                        // empty by default
dynamic_sidebar('Header');
                    ?>
                    </div>
                    <h1 id="site-header">
                        <a href="<?php bloginfo('url'); ?>" title="<?php
bloginfo('name'); ?>">
                            <img src="<?php header_image(); ?>"
alt="<?php bloginfo('name'); ?>" />
                        </a>
                    </h1>
                </div>
                <div id="header-bottom">
                    <?php wp_nav_menu('top-navigation'); ?>
                </div>
            </div>
        <div id="plate">
```

Just for the sake of it, let's view my theme as it looks right now (as seen in Figure 9-11). The default header is pre-loaded as previously defined in functions.php. Looks a bit out of place, but hey, it's better than the previous one, right?

CREATING ACTION HOOKS

Action hooks are cool little things. Basically, they let you attach functions (usually from your functions.php file) to various places in your theme, hence the name hooks. You create the action hooks yourself, in functions.php, and insert them where you want in your theme.

For Notes Mag, I want four action hooks. Other theme authors like to fill their themes with action hooks, but I prefer to keep them to a minimum. In fact, four is a bit much, but since this is meant to be a theme with which you can do a bunch of things, I feel it makes sense.

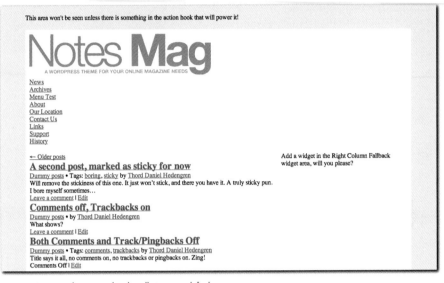

Figure 9-11: Now with a custom header, albeit a very default one

I'll have action hooks before the actual site really starts, outside the `div#wrap` but within the `div#site`, if you remember the site structure. That's one. The second one sits underneath the menu, between `div#header` and `div#plate`. The third one is only used in single-post view and is located between the post and the comments for easy insertion of whatever you might want there. The fourth and final hook is located just before `div#footer` kicks in.

I start by creating the hook above the site so that I can include it in the header.php file. This is done in functions.php:

```
// Create the above site hook
function notesmag_above_site() {
    do_action('notesmag_above_site');
}
```

Then I add it to header.php, inserting it just after `div#site`, like this:

```
<?php
    // Use this hook to do things above the actual site
    notesmag_above_site();
?>
```

Notice that my very own hook, called `notesmag_above_site()`, looks and acts like just about any template tag I've used thus far.

Now I can attach things to this hook. Let's say I want to output a "Hello world!" message above the site. I just create a function that does this, and then attach it to the hook. I'll start with the function, putting it in functions.php for testing purposes (I'll remove it later).

```
function hello_world() {
    echo '<p style="text-align:center;">Hello world!</p>';
}
```

This is a simple function that just echoes a p tag with some styling and the text "Hello world!" Now, I add this function to the `notesmag_above_site()` hook. This isn't done in the header.php template file but by using `add_action()` and thus adding the function to the hook.

```
add_action('notesmag_above_site', 'hello_world');
```

There, I added the `hello_world` function to my hook. Suddenly, I've got a nice Hello world! message on my site (see Figure 9-12).

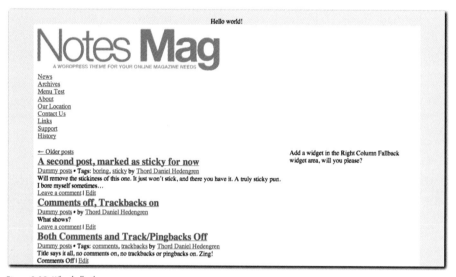

Figure 9-12: Why, hello there

The purpose of adding hooks to a theme is for easy addition of features in key places. In the case of Notes Mag, I want to be able to quickly insert things just above the site, below the menu, between post and comments, and just before the footer. So I create an action hook for every one of these places; then, when I need to, I can just write a function that inserts whatever it is I want to output there.

Removing the "Hello world!" function, here are the four hooks as they should look in functions.php:

```
// NOTES MAG HOOKS
// Create the above site hook
function notesmag_above_site() {
    do_action('notesmag_above_site');
}
// Create the below menu hook
function notesmag_below_menu() {
    do_action('notesmag_below_menu');
}
// Create the between post and comments hook
```

```
function notesmag_below_post() {
    do_action('notesmag_below_post');
}
// Create the above footer hook
function notesmag_above_footer() {
    do_action('notesmag_above_footer');
}
// <- ENDS
```

Now, I add notesmag_above_site(), notesmag_below_menu(), notesmag_below_post(), and notesmag_above_footer() to their appropriate places. All but notesmag_below_post() can be added now, but the single-post template isn't created yet. So I'll have to remember to add it later. Just to show you how simple this is, here is the header.php file with the added hooks, both above the site and below the menu:

```
<!DOCTYPE html>
<html <?php language_attributes(); ?>>
<head>
<meta charset="<?php bloginfo( 'charset' ); ?>" />
<title>
      <?php
            // Print the right title
            if (is_home () ) {
                bloginfo('name');
            } elseif (is_category() || is_tag()) {
                single_cat_title(); echo ' &bull; ' ; bloginfo('name');
            } elseif (is_single() || is_page()) {
                single_post_title(); } else { wp_title('',true);
            }
      ?>
</title>
<link rel="profile" href="http://gmpg.org/xfn/11" />
<link rel="stylesheet" type="text/css" media="all" href="<?php bloginfo( 'style-
  sheet_url' ); ?>" />
<link rel="pingback" href="<?php bloginfo( 'pingback_url' ); ?>" />
<?php
      // Kick off WordPress
      wp_head();
?>
</head>

<body <?php body_class(); ?>>

<div id="site">
      <?php
            // Use this hook to do things above the actual site
            notesmag_above_site();
      ?>
      <div id="wrap">
            <div id="wrap-inner">
```

271

```
                    <div id="header">
                        <div id="header-middle">
                            <div class="ad right">
                    <?php
                            // Adding the Header widget area,
                            // empty by default
        dynamic_sidebar('Header');
                        ?>
                        </div>
                        <h1 id="site-header">
                            <a href="<?php bloginfo('url'); ?>" title="<?php
        bloginfo('name'); ?>">
                                <img src="<?php header_image(); ?>"
        alt="<?php bloginfo('name'); ?>" />
                            </a>
                        </h1>
                    </div>
                    <div id="header-bottom">
                        <?php wp_nav_menu('top-navigation'); ?>
                    </div>
                </div>
                <?php
                        // Use this hook to do things between the menu and
                        // the main content
                        notesmag_below_menu();
                ?>
                <div id="plate">
```

None of these hooks does anything or outputs anything until you feed them a function, so you won't see them on your live site unless you put them to good use. For now, they're just lying there dormant.

VIEWING OUR FINAL FUNCTIONS.PHP

For clarity's sake, here is the final functions.php. Quite a lot longer than it was when I started out a while ago, but still pretty lean and mean:

```php
<?php // Here we go!

// The default content width
if ( ! isset( $content_width ) )
    $content_width = 640;

// Localization support, fetches languages files from /lang/
load_theme_textdomain( 'notesmag', TEMPLATEPATH . '/lang' );

// The visual editor will use editor-style.css
add_editor_style();

// Add default posts and comments RSS feed links
```

```php
add_theme_support( 'automatic-feed-links' );

// Adding support for featured images
add_theme_support( 'post-thumbnails' );

// Add custom background support
add_custom_background();

// Add the Top Navigation menu
register_nav_menus( array(
    'top-navigation' => __( 'Top Navigation', 'notesmag' ),
) );

// CUSTOM HEADER ->
// No header text please
define('NO_HEADER_TEXT', true );
// No text colors either, then
define('HEADER_TEXTCOLOR', '');
// The default header image, found in /img/header-default.gif
define('HEADER_IMAGE', get_bloginfo('stylesheet_directory') . '/img/header-default.
  gif');
// Width and height in pixels: 480x120 px
define('HEADER_IMAGE_WIDTH', 480);
define('HEADER_IMAGE_HEIGHT', 120);
// For our custom header admin needs
function notesmag_admin_header_style() {
    ?><style type="text/css">
      #headimg {
          width: <?php echo HEADER_IMAGE_WIDTH; ?>px;
          height: <?php echo HEADER_IMAGE_HEIGHT; ?>px;
          background: no-repeat;
      }
    </style><?php
}
// Add it to the hook for admin usage
add_custom_image_header('', 'notesmag_admin_header_style');
// <- ENDS

// WIDGET AREAS ->
// Front Page Top Right widget area
register_sidebar( array(
    'name' => __( 'Front Page Top Right', 'notesmag' ),
    'id' => 'front-page-top-right',
    'description' => __( 'Widget area on the top right, visible on the front page
  only', 'notesmag' ),
    'before_widget' => '<li id="%1$s" class="widget-container %2$s">',
    'after_widget' => '</li>',
    'before_title' => '<h2 class="widget-title">',
    'after_title' => '</h2>',
) );
// Front Page Columns Left widget area
```

```
register_sidebar( array(
    'name' => __( 'Front Page Columns Left', 'notesmag' ),
    'id' => 'front-page-columns-left',
    'description' => __( 'The left column in the lower part of the front page.',
  'notesmag' ),
    'before_widget' => '<li id="%1$s" class="widget-container %2$s">',
    'after_widget' => '</li>',
    'before_title' => '<h2 class="widget-title">',
    'after_title' => '</h2>',
) );
// Front Page Columns Middle widget area
register_sidebar( array(
    'name' => __( 'Front Page Columns Middle', 'notesmag' ),
    'id' => 'front-page-columns-middle',
    'description' => __( 'The middle column in the lower part of the front page.',
  'notesmag' ),
    'before_widget' => '<li id="%1$s" class="widget-container %2$s">',
    'after_widget' => '</li>',
    'before_title' => '<h2 class="widget-title">',
    'after_title' => '</h2>',
) );
// Front Page Columns Right widget area
register_sidebar( array(
    'name' => __( 'Front Page Columns Right', 'notesmag' ),
    'id' => 'front-page-columns-left',
    'description' => __( 'The right column in the lower part of the front page.',
  'notesmag' ),
    'before_widget' => '<li id="%1$s" class="widget-container %2$s">',
    'after_widget' => '</li>',
    'before_title' => '<h2 class="widget-title">',
    'after_title' => '</h2>',
) );
// Right Column Archive widget area
register_sidebar( array(
    'name' => __( 'Right Column Archive', 'notesmag' ),
    'id' => 'right-column-archive',
    'description' => __( 'The right column on date-based archive pages.', 'notesmag'
  ),
    'before_widget' => '<li id="%1$s" class="widget-container %2$s">',
    'after_widget' => '</li>',
    'before_title' => '<h2 class="widget-title">',
    'after_title' => '</h2>',
) );
// Right Column Category widget area
register_sidebar( array(
    'name' => __( 'Right Column Category', 'notesmag' ),
    'id' => 'right-column-category',
    'description' => __( 'The right column on category archive pages.', 'notesmag'
  ),
    'before_widget' => '<li id="%1$s" class="widget-container %2$s">',
    'after_widget' => '</li>',
```

```php
        'before_title' => '<h2 class="widget-title">',
        'after_title' => '</h2>',
) );
// Right Column Tag widget area
register_sidebar( array(
        'name' => __( 'Right Column Tag', 'notesmag' ),
        'id' => 'right-column-tag',
        'description' => __( 'The right column on tag archive pages.', 'notesmag' ),
        'before_widget' => '<li id="%1$s" class="widget-container %2$s">',
        'after_widget' => '</li>',
        'before_title' => '<h2 class="widget-title">',
        'after_title' => '</h2>',
) );
// Post Right Column widget area
register_sidebar( array(
        'name' => __( 'Post Right Column', 'notesmag' ),
        'id' => 'post-right-column',
        'description' => __( 'The right column on single posts.', 'notesmag' ),
        'before_widget' => '<li id="%1$s" class="widget-container %2$s">',
        'after_widget' => '</li>',
        'before_title' => '<h2 class="widget-title">',
        'after_title' => '</h2>',
) );
// Page Right Column widget area
register_sidebar( array(
        'name' => __( 'Page Right Column', 'notesmag' ),
        'id' => 'page-right-column',
        'description' => __( 'The right column on Pages.', 'notesmag' ),
        'before_widget' => '<li id="%1$s" class="widget-container %2$s">',
        'after_widget' => '</li>',
        'before_title' => '<h2 class="widget-title">',
        'after_title' => '</h2>',
) );
// Right Column Fallback widget area
register_sidebar( array(
        'name' => __( 'Right Column Fallback', 'notesmag' ),
        'id' => 'right-column-fallback',
        'description' => __( 'When all else fails, this widget area will be used for the
 right column.', 'notesmag' ),
        'before_widget' => '<li id="%1$s" class="widget-container %2$s">',
        'after_widget' => '</li>',
        'before_title' => '<h2 class="widget-title">',
        'after_title' => '</h2>',
) );
// Header widget area
register_sidebar( array(
        'name' => __( 'Header', 'notesmag' ),
        'id' => 'header',
        'description' => __( 'The widget area just beside the logo in the header.',
 'notesmag' ),
        'before_widget' => '<li id="%1$s" class="widget-container %2$s">',
```

```
        'after_widget' => '</li>',
        'before_title' => '<h2 class="widget-title">',
        'after_title' => '</h2>',
) );
// Footer widget area
register_sidebar( array(
        'name' => __( 'Footer', 'notesmag' ),
        'id' => 'footer',
        'description' => __( 'The footer widget area.', 'notesmag' ),
        'before_widget' => '<li id="%1$s" class="widget-container %2$s">',
        'after_widget' => '</li>',
        'before_title' => '<h2 class="widget-title">',
        'after_title' => '</h2>',
) );
// <- ENDS


// NOTES MAG HOOKS
// Create the above site hook
function notesmag_above_site() {
    do_action('notesmag_above_site');
}
// Create the below menu hook
function notesmag_below_menu() {
    do_action('notesmag_below_menu');
}
// Create the between post and comments hook
function notesmag_below_post() {
    do_action('notesmag_below_post');
}
// Create the above footer hook
function notesmag_above_footer() {
    do_action('notesmag_above_footer');
}
// <- ENDS
?>
```

With all the functionality added, it's time to get started on the actual design. This means CSS styling and creating a few new templates so that the Notes Mag theme behaves.

TEMPLATES, TEMPLATES, TEMPLATES

Now I can start creating all the necessary templates for the various parts of the site. So, without further ado, let's give the skeleton its legs so that I can get cracking and make this site look decent!

SETTING UP THE FRONT PAGE

Controlling the front page in the Notes Mag theme is home.php. This template takes precedence. Everything is a bit different on the front page (as you'll remember from the sketch), so it makes sense to start here.

I've opted not to use get_template_part() for home.php because it doesn't make all that much sense. The template breaks out of the rest of the site too much to be easily edited in a child theme anyway. Better to just overwrite the whole thing should you want to do that.

Anyway, here's the basic layout of the home.php template.

```php
<?php get_header(); ?>

    <div id="headline-main">
        <div class="featured-widget">
            widget area
        </div>
        <div class="featured-story">
            featured
        </div>
    </div>
    <div id="headline-stories">
        <div class="story column left">
            left
        </div>
        <div class="story column left">
            middle
        </div>
        <div class="story column right">
            left
        </div>
    </div>
    <div id="tag-line">
        tags search
    </div>
    <div id="headline-widgets">
        <div class="column left">
            left widgets
        </div>
        <div class="column left">
            middle widgets
        </div>
        <div class="column right">
            right widgets
        </div>
    </div>

<?php get_footer(); ?>
```

Obviously, this needs content, which is to say that I need loops and widget areas, but first I want to get the positioning right. This simple little styling will make things end up sort of where they should be:

```
div#headline-main, div#headline-stories,
div#tag-line {
```

```
        width: 100%;
        float: left;
        margin-bottom: 20px;
}
        div.featured-story {
                width: 640px;
                float: left;
        }
        div.featured-widget {
                width: 320px;
                float: right;
        }

div#headline-stories {}
        div.story {}

div#tag-line {}

div#headline-widgets {
        width: 100%;
        float: left;
}
```

Now that I've got the basic layout for the front page sorted (as shown in Figure 9-13), I can populate it with some content.

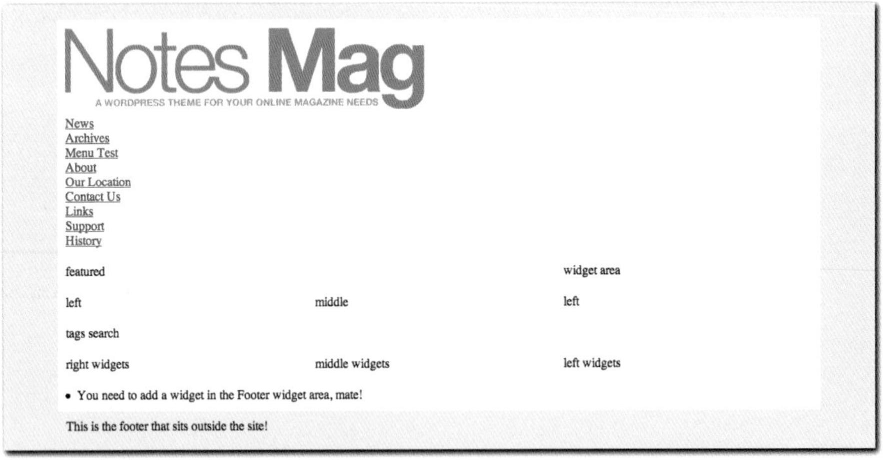

Figure 9-13: The front page with a somewhat completed layout

POPULATING THE FRONT PAGE WITH CONTENT

To populate that simple little code, I start with the obvious stuff, like the widget areas. You'll remember that there is a widget area to the right of the featured post section just below the menu, as well as three widget area columns just before the footer. I start by adding the appropriate widget code to these, picking from the areas I added previously to functions.php:

```php
<?php get_header(); ?>

    <div id="headline-main">
        <div class="featured-widget">
            <ul>
        <?php
            // The Front Page Top Right widget area
            if ( !dynamic_sidebar('front-page-top-right') ) : ?>
            <li>You need to put something in the Front Page Top Right widget
            area right about now.</li>
        <?php endif; ?>
            </ul>
        </div>
        <div class="featured-story">
            featured
        </div>
    </div>
    <div id="headline-stories">
        <div class="story column left">
            left
        </div>
        <div class="story column left">
            middle
        </div>
        <div class="story column right">
            left
        </div>
    </div>
    <div id="tag-line">
        tags search
    </div>
    <div id="headline-widgets">
        <div class="column left">
    <?php
        // The Front Page Columns Left widget area
        if ( !dynamic_sidebar('front-page-columns-left') ) : ?>
        <li>Put a widget in the Front Page Columns Left widget area please.
        </li>
    <?php endif; ?>
        </div>
        <div class="column left">
    <?php
        // The Front Page Columns Middle widget area
        if ( !dynamic_sidebar('front-page-columns-middle') ) : ?>
            <li>Put a widget in the Front Page Columns Middle widget area
            please.</li>
    <?php endif; ?>
        </div>
        <div class="column right">
    <?php
        // The Front Page Columns Right widget area
```

279

```
            if ( !dynamic_sidebar('front-page-columns-right') ) : ?>
            <li>Put a widget in the Front Page Columns Right widget area please.
            </li>
        <?php endif; ?>
          </div>
      </div>

<?php get_footer(); ?>
```

Now that I've got the widget areas where they should be, I tackle the next element. The `div#tag-line` block is supposed to be something of a divider between the top stories and the widget areas below, showing off the most popular tags, as well as having a default search form to the right. Now I add the necessary code for that, using `wp_tag_cloud()` and `get_search_form()`.

```
<div id="tag-line">
    <?php get_search_form(); ?>
    <div class="tags">
        <?php _e(,Hot tags:', ,notesmag'); ?> <?php wp_tag_cloud('smallest=16&larg
  est=16&unit=px&number=7'); ?>
    </div>
</div>
```

The parameters in `wp_tag_cloud()` set the size of each tag to 16 pixels and output the seven most used ones in a flat format, separated by spacing. Meanwhile, `get_search_form()` includes the default search form, which won't really work for us here. So I add my very own searchform.php instead:

```
<form action="<?php bloginfo('url'); ?>/" method="get" id="searchform"
  class="tag-line-search">
    <fieldset>
        <input type="text" name="s" id="search" value="<?php the_search_query(); ?>"
  />
        <input type="button" value="<?php _e('Search', 'notesmag'); ?>" />
    </fieldset>
</form>
```

To make this thing look even half decent, I added this to style.css:

```
div#tag-line {
    background: #e9e9e9;
}
    div.tags {
        padding: 10px;
        line-height: 24px;
        color: #888;
    }
        div.tags a {
            margin-left: 5px;
        }
```

```css
form.tag-line-search {
        float: right;
        padding: 10px;
        border-left: 1px solid #fff;
}
```

That's that; a working line of tags and a search form floating to the right. Now I output those three posts just above the tag object. The idea here is to output the three latest posts that have a certain tag, suitably enough called "featured." So what I'll get is the latest three posts with the tag featured. I'll achieve this with the loop:

```php
<div id="headline-stories">
<?php
    // Custom loop time - fetch three posts tagged "featured"
    $loop = new WP_Query( array(
            'tag' => 'featured',
            'posts_per_page' => 3
    ) );
    while ( $loop->have_posts() ) : $loop->the_post(); ?>
        <div class="story column left">
            <div class="post-thumbnail">
                <a href="<?php the_permalink(); ?>" title="<?php the_title_
attribute(); ?>">
                    <?php the_post_thumbnail(); ?>
                </a>
            </div>
            <h2>
                <a href="<?php the_permalink(); ?>" title="<?php the_title_
attribute(); ?>">
                    <?php the_title(); ?>
                </a>
            </h2>
            <div class="story-entry">
                <?php the_excerpt(); ?>
            </div>
        </div>
<?php
    // Loop ends
    endwhile;
?>
</div>
```

Here I'm using WP_Query, which takes the query_posts() parameters and stores them in $loop, which I then loop. The parameters are set to just display posts tagged with "featured," just three of them (see Figure 9-14). Each post sits in a div that will float appropriately. I also added a post thumbnail, which sits above the headline, if available, but does not specify its size just yet — that depends on how I style it later on.

Now there's just one final thing left for the front page, and that's the big featured blurb on the top left. There are many ways to solve this "problem," but the most obvious one is usually the best.

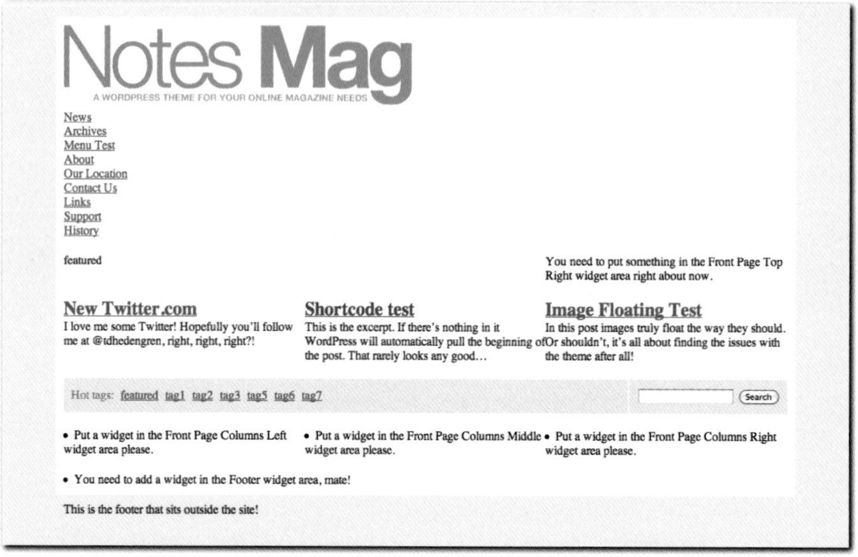

Figure 9-14: Showing three posts tagged "featured"

There are a bunch of plugins that can do this, and which one you'll use is up to you. Person-ally, I'm not a big fan of content sliders, but I know a lot of people are. So if you want to populate this area with one of those, I recommend that you take a look around. You'll get the best result if you modify one of the jQuery or MooTools sliders yourself. But if that's not for you, go with one of the plugins. Featured Content Gallery () is popular, but forces you to use custom fields. A simpler option is JQuery Featured Content Gallery (), also free to use. There are many options in this sphere, so it all boils down to which one you prefer (see Figure 9-15).

Figure 9-15: A simple jQuery slider

Depending on your preferences, you might want to alter this area to make it widget ready or put the plugin's PHP snippet in there to start using it. When released, Notes Mag will come with its own solution; but for now, I'm left with plugins.

SINGLE POSTS AND PAGES

The single-post template is actually really simple. It features a full-width top with the post title and some meta data. The content then flows to the left and the proper right column (thanks to the conditional tags in sidebar.php) obviously sits to the right. I rely on the default comment template for both single.php and page.php.

That's about it, so here's single.php:

```php
<?php get_header(); ?>
<?php
    // The basic loop
    while ( have_posts() ) : the_post(); ?>
 <div id="single-header" class="fullcolumn">
        <div class="entry-meta-top category">
                <?php _e('Written by ', 'notesmag'); the_author_posts_link(); ?>
        </div>
        <h1 class="entry-title">
                <?php the_title(); ?>
        </h1>
</div>
<div id="content" class="widecolumn">
        <div id="post-<?php the_ID(); ?>" <?php post_class(); ?>>
                <div class="entry-content">
                    <?php the_content(); ?>
                    <?php wp_link_pages( array( 'before' => '<div class="page-
link">' . __( 'Sidor:', 'notesmag' ), 'after' => '</div>' ) ); ?>
                </div>
                <div class="entry-meta-lower">
                    <?php _e('Filed in', 'notesmag');?> <?php the_category(',
'); ?>
                    <?php _e('on', 'notesmag'); ?> <?php the_date(); ?>
                    <?php
                        // Check for tags, output if any
                        if ( has_tag() ) {
                            echo '<br />';
                            _e("Tagged with ", "notesmag");
                            the_tags('<span class="meta-tags">', ', ',
'</span>');
                        } ?>
                    <?php edit_post_link( __( 'Edit', 'notesmag' ), '<span
class="meta-sep">&bull;</span> <span class="edit-link">', '</span>' ); ?>
                </div>
        </div>
```

```php
<?php

            // Use this hook to do things between the content and
            // the comments
            notesmag_below_post();

        ?>

        <?php
            // If the comments are open we'll need the comments template
            if (comments_open()) {
                comments_template( '', true );
            }
        ?>
    </div>
<?php
        // End the loop
endwhile; ?>
<?php get_sidebar(); ?>
<?php get_footer(); ?>
```

Note that the `div#single-header` has the `fullcolumn` class, which means that it takes up the full width. As you can see, I've opted to put the full loop in single.php this time around. This is because it has a slightly different layout with the post title and author name above the actual loop, which would've caused some issues if it were to be outside the loop.

Note the action hook below the post `div`, before the comment check. Otherwise, it is pretty straightforward (see Figure 9-16). Page.php is all but identical. The only differences are no category, tag, or author tags in the Page-related templates; so, I'll skip those.

Figure 9-16: The single-post template is in need of some styling

THE ARCHIVES

The three kinds of archives, date-based, category, and tags, are all treated equally, which means that I can rely on archive.php for this. You might remember the sketch in Figure 9-2, which features the archive title at the very top, in a similar fashion as the single-post and Page view. The actual content listing consists of the title with a description, some meta data, and a right column; but I've already taken care of that, as you may recall.

There's a twist on category archives. I output the top three latest stories within the category that are also tagged with "featured." This is much like the front page (home.php), but for the active category only.

Here's archive.php:

```php
<?php get_header(); ?>

<?php
    // We'll only use headlines on category archives
    if ( is_category()) { ?>

    <div id="headline-stories">
    <?php
        // Custom loop time - fetch three posts from the current archive
        // all tagged "featured"
        $categoryvariable=$cat;
        $loop = new WP_Query(array(
            'cat' => $cat,
            'tag' => 'featured',
            'posts_per_page' => 3
        ));
        while ( $loop->have_posts() ) : $loop->the_post(); ?>
            <div class="story column left">
                <div class="post-thumbnail">
                    <a href="<?php the_permalink(); ?>" title="<?php
the_title_attribute(); ?>">
                        <?php the_post_thumbnail(); ?>
                    </a>
                </div>
                <div class="post-content">
                    <h2>
                        <a href="<?php the_permalink(); ?>" title="<?php
the_title_attribute(); ?>">
                            <?php the_title(); ?>
                        </a>
                    </h2>
                    <div class="story-entry">
                        <?php the_excerpt(); ?>
                    </div>
```

```php
                                    </div>
                                </div>
                    <?php
                        // Loop ends
                        endwhile;
                    ?>
                    </div>
            <?php } ?>
                <div id="archive-header" class="fullcolumn">
                        <h1 class="archive-title">
                        <?php
                                // Output the category title
                                if ( is_category() ) {
                                        single_cat_title();
                                }
                                // Output the tag title
                                elseif ( is_tag() ) {
                                        single_tag_title();
                                // For everything else
                                } else {
                                        _e('Browsing the Archive', 'notesmag');
                                }
                        ?>
                        </h1>
                </div>
                <div id="content" class="widecolumn">
                        <?php
                                // Look for loop-archive.php, fallback to loop.php
                                get_template_part( 'loop', 'archive' );
                        ?>
                </div>

<?php get_sidebar(); ?>
<?php get_footer(); ?>
```

You'll recognize the loop from `div#headlines-stories`; it is more or less the same as the one on home.php, with the addition of `$cat fetching`, the category ID, so that I can pass that to the `WP_Query` and hence limit the output to the active category, the tag "featured," and three posts.

Further on you find a simple conditional `if else` thingy that outputs different headings depending on where on the site you are.

Finally, I'm moving on to the actual loop that shows the posts within the archive. I include it with `get_template_part()` that looks for loop-archive.php first, and defaults to loop.php, which in fact is what I use.

And you know what, that's it! Now let's style this baby.

MAKING NOTES MAG LOOK GOOD

Although the Notes Mag theme may seem a bit crude right now, it is in fact on pretty solid ground. The only thing left to do before releasing the 1.0 version of the theme is to make it look good, and I use CSS for that — as do all good WordPress coding folks.

I won't go through every little thing here as you already know a bunch of CSS by now. Instead, I dive into certain parts of the site and solve those problems. The complete stylesheet is available from the book's companion Web site at www.wiley.com/go/ smashingwordpressthemes.

STYLING THE MENU

Custom menus are great, but styling them can be a bore. At least until you learn how they are built. By default, the menu lands in a div, which in turn consists of a ul with li items inside. That's why your pretty horizontal menu won't look great unless you float them.

```
div#header-bottom {
    width: 100%;
    float: left;
    margin-bottom: 20px;
    background: #444;
}
    ul.menu {}
        ul.menu li {
            float:left;
            padding: 10px 5px;
            border-right: 1px solid #777;
        }
            ul.menu li:hover {
                background: #000;
            }
            ul.menu li a {
                padding: 10px 5px;
            }
```

With these few lines of code, you can make a boring menu a lot more appealing and user-friendly (as shown in Figure 9-17).

Speaking about menus, a word of advice: Avoid menus based solely on a hover effect, such as drop-downs. It is all well and good to hover with the mouse pointer on a computer screen, but try to hover when using a touchscreen device. That's right, every iPad, iPhone, Android, and so on will fail miserably when forced to navigate hover elements because you can't hover with your finger. Either you touch the device or you don't. If you want to use a hover effect, be sure you're not using it for something essential to the menu's function.

Figure 9-17: The Notes Mag styled menu

POSITIONING POST COLUMNS

Another thing worth taking a look at is the positioning of the featured post columns, which are consistent with the three columns with widget areas just above the footer. I'm talking front page here (home.php), as you've probably gathered. This is for the three latest posts tagged with "featured" found in `div#headline-stories`.

```
div#headline-stories {
     background: url(img/headline-stories-bg.gif) repeat-y;
}
     div.story {}
          div.post-thumbnail {
               width: 300px;
               height: 120px;
               margin: 0 10px 5px 10px;
               background: #444;
          }
          div.story h2, div.story-entry {
               padding: 5px 15px;
          }
```

Although 960 pixels is great for columns, it can be a bit tricky to get things to align properly when outputting it in a loop like this without hands on fixes on a per-column basis. I didn't want that here, so that's why the margins and paddings are the way they are.

The same concept is applied to the three columns just above the footer:

```
div#headline-widgets {
     width: 100%;
     float: left;
}
     div#headline-widgets ul {}
          div#headline-widgets ul li.widget-container {
               padding: 5px 10px;
          }
```

Usually I tend to group similar objects like these together, but I've got something planned for future versions of Notes Mag, so I'm keeping them apart for now.

A QUICK LOOK AT THE ARCHIVES

The archive pages borrow from the front page in terms of the three featured posts, which only show up if it is a category archive (see Figure 9-18). They are treated exactly the same. Other than that, the styling is pretty simple, with the wrapping elements making sure I've got enough space everywhere.

The archive title is worth mentioning as a design element. I'm using it to break off with the three-featured posts on top, if there are any (category archives, again); but at the same time, I'm maintaining the look for the single post and Page view, which is similar, in terms of titling.

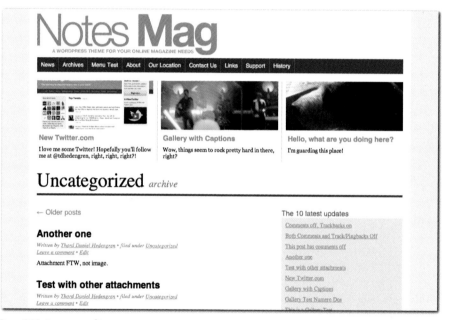

Figure 9-18: A category archive

The archive header isn't much in terms of CSS, but here it is for consistency's sake.

```
div#archive-header {}
    h1.archive-title {
        margin: 0 10px 30px 10px;
        padding-bottom: 5px;
        border: 1px solid #444;
        border-width: 1px 0 5px 0;
    }
        span.archive-meta {
            color: #888;
        }
```

SINGLE POSTS AND PAGES

Finally, take a look at the single posts and Pages (see Figure 9-19). They are essentially the same, with minor differences in template files (single.php and page.php with their loops, respectively). The stylesheets are more or less the same, with some things, such as categories, not being used on Pages at all.

Figure 9-19: Single-post view

```css
div.post, div.page {
    margin-bottom: 30px;
    padding-right: 20px;
}
    div.entry-content p {
        margin-bottom: 18px;
    }
    .entry-title, div.entry-meta, div.entry-meta-lower,
    div.entry-content p, div.entry-summary p {
        margin-left: 10px;
    }
    div.entry-meta, div.entry-meta-lower {
        margin-top: 5px;
        margin-bottom: 10px;
        color: #888;
    }
    div.entry-meta-top {
        margin: 20px 20px 0 10px;
        color: #888;
    }
    div.entry-meta-lower {
        padding: 10px;
```

```
        border: 1px solid #e9e9e9;
        border-width: 1px 0;
    }
div.navigation {
    margin: 0 20px 0 10px;
}
    div#nav-above {
        margin-bottom: 50px;
    }
    div#nav-below {
        padding-bottom: 50px;
    }
    div.nav-previous {
        float: left;
    }
    div.nav-next {
        float: right;
    }
```

Nothing fancy here either. The comment section is worth a look though.

```
ol.commentlist {
    width: 610px;
}
    h3#comments, ol.commentlist, div#respond {
        margin-left: 10px;
        margin-bottom: 20px;
    }
        li.comment {
            margin-left: 10px;
            padding: 0 0 20px 20px;
            border: 1px solid #888;
            border-width: 0 0 1px 1px;
            color: #444;
        }
        li.depth-1 {
            margin-top: 10px;
            padding-top: 20px;
        }
        li.bypostauthor {}
            li.bypostauthor div.comment-author img {
                padding-left: 5px;
                border-left: 5px #1895a8 solid;
            }
            li.comment p {
                margin-top: 10px;
            }
            div.reply {
                text-align: right;
                margin: 2px 0;
            }
```

```
            div.comment-author, div.comment-meta {
                    line-height: 16px;
            }
            div.comment-author {
                    margin-bottom: 2px;
            }
                    div.comment-author img {
                            float: left;
                            margin-right: 10px;
                    }
                    cite.fn {
                            font-style: normal;
                            font-weight: bold;
                    }
div#respond {
        width: 605px;
        margin-left: 10px;
        padding: 20px 0;
        border-left: 5px solid #888;
        background: #e9e9e9;
}
        div#respond h3, form#commentform, div#cancel-comment-reply {
                padding: 0 20px;
        }
        div#respond p {
                margin-top: 10px;
        }
        textarea#comment {
                width: 520px;
                padding: 10px;
        }
```

There are two main elements to keep an eye out for when styling comments. The ol.commentlist element contains all the comments, and the div#respond holds the reply box. You'll obviously want to position headers and comments as well, and make sure to style li.bypostauthor so that the post author's comments will stand out (as in Figure 9-20).

You can download the complete stylesheet from the book's companion Web site at www.wiley.com/go/smashing wordpressthemes.

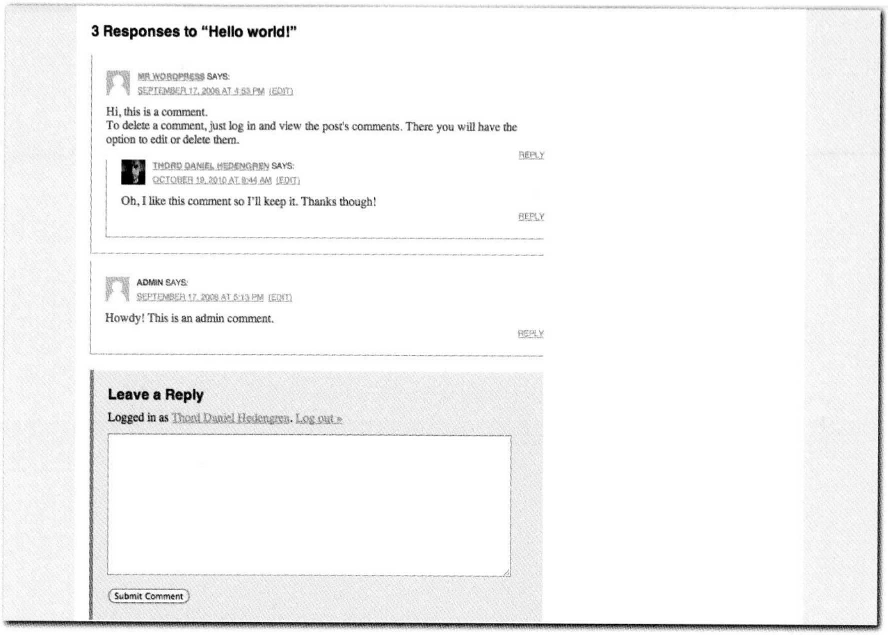

Figure 9-20: Here there be threaded comments

WRAPPING IT UP

That's it for the Notes Mag theme. As I'm turning in these words, the site is out for beta testing. You can get the latest version from `http://notesblog.com/mag` anytime, free of charge, of course. There may be some changes when you download it, all good themes evolve over time, but rest assured that you've got a good idea of the core.

On a slightly wider scale, I hope this chapter has provided some insight into how to build a theme from scratch. In the remaining chapters of the book, I focus on adding that little something extra.

IV

TAKING THEMES FURTHER

10 THE BUDDYPRESS COMMUNITY

IT SHOULD COME as no great surprise that you can use WordPress to power a full-fledged social networking community. There are several ways to do this, more or less advanced. But one solution stands on its own, and that's the BuddyPress plugin. This one's backed by the WordPress core developers and is a truly promising tool for extending your site with member functionality. With a few simple steps, you can have your users exchange direct messages, start discussion groups, and interact with the site in a whole new way.

This chapter shows how you can add some community features to just about any WordPress Web site, using BuddyPress.

WHAT IS BUDDYPRESS?

So what is BuddyPress? Well, first of all, it is a plugin, which means that it resides in the WordPress plugins folder. You can install it from the WordPress plugin directory, either from `http://wordpress.org/extend/plugins` or from within your admin panel.

BuddyPress has its own Web site too, at `http://buddypress.org`, where you can register (see Figure 10-1), and talk to your fellow BuddyPressers about how this and that works. There's even a dedicated BuddyPress plugins directory, so that you can find plugins created solely for use with BuddyPress.

That's right, there's a complete ecosystem around this one plugin, almost as if it was a stand-alone system. But it is not; you need WordPress to run BuddyPress.

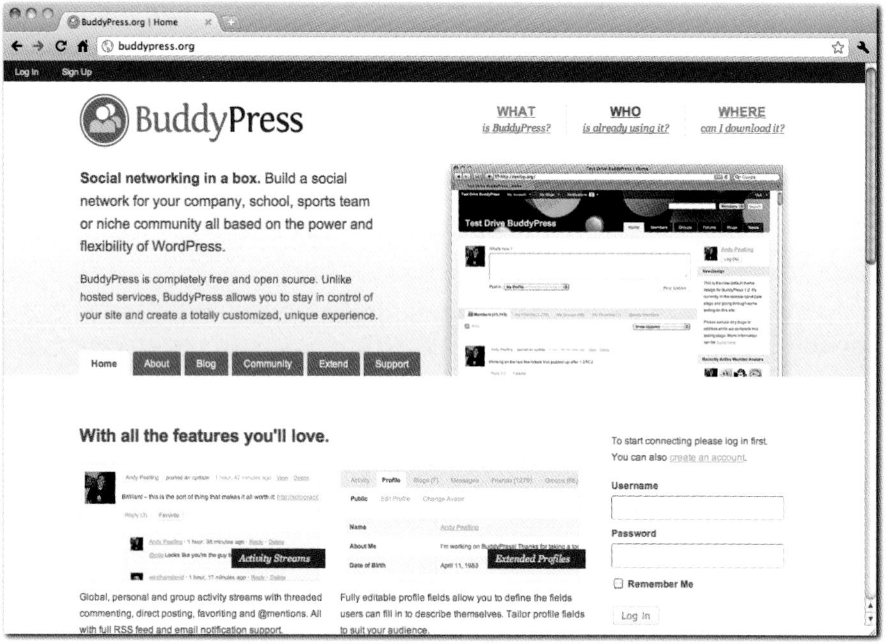

Figure 10-1: The BuddyPress Web site at http://buddypress.org

BUDDYPRESS, THEMES, AND PLUGINS

I'll show you how to upload BuddyPress to your theme in a little bit. For now, you just need to know that BuddyPress adds a bunch of social networking features that you can enjoy. This means that the themes you use today most likely don't include BuddyPress; the features need to be added. That's why there are BuddyPress themes, which I'll touch on later, created solely to work with WordPress sites running the community plugin.

It is crucial to understand that BuddyPress differs from other plugins. You can't just install it, activate it, and then think it will work. You need to work with your theme, at least a wee little bit, to make it work. Luckily this is easy enough.

These additional plugins (see Figure 10-2) are for BuddyPress only; they require the Buddy-Press plugin in order to work. That means that your theme needs to be ready for the additional plugins as well, which in turn means that the theme first needs to work with BuddyPress. For example, if you're getting a nasty PHP error, you'll miss out on your Buddy-Press add-on plugin's functionality because it just won't find the BuddyPress specific hooks to get it to work.

Figure 10-2: Plugin directory found on the official BuddyPress site

Adding BuddyPress functionality to your site brings it up a notch feature-wise, but it is not without work.

SHOULD I USE BUDDYPRESS?

The answer to this question depends, obviously, on your goals. Do you need the functionality? Why have people registered on your site if there is no incentive for them to stick around? Or why add features that no one will use?

As always, it is important to keep things simple, and as lean and mean as possible. If you don't need a particular feature, no matter where it comes from, then don't use it. Feature overload is the same as clutter, and we all want to stay clear of that, right?

There's another part to the question, and that involves the plugin itself. It is getting better and better all the time, but it isn't perfect. The documentation, shown in Figure 10-3 and found at http://codex.buddypress.org/home, is obviously a work in progress, as is the WordPress Codex. While it is hard to know how far the documentation team will have gotten when you read this, at this time it is a bit of a steep learning curve to get started with Buddy-Press. As is common in open source projects, adding more advanced tweaks (in your theme of course) often means you'll have to read the plugin code or ask for help within the community. This isn't necessarily a problem; it is just worth mentioning that BuddyPress is still in the early stages. If you can, do contribute!

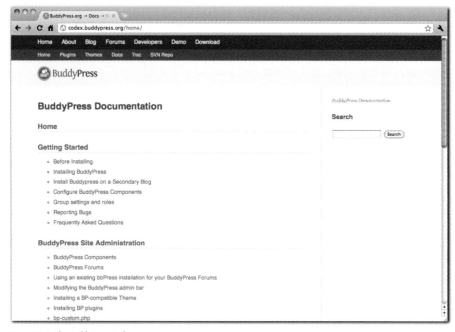

Figure 10-3: The BuddyPress Codex

Another problem with the plugin is that a lot of the design is embedded in the code. That means that it isn't as easy to alter the look and feel of features as we're used to, which is a shame, to say the least. BuddyPress is actively being developed and you can expect this to change as new versions roll out.

All that being said, BuddyPress is still a great tool to take your site up a notch. If you want to engage the users on your site, and think you can get them to play along, then BuddyPress is the way to go.

THE BUDDYPRESS TEMPLATE PACK

The BuddyPress Template Pack is your best friend when it comes to adding BuddyPress functionality to an existing site. Chances are you already have a theme that you're pleased with and want to build upon, and that's where the BuddyPress Template Pack comes in. It's a plugin, and it will help you add the BuddyPress functionality into your theme.

I tell you how to install it in a little bit, but let's take a closer look first.

THE BUDDYPRESS TEMPLATE FILES OVERVIEW

What the BuddyPress Template Pack really does is add a bunch of new template files to your active theme, for use with BuddyPress. It won't overwrite anything (unless you have files with the BuddyPress template filenames) and if you want to, you can always just delete the added files and folders, and then deactivate the plugin.

The added template files (and there's a lot of those) are copied to your theme folder. You will probably want to style them a bit to make them fit your theme, but overall they are pretty much ready for use, albeit a bit crude. The idea is that these newly added template files are as simple as possible so that you can easily alter them to fit your needs. Most of the time you can just add some CSS to your theme's style.css file to get the look and feel you like on the BuddyPress parts of your site.

It's worth mentioning that while the BuddyPress Template Pack is a plugin, you can't just deactivate it when you have run the plugin and gotten the template files copied to your theme. The plugin also acts as a bridge with BuddyPress and adds things like the top admin bar, and so on. Obviously you can add that to your theme manually as well, but the BuddyPress Template Pack is an easy way to accomplish this.

ADDING THE BUDDYPRESS TEMPLATE PACK TO A WORDPRESS SITE

In this section, you add the BuddyPress Template Pack to an existing WordPress site (using the Twenty Ten theme) and see what happens. Obviously you need to have the BuddyPress plugin installed. You'll find that at `http://buddypress.org`, or by searching for "Buddy-Press" in the WordPress admin panel where you add new plugins.

1. **Download and install the plugin.** Log in to your WordPress Web site, browse to Plugins, and then click Add New. Search for "BuddyPress Template Pack" to find the plugin (see Figure 10-4). Click Install Now.
2. **Activate the BuddyPress Template Pack.** Activate the plugin after installing the Template Pack, either directly from the "install succeeded" page or from the Plugins page in the admin panel. Then go to Appearance, click BP Compatibility, and get ready to run the compatibility guide (see Figure 10-5).

Figure 10-4: Installing the BuddyPress Template Pack plugin

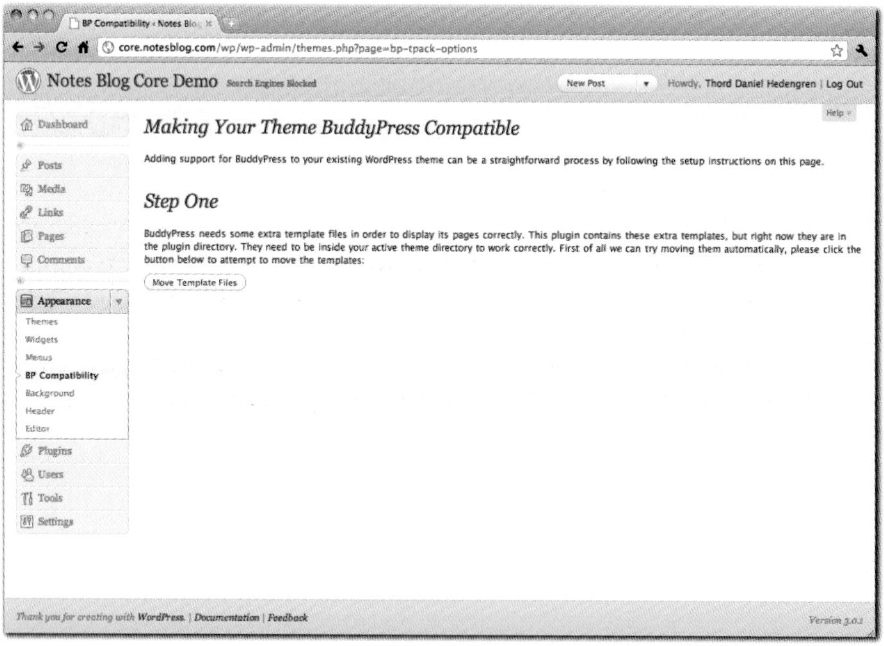

Figure 10-5: The BP compatibility page

3. **Move the necessary template files.** Click the Move Template Files button on the BP compatibility page for the BuddyPress Template Pack plugin to move the necessary template files to your active theme's folder. Most likely you'll get a fancy success message (see Figure 10-6) and be prompted to move on to the next step. If not, see what went wrong and remedy it; usually it is your writing permission on the theme folder.

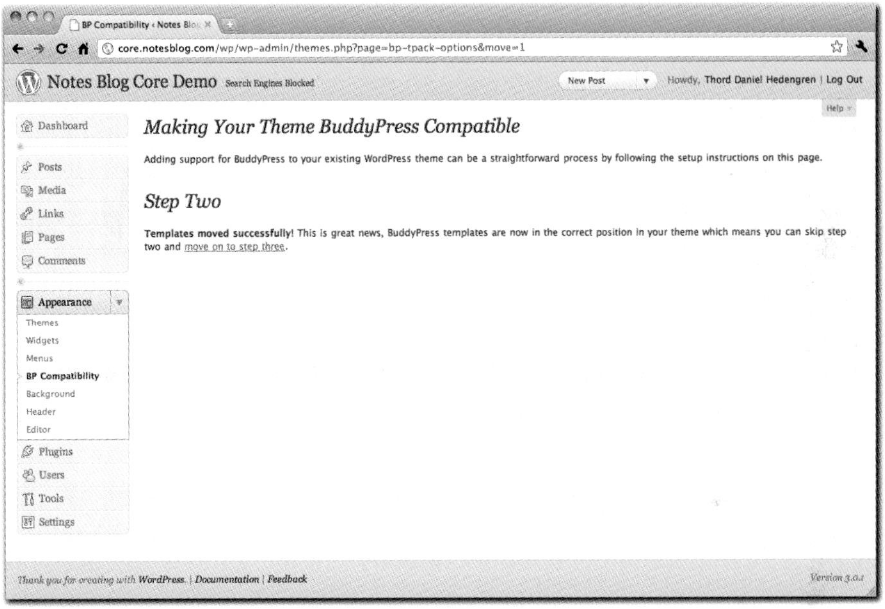

Figure 10-6: Templates moved successfully!

4. **And you're done (sort of).** Click the link to "move on to step three" (Figure 10-7) on the success page. You'll get a confirmation message about what's been done and a lot of information about what's been done, how BuddyPress templates should be built, and what files have been added.

When you've read it all, and verified that the folders and files really are where they should be, click the Finish button at the bottom of the page. The result is shown in Figure 10-8.

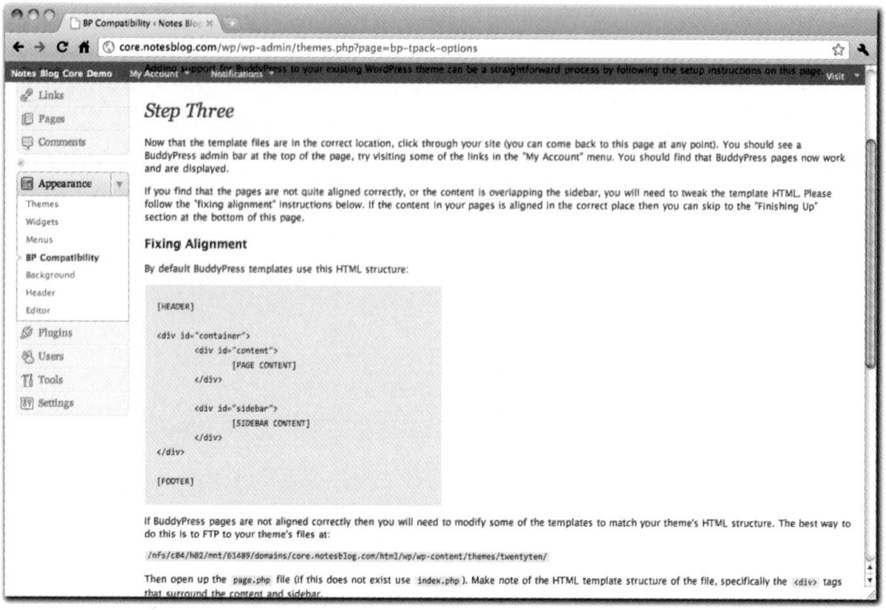

Figure 10-7: Sort of done

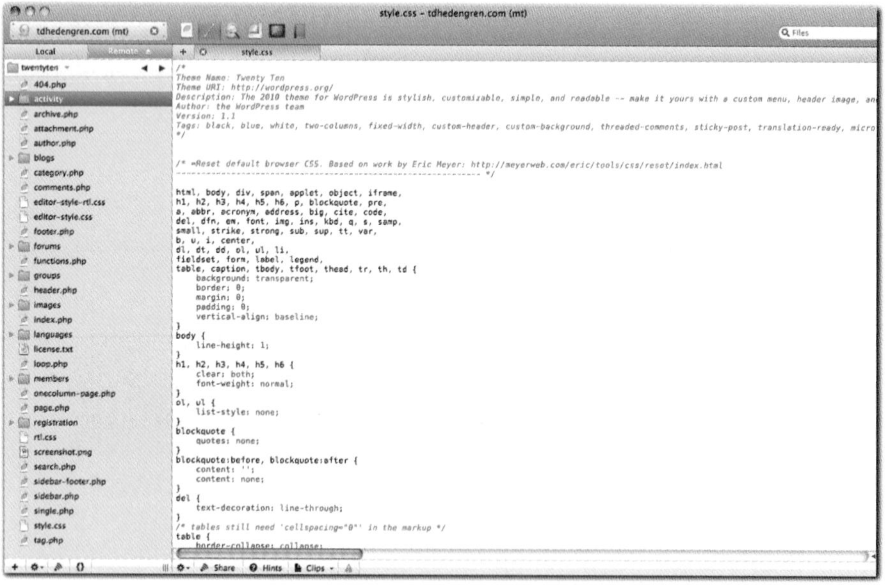

Figure 10-8: A bunch of folders containing BuddyPress template files have been added to the Twenty Ten theme

5. **Finally, you need to adjust some final settings.** Now the BP compatibility page looks quite different in your admin panel. You have settings for disabling stylesheets that help format how your BuddyPress pages look, as well as semi-necessary JavaScript files (see Figure 10-9). You probably want these turned on, otherwise you'll have to fiddle more with your theme.

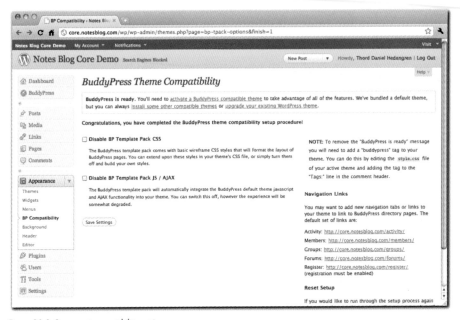

Figure 10-9: Some post-compatibility settings

Oh, and you might want to add the tag "buddypress" to your theme's style.css theme tag listing in the theme declaration on top. Otherwise, you'll get a "BuddyPress is ready" warning on every page in the admin panel despite your theme being BuddyPress ready. Take a look at Figure 10-10 with the BuddyPress feature installed.

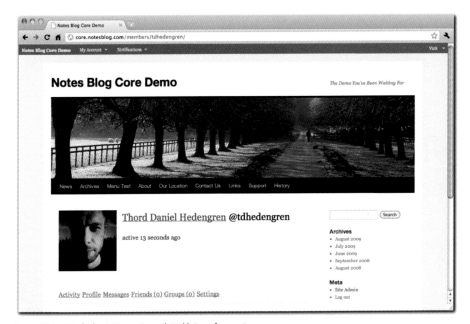

Figure 10-10: Hey look, it's Twenty Ten with BuddyPress features!

CASE STUDY: ADDING BUDDYPRESS COMMUNITY FEATURES TO A SITE

The best way to show how to add community functionality to a site using BuddyPress is, of course, to actually do it. So in this section I do just that, using the BuddyPress Template Pack previously mentioned, and a well-established Web site I'm running that actually would benefit from revamped (or in this case, actual) members functionality.

Go to my Spelbloggen site (`http://spelbloggen.se`), a blog about computer and video games running WordPress (see Figure 10-11). The blog was built during an event called 24 Hour Business Camp early 2010, and is alive and kicking. By the end of this section, it'll be a little bit more alive, and kicking even harder.

Figure 10-11: Spelbloggen, prior to BuddyPress additions

ADD THE BASIC FEATURES

It is easy enough to get the basic BuddyPress features in on Spelbloggen. Because I'm the cautious type, I have a test site set up that contains a copy of the database, but otherwise is identical to the original site. This is always a good idea as you don't want to mess up a live site, especially when working with things like this. After all, there'll be quite some template file fiddling during this process. Always test plugins that add stuff to your database in a secluded area. You don't want unnecessary database clutter. By testing plugins by themselves, you avoid these problems.

Also, while Spelbloggen is a Swedish language site, I'm holding off localizing it for now. In part this is to make sure that those of you who don't know the language of kings can keep up with all these admin screenshots, but also because I'll be adding the BuddyPress localization files last.

Right. So the first thing I do is install the BuddyPress plugin and activate it. Not much will happen as my theme doesn't show BuddyPress features, but I will get the annoying "Buddy-Press is ready" warning in the WordPress admin panel (as portrayed in Figure 10-12).

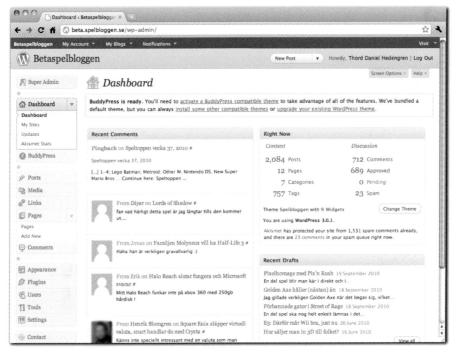

Figure 10-12: The pesky BuddyPress alerts

Next I get the BuddyPress Template Pack in and run the install guide. You saw all that previously, so there's not much to add after that.

With BuddyPress installed and the BuddyPress Template Pack guide ready, which means that my theme has gotten the template files copied to the theme folder, the functionality is actually up and running (see Figure 10-13). How about that?

Figure 10-13: Look at that default BuddyPress admin bar!

A CLOSER LOOK AT THE BUDDYPRESS TEMPLATE FILES

The BuddyPress template files are just like your theme's regular template files, which means that they are PHP using WordPress template tags, as well as new tags added by BuddyPress. You'll find them in your theme's folder, thanks to the BuddyPress Template Pack plugin. All of the BuddyPress template files reside in folders within your theme folder, which makes them easy to spot, and to delete, should you want to clean up your theme.

These are the new folders I should see in my theme folder now, containing everything I need to BuddyPress my site:

/activity

/blogs

/forums

/groups

/members

/registration

Now, inside these folders are a bunch of files, and even more folders. For better or for worse, BuddyPress contains a lot of files. Sometimes that's a good thing, making it easy to find exactly what you need to alter; but sometimes it is not, and then it'll be tedious at best to make the same change in several places.

You might remember that the BuddyPress Template Pack plugin said that you might have to alter a few of the new template files to fit your theme structure. These are as follows:

/activity/index.php

/blogs/index.php

/forums/index.php

/groups/index.php

/groups/create.php

/groups/single/home.php

/groups/single/plugins.php

/members/index.php

/members/single/home.php

/members/single/plugins.php

/registration/register.php

BuddyPress is built under the assumption that your theme follows a simple and fairly common layout. First is your header, which BuddyPress won't mess with design-wise. Then there's a `div#container` in which both `div#content` (for the main content, as usual) and `div#sidebar` (for the sidebar) sits. And finally, there's the footer, again usually not something you need to alter.

This is how the BuddyPress template files are built. If that doesn't work with your theme, then you need to make some changes. Which I will, in fact, do now for Spelbloggen!

A FEW WORDS ABOUT BUDDYPRESS UPGRADES

Before I start applying the basic changes to make things look decent in the Spelbloggen theme, here's a point to keep in mind: I'm not hacking a theme here, I'm editing copied files. In some cases, it might even be a good idea to keep the BuddyPress parts of a theme separate, in a child theme perhaps. This is not what I'm doing in this case, but it is something to consider. Over the years, a lot of BuddyPress users have ended up hacking the actual plugin, or doing things that would break with BuddyPress upgrades. That's a bad thing, of course; you want to keep your edits separate from anything that could be overwritten by an upgrade. That could be true for your theme, unless you're the one doing the upgrades, in which case you want to keep the alterations in a child theme. View the BuddyPress folders in Figure 10-14.

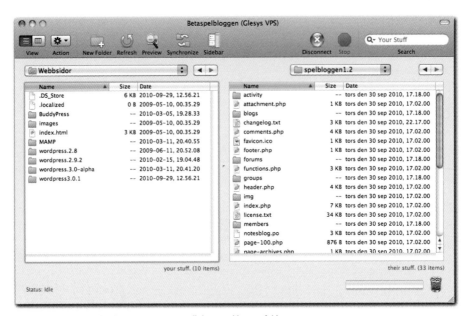

Figure 10-14: Browsing the theme via FTP, seeing all those BuddyPress folders

When it comes to the Spelbloggen theme, that's not a problem; it is the only one of its kind and will be upgraded as such. If you build on a theme you downloaded, it's a different story. Make sure you've got your upgrade strategy in place!

MODIFYING THE TEMPLATE FILES TO FIT A SITE

First, I need to make sure that my BuddyPress files have the right layout. In Spelbloggen's case, that means slight alterations to the structure. For starters, there is no `div#container` in Spelbloggen's design, which I could let sit there, but I'll remove it instead. Also, I need to add the class `"widecolumn"` to the `div#content` element so that the right width will be used.

To demonstrate, Figure 10-15 shows the BuddyPress members index.php template, located in `/members/index.php` and showing the members directory. It's a bit empty now, but you get the picture.

Figure 10-15: Ugly, unfixed members directory

```php
<?php get_header() ?>

<div id="container">
        <div id="content">

                <form action="" method="post" id="members-directory-form"
 class="dir-form">

                        <h3><?php _e( 'Members Directory', 'buddypress' ) ?></h3>

                        <?php do_action( 'bp_before_directory_members_content' ) ?>

                        <div id="members-dir-search" class="dir-search">
                                <?php bp_directory_members_search_form() ?>
                        </div><!-- #members-dir-search -->

                        <div class="item-list-tabs">
                                <ul>
                                        <li class="selected" id="members-all"><a
href="<?php bp_root_domain() ?>"><?php printf( __( 'All Members (%s)', 'buddypress'
), bp_get_total_member_count() ) ?></a></li>
```

```php
                                        <?php if ( is_user_logged_in() && function_
exists( 'bp_get_total_friend_count' ) && bp_get_total_friend_count( bp_loggedin_
user_id() ) ) : ?>
                                                <li id="members-personal"><a
href="<?php echo bp_loggedin_user_domain() . BP_FRIENDS_SLUG . '/my-friends/'
?>"><?php printf( __( 'My Friends (%s)', 'buddypress' ), bp_get_total_friend_count(
bp_loggedin_user_id() ) ) ?></a></li>
                                        <?php endif; ?>

                                        <?php do_action( 'bp_members_directory_mem-
ber_types' ) ?>

                                        <li id="members-order-select" class="last
filter">

                                                <?php _e( 'Order By:', 'buddypress'
) ?>
                                                <select>
                                                        <option value="active"><?php
_e( 'Last Active', 'buddypress' ) ?></option>
                                                        <option value="newest"><?php
_e( 'Newest Registered', 'buddypress' ) ?></option>

                                                        <?php if ( bp_is_active(
'xprofile' ) ) : ?>
                                                                <option
value="alphabetical"><?php _e( 'Alphabetical', 'buddypress' ) ?></option>
                                                        <?php endif; ?>

                                                        <?php do_action( 'bp_mem-
bers_directory_order_options' ) ?>
                                                </select>
                                        </li>
                                </ul>
                        </div><!-- .item-list-tabs -->

                        <div id="members-dir-list" class="members dir-list">
                                <?php locate_template( array( 'members/members-loop.
php' ), true ) ?>
                        </div><!-- #members-dir-list -->

                        <?php do_action( 'bp_directory_members_content' ) ?>

                        <?php wp_nonce_field( 'directory_members', '_wpnonce-member-
filter' ) ?>

                        <?php do_action( 'bp_after_directory_members_content' ) ?>
```

```
                    </form><!-- #members-directory-form -->

            </div><!-- #content -->
</div><!-- #container -->

<?php locate_template( array( 'sidebar.php' ), true ) ?>

<?php get_footer() ?>
```

Notice how it starts with div#container and then div#content for the actual content? That's what I'm after; I want to remove the div#container part, so I'll do just that, and not forget to remove the code that closes it either. It opens on line 3, and closes on line 56, so the contents of those will have to go. I'll also add class="widecolumn" to the div#content element to get the widths right.

```
<?php get_header() ?>

<div id="content" class="widecolumn">

    <form action="" method="post" id="members-directory-form" class="dir-form">

        <h3><?php _e( 'Members Directory', 'buddypress' ) ?></h3>

        <?php do_action( 'bp_before_directory_members_content' ) ?>

        <div id="members-dir-search" class="dir-search">
                <?php bp_directory_members_search_form() ?>
        </div><!-- #members-dir-search -->

        <div class="item-list-tabs">
                <ul>
                        <li class="selected" id="members-all"><a href="<?php bp_
root_domain() ?>"><?php printf( __( 'All Members (%s)', 'buddypress' ), bp_get_
total_member_count() ) ?></a></li>

                        <?php if ( is_user_logged_in() && function_exists( 'bp_get_
total_friend_count' ) && bp_get_total_friend_count( bp_loggedin_user_id() ) ) : ?>
                        <li id="members-personal"><a href="<?php echo
bp_loggedin_user_domain() . BP_FRIENDS_SLUG . '/my-friends/' ?>"><?php printf( __(
'My Friends (%s)', 'buddypress' ), bp_get_total_friend_count( bp_loggedin_user_id()
) ) ?></a></li>
                        <?php endif; ?>

                        <?php do_action( 'bp_members_directory_member_types' ) ?>

                        <li id="members-order-select" class="last filter">
```

```php
                                <?php _e( 'Order By:', 'buddypress' ) ?>
                                <select>
                                        <option value="active"><?php _e( 'Last
Active', 'buddypress' ) ?></option>
                                        <option value="newest"><?php _e( 'Newest
Registered', 'buddypress' ) ?></option>

                                        <?php if ( bp_is_active( 'xprofile' ) ) : ?>
                                                <option value="alphabetical"><?php
_e( 'Alphabetical', 'buddypress' ) ?></option>
                                        <?php endif; ?>

                                        <?php do_action( 'bp_members_directory_
order_options' ) ?>
                                </select>
                        </li>
                </ul>
        </div><!-- .item-list-tabs -->

        <div id="members-dir-list" class="members dir-list">
                <?php locate_template( array( 'members/members-loop.php' ), true )
?>
        </div><!-- #members-dir-list -->

        <?php do_action( 'bp_directory_members_content' ) ?>

        <?php wp_nonce_field( 'directory_members', '_wpnonce-member-filter' ) ?>

        <?php do_action( 'bp_after_directory_members_content' ) ?>

    </form><!-- #members-directory-form -->

</div><!-- #content -->

<?php locate_template( array( 'sidebar.php' ), true ) ?>

<?php get_footer() ?>
```

Removing div#container really didn't do much, but since it's not on other parts of the site, it could be a nuisance later on. However, the simple class="widecolumn" contains the necessary styling to give the content column its correct width and fix the general layout. The members directory still isn't pretty (as you'll see in Figure 10-16), but at least it uses the correct layout.

I need to do this on all the previously mentioned BuddyPress PHP template files, otherwise their respective features won't fit in on the site as they should. A few minutes of copying and pasting later (or a quick search and replace across multiple files using a favorite text editor) and I'll have everything from members pages to groups to user pages fitting nicely into my site, as shown in Figure 10-17.

Figure 10-16: The correct widths are in, still not pretty though

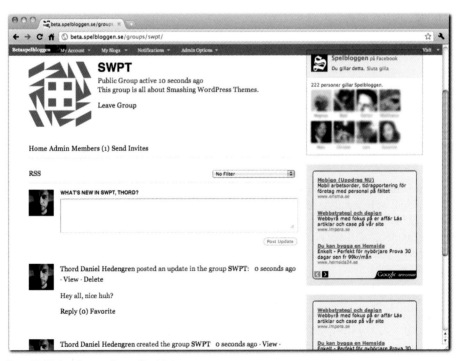

Figure 10-17: A newly created group fits right in

An optional solution to the width problem would obviously be to just give #container the width as well, along with the widecolumn class. Either way is fine. In this case I wanted to stay consistent with the rest of the site (Spelbloggen is quite extensive). You'll decide what works best for you; it is nice to not have to copy and paste all those edits, of course.

In essence, this is what you need to do to get started with BuddyPress on an existing site. The rest can be done by styling the elements like you usually do, in your stylesheet. It's all there; all you need to do is go through the various new pages and style them accordingly. I won't go into that; it's just basic CSS, and you know that already.

But why stop there? Let's fiddle some more!

WHAT ARE ALL THOSE NEW TAGS?

The BuddyPress template files look a bit different from regular theme template files. They are not only filled with WordPress template tags, but with new ones that just won't work without having BuddyPress installed.

Take a look at the BuddyPress template file for viewing a member page, /members/single/home.php. It looks like this (with div#container removed, and so on; I'm still fiddling with Spelbloggen here):

```php
<?php get_header() ?>

<div id="content" class="widecolumn">

    <?php do_action( 'bp_before_member_home_content' ) ?>

    <div id="item-header">
        <?php locate_template( array( 'members/single/member-header.php' ), true )
    ?>
    </div><!-- #item-header -->

    <div id="item-nav">
        <div class="item-list-tabs no-ajax" id="object-nav">
            <ul>
                    <?php bp_get_displayed_user_nav() ?>

                    <?php do_action( 'bp_members_directory_member_types' ) ?>
            </ul>
        </div>
    </div><!-- #item-nav -->

    <div id="item-body">
        <?php do_action( 'bp_before_member_body' ) ?>
```

```php
<?php if ( bp_is_user_activity() || !bp_current_component() ) : ?>
        <?php locate_template( array( 'members/single/activity.php' ), true
) ?>

        <?php elseif ( bp_is_user_blogs() ) : ?>
            <?php locate_template( array( 'members/single/blogs.php' ), true )
?>

        <?php elseif ( bp_is_user_friends() ) : ?>
            <?php locate_template( array( 'members/single/friends.php' ), true )
?>

        <?php elseif ( bp_is_user_groups() ) : ?>
            <?php locate_template( array( 'members/single/groups.php' ), true )
?>

        <?php elseif ( bp_is_user_messages() ) : ?>
            <?php locate_template( array( 'members/single/messages.php' ), true
) ?>

        <?php elseif ( bp_is_user_profile() ) : ?>
            <?php locate_template( array( 'members/single/profile.php' ), true )
?>

        <?php endif; ?>

        <?php do_action( 'bp_after_member_body' ) ?>

    </div><!-- #item-body -->

    <?php do_action( 'bp_after_member_home_content' ) ?>

</div><!-- #content -->

<?php locate_template( array( 'sidebar.php' ), true ) ?>

<?php get_footer() ?>
```

Every PHP snippet starting with bp_ is BuddyPress related, which makes sense. A good (and simple) example is the bp_get_displayed_user_navi() template tag, which outputs the user navigation.

You'll also notice a lot of do_action() snippets. These are creating hooks that I can attach an action to, so if I want to cram something special into a specific spot on a page, and there is a hook, I can do so with the add_action(). Basically, add_action() attaches functions to do_action().

I'll illustrate this by adding an annoying box to do_action('bp_before_member_body'). First I need to write a function, which resides in functions.php, residing within PHP tags of course (just like most things in functions.php, albeit not necessarily all).

```
function annoying_box() {
            echo '<div style="padding:10px; background:yellow; color:red;
 font-weight:bold;">
                        Hey there! Annoyed yet?
            </div>';
    }
add_action('bp_before_member_body', 'annoying_box');
```

First I create the function, called `annoying_box()`. Within it is a simple `echo` that outputs a `div` with some annoying text and just as annoying styles. Nope, this won't be pretty . . . After that I need to add this function to a hook, which is the `bp_before_member_body` one mentioned earlier. I do this with `add_action()`, first passing the hook I want to hook on to (again, `bp_before_member_body`), and then the function I want to hook on with (which is `annoying_box`). I could have passed two more parameters to `add_action()`, priority and number of arguments, but they don't do any good here so I just left them out.

Figure 10-18 shows the end result.

Figure 10-18: An annoying box added with a simple action hook

BuddyPress has a lot of hooks you can play with, which helps a lot. The number of hooks can help when you need to insert something in a particular place, which is handy. Also, there's always the option to rearrange the template files altogether to get the look and feel you're after.

FIXING PERMALINKS AND LOCALIZATION

The default permalinks for the various BuddyPress pages might not suit your needs. Maybe you don't want your members to reside under /members/ username, but rather /superstars/username. You can change this by adding a few lines of code to your wp-config.php file. That's right, the one with all the database information and whatnot in your Word-Press install.

The Action Reference page in the BuddyPress Documentation is a good place to start if you want to hook into BuddyPress: http://codex.buddypress.org/developer-docs/action-reference/.

These are the strings that you can alter:

```
define( 'BP_ACTIVATION_SLUG', 'activate' );
define( 'BP_ACTIVITY_SLUG', 'activity' );
define( 'BP_BLOGS_SLUG', 'blogs' );
define( 'BP_FORUMS_SLUG', 'forums' );
define( 'BP_FRIENDS_SLUG', 'friends' );
define( 'BP_GROUPS_SLUG', 'groups' );
define( 'BP_MEMBERS_SLUG', 'members' );
define( 'BP_MESSAGES_SLUG', 'messages' );
define( 'BP_REGISTER_SLUG', 'register' );
define( 'BP_SEARCH_SLUG', 'search' );
define( 'BP_SETTINGS_SLUG', 'settings' );
define( 'BP_XPROFILE_SLUG', 'profile' );
```

Suppose you really want to change "members" to "superstars." Easy, just find the row with BP_MEMBERS_SLUG and change 'members' to 'superstars', like this:

```
define( 'BP_MEMBERS_SLUG', 'superstars' );
```

Simple, huh? When it comes to Spelbloggen, I don't want English in my URLs, if I can help it, so I've translated all these to Swedish. This is what I'm using for Spelbloggen:

```
define( 'BP_ACTIVATION_SLUG', 'aktivera' );
define( 'BP_ACTIVITY_SLUG', 'aktivitet' );
define( 'BP_BLOGS_SLUG', 'bloggar' );
define( 'BP_FORUMS_SLUG', 'forum' );
define( 'BP_FRIENDS_SLUG', 'vanner' );
define( 'BP_GROUPS_SLUG', 'grupper' );
define( 'BP_MEMBERS_SLUG', 'medlemmar' );
define( 'BP_MESSAGES_SLUG', 'meddelanden' );
define( 'BP_REGISTER_SLUG', 'registrea' );
define( 'BP_SEARCH_SLUG', 'sok' );
define( 'BP_SETTINGS_SLUG', 'installningar' );
define( 'BP_XPROFILE_SLUG', 'profil' );
```

Speaking of localization, you can get BuddyPress in your language, just like you can with WordPress. All you need to do is download the language files and then upload them to the `bp-languages` folder within the `buddypress` folder, which in turn resides in your plugins folder. That's right; you upload the BuddyPress language files to the plugin's folder, which means they'll most likely get overwritten when there's an upgrade. It's not ideal, but that's the way it is.

Find your language file at `http://codex.buddypress.org/developer-docs/translations`.

ADDING BBPRESS TO YOUR GROUPS

You can get BuddyPress to do even cooler things by adding the bbPress forum to your install. This will give you a lean discussion forum for your groups. And you know what, it is really easy to add. Here's how!

1. **Start the install.** Go to BuddyPress and then Forums Setup in the WordPress admin panel, shown in Figure 10-19. Click the Set up a new bbPress installation button. (If you already have a stand-alone bbPress installation, click the Use an existing bbPress installation button.)

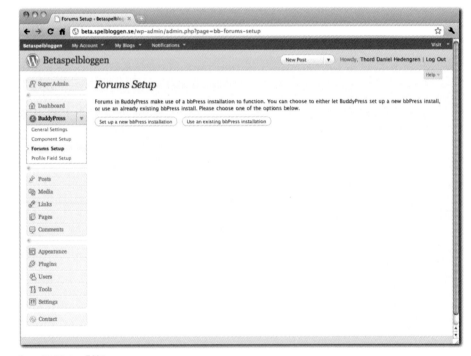

Figure 10-19: Install bbPress

2. **Complete the install.** On the second page (Figure 10-20), click the Complete Installation button. You'll get a success message, as shown in Figure 10-21.

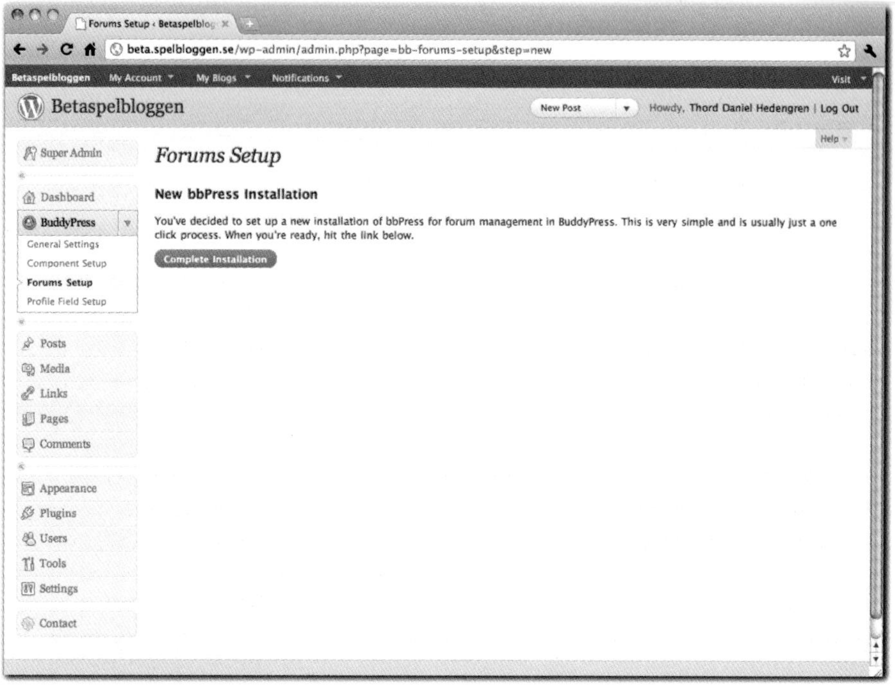

Figure 10-20: Click the button to complete the installation

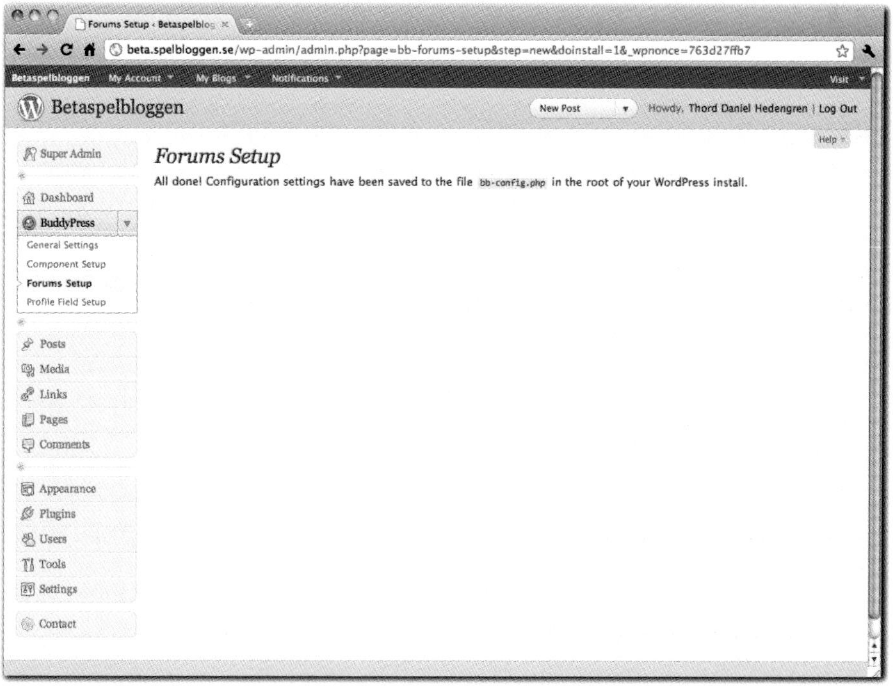

Figure 10-21: Success!

3. **Create a group.** Now go to your site's groups page (usually at `yourdomain.com/groups` unless you've changed it) and create a group. Make sure that the Enable discussion forum option is checked when creating the group (see Figure 10-22).

Figure 10-22: You need to enable forums on a per-group basis

4. **And here's your group with a forum.** There you go! Now you've got basic forum functionality for your groups, as shown in the Spelbloggen page in Figure 10-23!

So what happened? Well, the bbPress forum system ships with BuddyPress, and the only thing that's happening is that your WordPress database now hosts a forum as well. As you can see in Figure 10-24, all the files are already there, in the `wp-content/buddypress/bp-forums/bbpress` folder.

Read more about bbPress at `http://bbpress.org`.

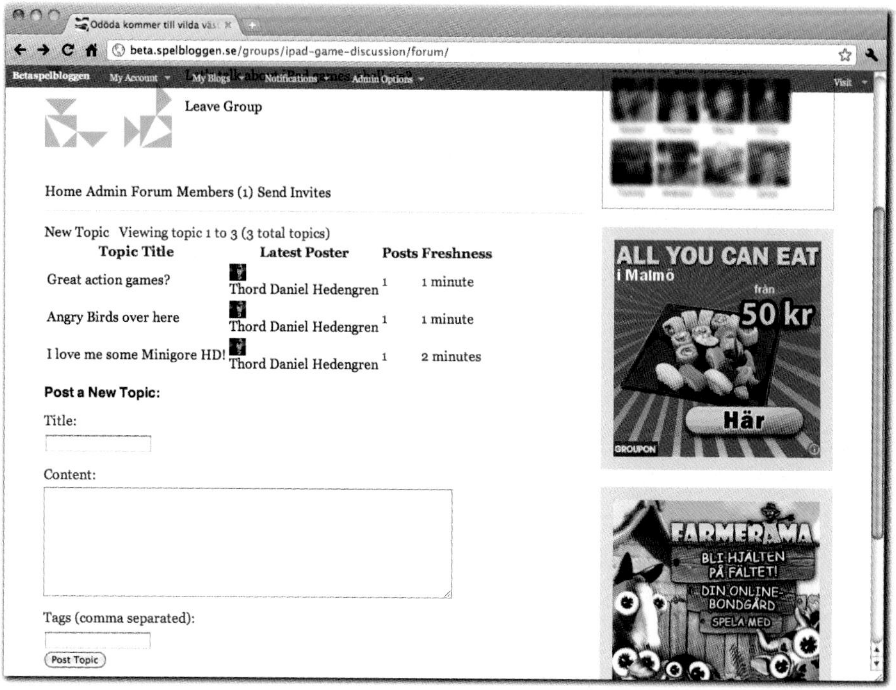

Figure 10-23: Let the discussions begin

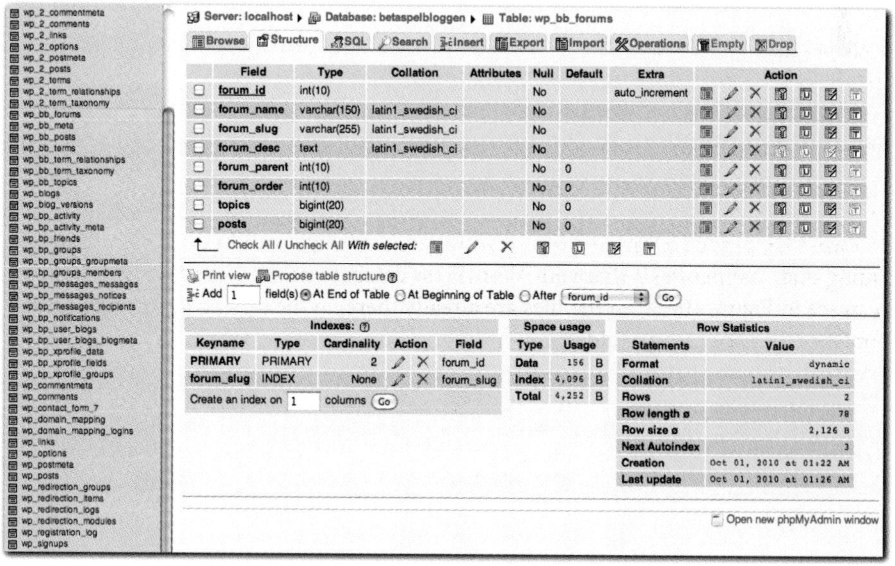

Figure 10-24: Screenshot showing bbPress tables from PhpMyAdmin

ABOUT BUDDYPRESS THEMES

A few words about BuddyPress themes are in order. I don't mean any old theme that you've made BuddyPressed using the BuddyPress Template Pack and some fancy styling in your theme folder, but themes created solely for BuddyPress usage. Some might not even work without the plugin, although most will.

FOCUS ON COMMUNITY FEATURES

The thing with BuddyPress themes overall is that they usually focus on the community features. This makes sense, of course; it is what BuddyPress is there for after all, but it also means that most of these themes are pretty linear in their content flow. The same thing over and over again, but with a slightly different approach.

This isn't necessarily a problem, especially if you're building a site from scratch where the community features are key. It is a bit more of an issue if you want to take your plain old site and move it to BuddyPress, while not planning on making any additions to your theme. Just switching themes can be hard because these BuddyPress themes are so focused on the community content flow, and chances are your old theme wasn't. That means it may be quite a big leap and something that will confuse your current readers and/or users. It's something to keep in mind when browsing for BuddyPress themes. The best solution is usually to take a theme of your own and add the functionality to it.

You'll find BuddyPress themes here and there. Most of the really good ones, unfortunately, are paid themes, but there are a few free ones out there. The BuddyPress themes page (`http://buddypress.org/extend/themes`) isn't exactly packed with options, but you'll find some there. The links lead to the official directory so you'll get all the benefits of automatic upgrades and whatnot.

One might say that the BuddyPress theme community hasn't taken full flight yet, but that isn't all that surprising. After all, since you can add BuddyPress functionality to any theme, people do that rather than build something new to release. That being said, I'm sure we'll see more themes with BuddyPress support out of the box as the plugin gains more ground in the future.

CHILD THEMING BUDDYPRESS THEMES

Despite the fact that they rely on a plugin (that is, BuddyPress themes, of course), there is no reason whatsoever not to create child themes on top of a BuddyPress theme. If you find a theme you like, create a child theme for it to hold your alterations and custom stuff, just like you would with a regular theme. These are WordPress themes with added features, nothing more than that, so the same principles apply.

As always, child themes can be a true time saver, especially if you intend to launch a new site quickly, but don't want to muck around too much with BuddyPress functions in a theme of your own. Just find a BuddyPress theme that gets the job done well enough, and then style and twist it to your needs with a child theme.

324

WRAPPING IT UP

Isn't it nice how easily you can add new features to your WordPress site with a simple plugin? Granted, BuddyPress isn't all that simple when it comes to functionality or extreme customization, but it surely adds a bunch of new options for you and your visitors. This chapter just touches on some of the things you can do with the plugin, and chances are it'll be even better in the months to come. After all, it has come a long way since it first launched.

Now, there's bound to be some more plugins you can use to charge your themes, right? Let's dig into that in the next chapter.

11

EXTENDING WITH PLUGINS

PLUGINS ARE GREAT for extending the functionality of your site beyond what you can get out of a WordPress theme itself. The real beauty of it is that someone most likely has already solved your potential problem and saved you much time and aggravation.

In this chapter, I look at which plugins are good to rely on in theme development and WordPress site building.

WHEN SHOULD YOU USE PLUGINS?

Sometimes you want to do things that just aren't supported in WordPress by default, and that's when plugins come in handy. As you probably know already, there are a huge number of plugins available from the official plugin directory at http://wordpress.org (see Figure 11-1). All plugins that you find there are free to download and use, and there's also some sort of quality control; at least you can rest assured that these plugins aren't poorly disguised malware for your site.

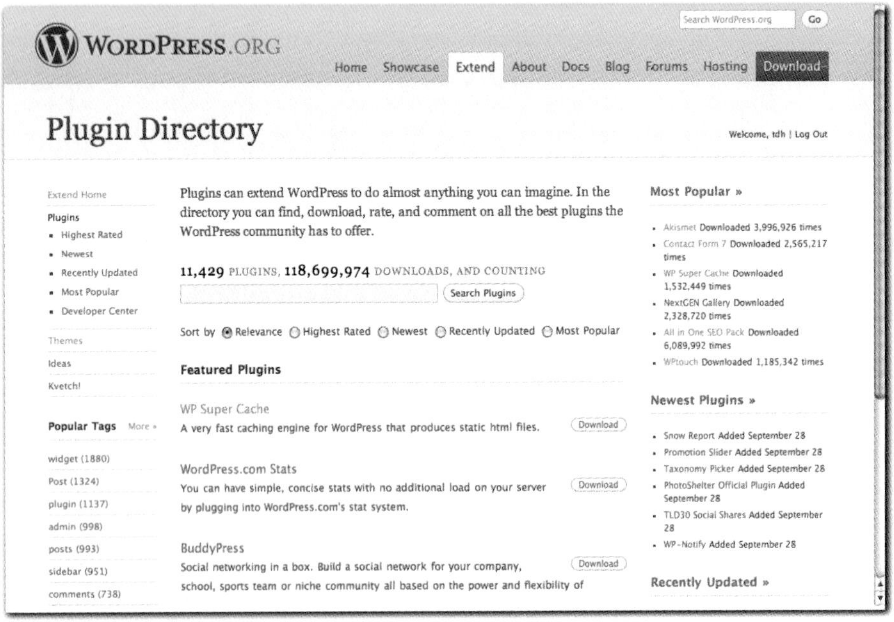

Figure 11-1: The plugins page on wordpress.org

THE PROBLEM WITH PLUGINS

Don't be afraid to use plugins. The fact that you can add features to a WordPress site as easily as activating a plugin is a great thing. As long as the plugin is decently written it shouldn't affect your site much.

Plugins are great, but you should definitely use them with caution. First, they offer even more overhead for your WordPress site. Adding functionality is fine, but consider how it is added. A poorly written plugin could put unnecessary strain on the database, or have a lot of http requests, for example, and that would make your site slower to load for your users. That's a bad thing in SEO terms as well, as search engines take into account how fast your site is loading as well these days.

Another thing you really need to be wary of is feature clutter. Adding cool functionality is tempting, especially since it is so easy to activate yet another plugin. However, you need to ask yourself if you really need that functionality and if your users will find it useful. What's the point of adding a feature no one uses? Keep your WordPress site lean and mean by keeping it as free of plugins as possible, while still achieving the functionality you need obviously (see Figure 11-2).

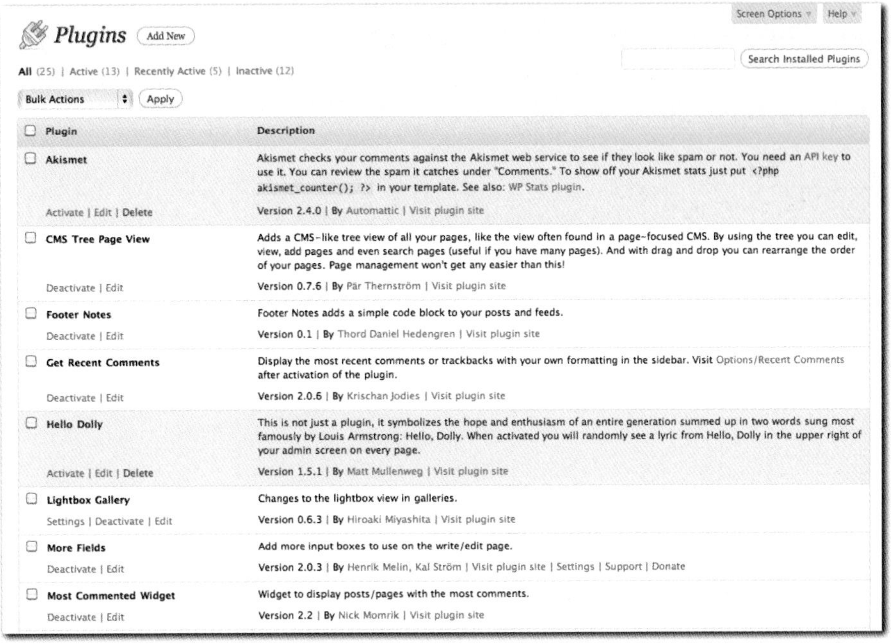

Figure 11-2: The Plugins page in the WordPress admin panel

Database bloat is another issue that sometimes comes with plugins. A lot of plugins (as well as themes, mind you) store data in the database. Sometimes it is just some innocent settings, but at other times you get a bunch of tables. If you run a plugin that adds a lot to the database, you definitely need to make sure to check up on it frequently. This is especially important on larger sites; smaller ones rarely have problems just because their databases have grown a bit due to plugins. Do a bit of database house cleaning every now and then and you'll be fine.

Speaking of databases, plugins that are storing stuff in the database sometimes leave a footprint, even after you have uninstalled them. Plugins written the way they should be written will have uninstall features that clear out the database entries the plugin is responsible for when you uninstall the plugin. But not all plugins do this (which is a shame, since adding the feature is simple enough). You might want to check your database, the wp_options table in particular, for unnecessary data left by plugins that you don't use anymore.

DEVELOPING THEMES THAT RELY ON PLUGINS

One thing you need to decide is whether you should rely on a plugin when developing your theme. There's a huge different between adding theme support for something, and actually depending on it. After all, a theme that won't work without a specific plugin isn't all that useful in an environment where said plugin won't work.

In almost every case, when a specific plugin is needed, it is a good idea to add theme support for it, but make sure that the site won't break when the plugin isn't available. This is really simple: just make a check to see if the plugin function is present where you need it, as follows:

```php
<?php
        // Check for function named foo
        if (function_exists('foo')) {
                foo();
        }
?>
```

Worth the extra code, wouldn't you say? This is how the code would look when calling a related-posts plugin, normally just executed with the plugin-specific `related_posts()` tag:

```php
<?php
        // Check for related_posts
        if (function_exists('related_posts')) {
                related_posts();
        }
?>
```

HOW TO PICK THE RIGHT PLUGIN

There are three things you can do to make sure you're picking the right plugin for the job.

First, read up on what the developer says about the plugin, and possibly about the developer as well. What does the plugin support (for example, which versions of WordPress), and how often is it updated? You'll find a lot of this information in the readme files of the various plugins you're considering, but sometimes you need to dig deeper.

Second, read up on what other users are saying about the plugin. You should be wary of plugins that are getting a lot of heat for bugs or error messages. However, just because some people have issues with a plugin doesn't mean that you will. Remember, it is a lot easier for most people to post a negative comment than a positive one. A total lack of comments on a plugin downloaded hundreds of times is actually a good thing. It might very well mean that the plugin does exactly what it is supposed to. Another thing to keep in mind when looking at community feedback on a plugin is how difficult it is to set it up. If the plugin requires a lot of steps, or if there are a bunch of settings, it can get a lot of negative feedback online solely based on the fact that it isn't for everybody, and some people just didn't understand how to use it.

Third, try the plugin yourself. This is a must for every plugin that's even remotely interesting. You should not, however, test new plugins on a live site. Set up a local sandbox WordPress install that can break without giving you any more problems than reinstalling WordPress. It might also be a good idea to have a test area on your server, a subdomain to your regular site, or something like that, so you can see how the plugin performs in the live environment.

Testing things yourself is important, because no matter how much others are telling you that this or that rocks, you won't know what you think of it until you give it a spin.

There are no shortcuts to picking the right plugin. Focus on the features you're looking for (see Figure 11-3), and then start playing with it. Do your research, both on your own needs and on the plugins you're considering, and you'll be just fine.

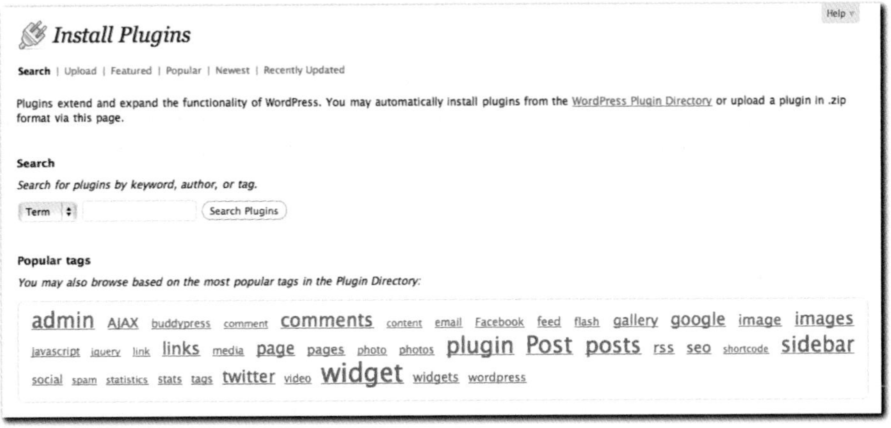

Figure 11-3: Installing plugins from the WordPress admin panel

IS IT REALLY A PLUGIN I NEED?

Sometimes you may want to add simple functionality to your site, and you start looking for plugins. But maybe that's not the way for you to go. Maybe you should look at functions.php instead?

The thing is, functions.php is a truly powerful template file. In theory, you can put just about any plugin in your functions.php file and run it from there. That, however, would not be a good idea. It makes sense to put features that are truly theme-specific in the theme's functions.php template.

Let's say you've constructed a nifty little shortcode (for example, something like the [gallery] shortcode that you can use in your post, but with your own functionality). This shortcode is only interesting for your particular theme because it does something truly theme-specific. You could put the feature in a plugin and activate it, of course, but it makes a lot more sense to just have it in functions.php (hence it is always active, so to speak) since there's no point in using it outside of the theme.

You'll have to decide whether you're looking for a plugin or are in need of something stand-alone when adding functionality. Small stuff usually works just as well in the functions.php template file, but then again, you shouldn't bloat it with features just because you can. There are no hard rules here: use your common sense is the only truly good advice. Scary, huh?

25 TRULY GREAT PLUGINS

You can find a lot of truly excellent plugins out there. Some are multi-purpose features, others fill a specific need that a lot of WordPress users have, and yet others solve one little issue that almost nobody knew existed. My point is that the plethora of plugins out there means that you not only have a lot to choose from, but also need to wade through them when in search of the solutions that you are after. See the plugin post from Think Vitamin in Figure 11-4.

Figure 11-4: A plugin list post from Think Vitamin, http://thinkvitamin.com/code/20-must-have-wordpress-plugins-for-every-website

Plugin list posts are popular online, and while the Internet has the upper hand over a static medium such as a book, I can still offer some plugins that stand above the rest. Hence the following list, with a short motivation for including the plugin in the first place. Do keep in mind that my list is by no means complete. Tons of options are available for the plugins that I list here, and many other respectable plugins are available as well.

With that said, you really should check out these plugins.

COMMENTING PLUGINS

WordPress has built-in comments functionality that is great on its own. Comment spam is an issue, unfortunately, so you want to be able to tackle that. There are also great plugins for displaying recent comments which is a commonly requested feature.

Akismet

While many plugins can be used with your comments section, the most obvious one to use is Akismet (`http://wordpress.org/extend/plugins/akismet`), which even ships with WordPress. This is a solution to stop spammers, and you're probably using it already so let's move on to another option.

WordPress Hashcash

WordPress Hashcash (`http://wordpress.org/extend/plugins/wp-hashcash`) is another tool that can help you manage comment spam, thanks to some JavaScripting (see Figure 11-5). It can solve your comment spam problem if Akismet just doesn't cut it; the two plugins work perfectly well together.

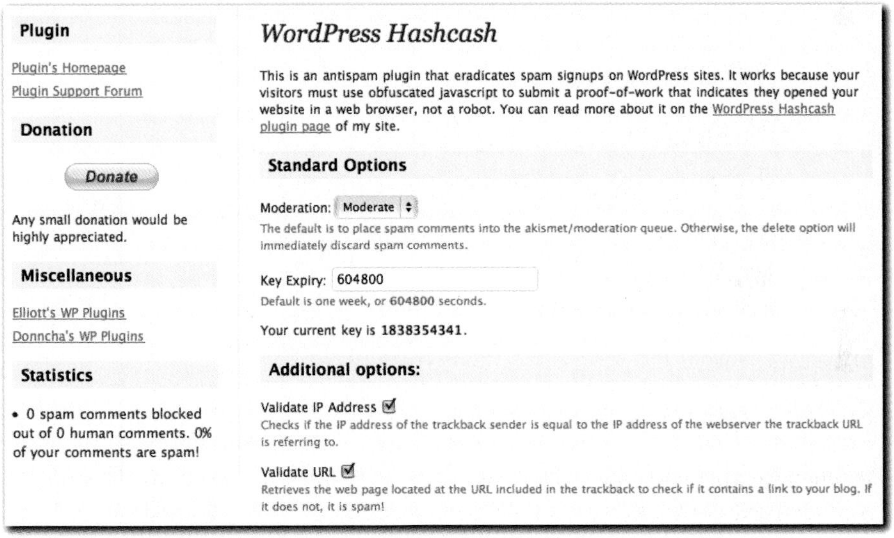

Figure 11-5: WordPress Hashcash

DISQUS

Another solution to comment spam is to outsource it. There are two major players in this field; DISQUS is the larger one (the other one is IntenseDebate). With the DISQUS Comments system (`http://wordpress.org/extend/plugins/disqus-comment-system`), you'll easily integrate with DISQUS and replace all your WordPress comments with the DISQUS system (see Figure 11-6). This works on both new and old sites since you can import your old comments. At times this means a lot of re-running the import script from within the plugin, since it can time out. Besides that, the DISQUS Comments system is a great solution if you want to run DISQUS Comments on your site.

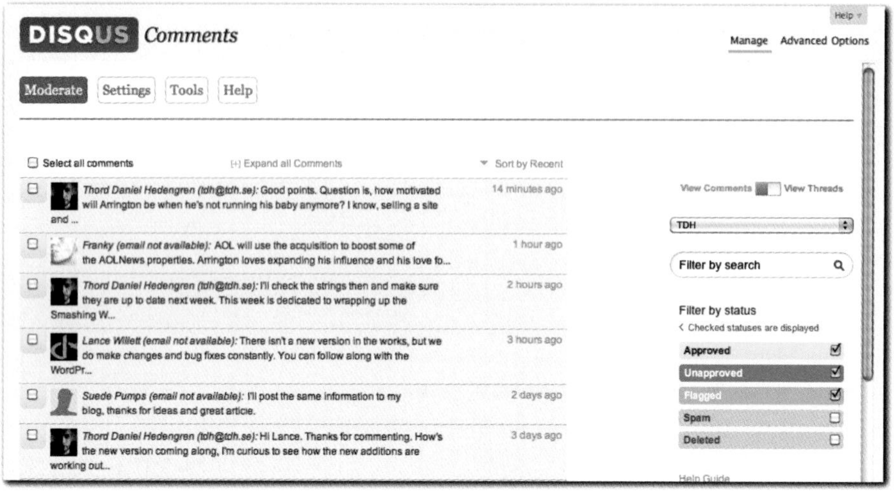

Figure 11-6: DISQUS Comments system

Subscribe to Comments

The Subscribe to Comments plugin (`http://wordpress.org/extend/plugins/subscribe-to-comments/`) is one of the more important plugins available. It adds a check box that lets commenters subscribe to new comments to a post or Page, getting notifications via e-mail.

Get Recent Comments

Get Recent Comments is another nice plugin related to comments (`http://wordpress.org/extend/plugins/get-recent-comments/`). It lets you output nice, recent comment listings beyond those that the standard widget can provide. The plugin (see Figure 11-7) can be inserted with code, or by using the widget. The thing that makes this plugin great is the control it gives you over your comments, with pseudo-tags for various types of data about the comment, comment author, post, time and date, and so on.

Most Commented Widget

Another recent comments plugin is the Most Commented Widget (`http://wordpress.org/extend/plugins/most-commented`), which adds a widget that displays the most frequently commented on posts and/or Pages (see Figure 11-8). There's not much to go on here in terms of settings, but it can be a bit fun at times.

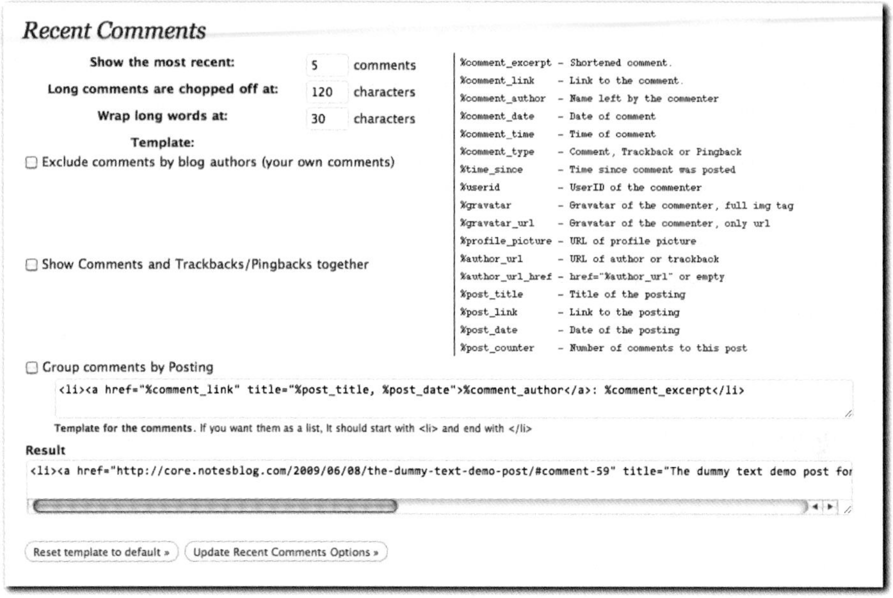

Figure 11-7: Get Recent Comments

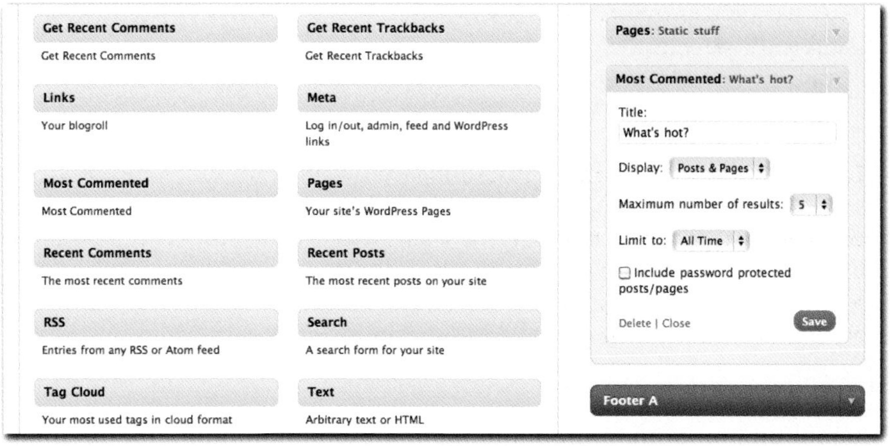

Figure 11-8: Most Commented Widget

Simple Trackback Validation

I'll wrap up the comments section with Simple Trackback Validation (`http://wordpress.org/extend/plugins/simple-trackback-validation`), a truly excellent plugin that gets rid of trackback spam (see Figure 11-9). By checking the IP of where the trackback is from and comparing it to where the trackback link is pointing to, the plugin deduces if it is spam or not. The theory is that most trackback spam are made by bots, and those rarely reside on the same server as the target site. A second layer of protection checks whether there really is a link back to your site from the trackback link sent. Since most trackback spam isn't contrived from actual spam sites containing a link, this usually gets rid of the worst.

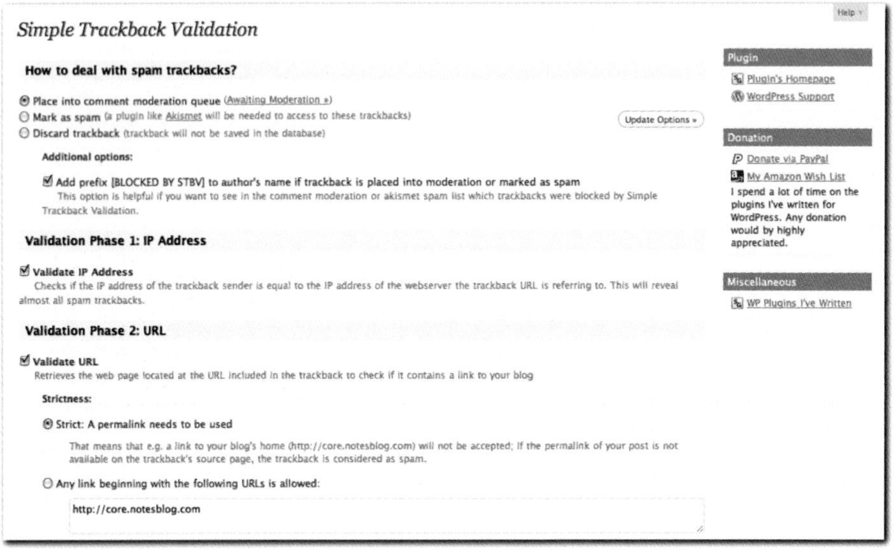

Figure 11-9 Simple Trackback Validation

SOCIAL MEDIA PLUGINS

Promoting your content using social media is important today, and a surefire way to get more readers. At least when done right, I might add, since spamming Twitter most likely won't get you anything other than aggravated ex-followers, and a lot of blocks and report-as-spams. Not a good thing at all, so use social media sharing solutions with caution.

Sociable

Sociable (`http://wordpress.org/extend/plugins/sociable`) is a nice and easy solution for adding social sharing icons to your site (see Figure 11-10). It supports a huge number of social sharing sites (pick the ones that are relevant for you, and omit the rest to avoid clutter) and is decent enough in its original state. What's nice is that you don't have to use Sociable's icons and you can style it yourself as well. A great options page and nice functionality makes this a nice quick and dirty option of getting your social sharing links onto your site.

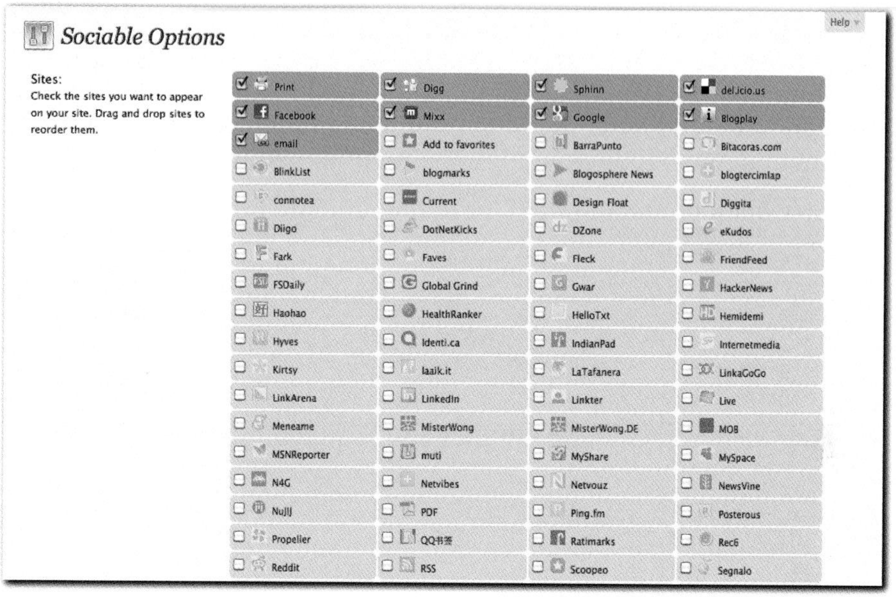

Figure 11-10: Sociable

Share This

Another easy way of adding sharing solutions to your site is the Share This (`http://wordpress.org/extend/plugins/share-this`) plugin, which works with the Share This Web site. In other words, it's a hosted solution where you'll get stats and everything, if you like. There are a bunch of hosted solutions like this, so Share This might not be the perfect plugin for your site, but it's a nice choice if you want a hosted solution rather than something that sits on your own server.

Lifestream Feeds

Lifestream Feeds (`http://wordpress.org/extend/plugins/lifestream`) is a cool way to fetch all your social media activities and store them in your WordPress database (see Figure 11-11). The plugin can pull in your tweets from Twitter, bookmarks for Delicious, pictures from Flickr, and so on. You can show off your social media activities on a page by itself. A word of caution though: The plugin can be pretty heavy on the server, so keep an eye out for dips in performance. Still, it's the best solution for these things out there as I'm writing this. With a decent setup it works perfectly well, so I still recommend it.

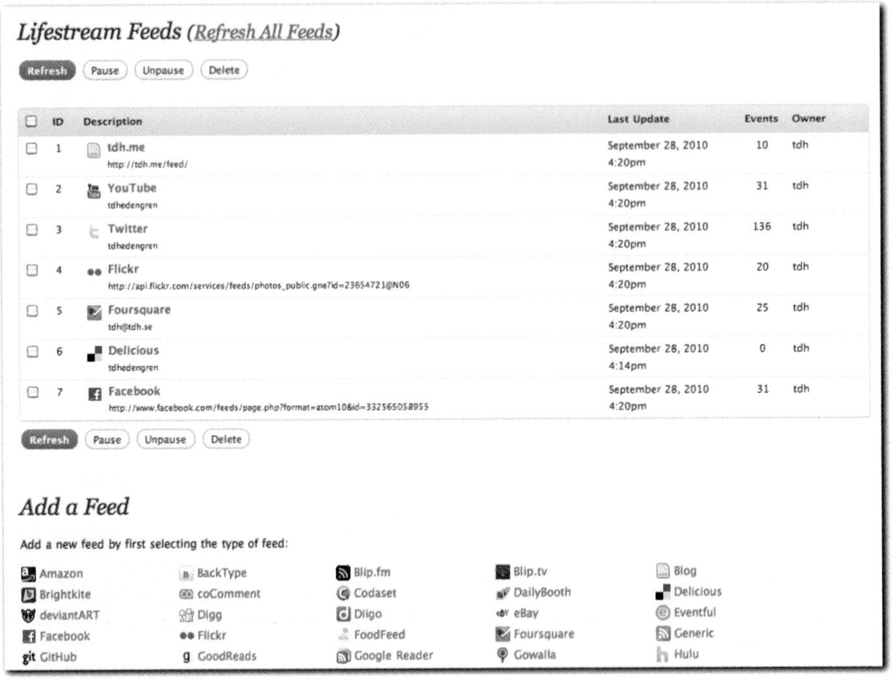

Figure 11-11: Lifestream Feeds

CONTENT RELATED STUFF

One way to get people to keep reading on your site is to use a related posts plugin.

Yet Another Related Posts Plugin Options

One great choice, and there are quite a few mind you, is Yet Another Related Posts Plugin Options (`http://wordpress.org/extend/plugins/yet-another-related-posts-plugin`), shown in Figure 11-12. This not only features a lot of setting options, but also has the option for separate template files. The plugin not only outputs related posts where you want them (easily added with a template tag or a widget), it also displays which ones are relevant on the Edit Post screen, which might help you in your writing.

Popularity Contest

Popularity Contest (`http://wordpress.org/extend/plugins/popularity-contest`) is another way to keep people browsing your site. Based on your settings, similar to the weighing method used in Yet Another Related Posts Plugin Options, you'll get a list of your most popular content (see Figure 11-13). You can display the list using the widget or by using plugin-specific template tags, along with your posts.

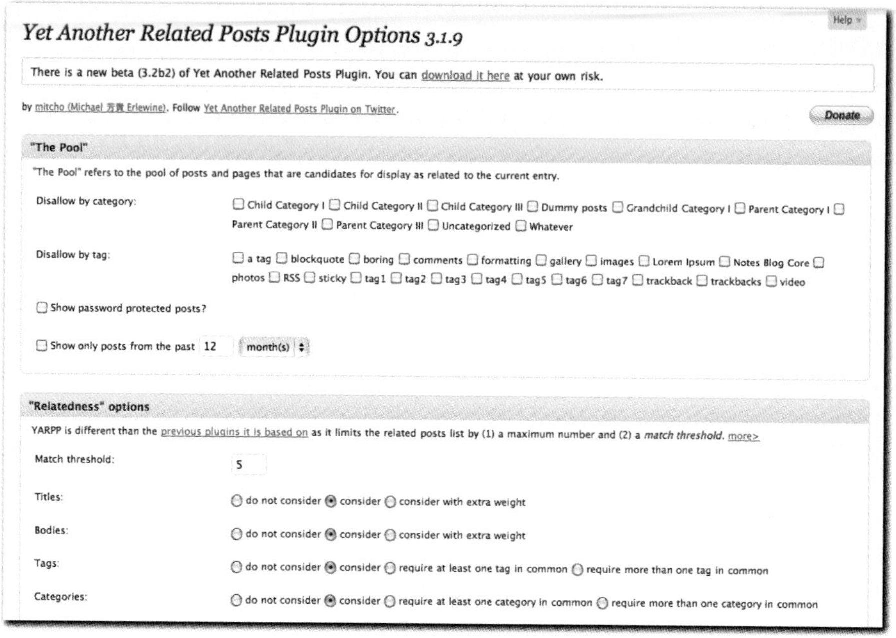

Figure 11-12: Yet Another Related Posts Plugin Options

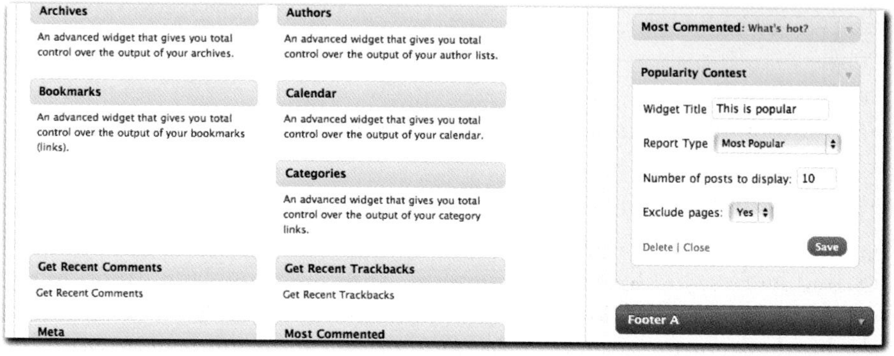

Figure 11-13: Popularity Contest

Contact Form 7

Contact Form 7 (http://wordpress.org/extend/plugins/contact-form-7) is probably the solution for you. It's one of a whole lot of form plugins that lets you set up anything from easy contact forms to more elaborate ones.

TDO Mini Forms

Another form-related plugin is the excellent TDO Mini Forms (http://wordpress.org/extend/plugins/tdo-mini-forms), which lets you set up forms where the user can submit content to be stored as posts, which you can approve (or not) at your own whim. The plugin offers a ton of settings, and is really quite powerful whenever you need to involve people from outside of WordPress. Unfortunately it is not actively developed as I'm writing this, although it works perfectly well, and is by no means discontinued.

Gravity Forms

A commercial alternative is Gravity Forms (`http://www.gravityforms.com`), although yet again, paying for plugins (and themes) is a grey area that you might not want to fiddle with. Gravity Forms is very popular, though, and might fit your needs so by all means check it out.

SyntaxHighlighter Evolved

If you ever intend to publish code on your site (for reading and not execution, that is) then SyntaxHighlighter Evolved (`http://wordpress.org/extend/plugins/syntax highlighter`) is a must. This plugin formats your code and lets the user save it to the clipboard easily. You can even style the code viewer, and there's support for several different languages, including PHP and HTML for your cool WordPress snippet sharing needs. Figure 11-14 shows the tool in action.

Figure 11-14: SyntaxHighlighter Evolved

Regenerate Thumbnails

Regenerate Thumbnails (`http://wordpress.org/extend/plugins/regenerate-thumbnails`) is a potential lifesaver when switching from one theme to another where the default content width differs. Let's say you have a lot of full width images, full content width, that is. Now, your new theme is 20 pixels wider, so the images you designed and placed in a manner tailored to occupy the full content width now look weird. Enter Regenerate Thumbnails, which will parse through all your images and create new thumbnails, as well as small, medium, and large versions of your images where it applies. The plugin fetches your image settings from the Media Settings screen, so make sure you got those right before kicking it off. And also, put on a kettle because it can take some time redoing all your images.

LIGHTBOX PLUGINS

There are a ton of lightbox plugins, those plugins that make images (and sometimes other media, too) load in an overlay above your site. You know the type; this is a popular technique to display images these days.

Shadowbox JS

Shadowbox JS (`http://wordpress.org/extend/plugins/shadowbox-js`) is perhaps the best of the breed, but it requires a license for commercial use, which makes it a somewhat doubtful choice.

Lightbox 2

Lightbox 2 (`http://wordpress.org/extend/plugins/lightbox-2`) is another popular plugin that does more or less the same thing, but it is reported that it clashes with some other plugins, so check your setup before going with this one.

CMS PLUGINS

WordPress is not just a blog platform anymore; it's a CMS, or just a publishing platform, if you will. Traditional CMSs have some features that WordPress is missing, such as nice tree views for pages.

CMS Tree Page View

CMS Tree Page View (`http://wordpress.org/extend/plugins/cms-tree-page-view`) adds a tree view page under Pages in the WordPress admin panel, as well as on your dashboard, if you like (see Figure 11-15). It's really neat, and makes it a bit easier to get a decent overview of things.

More Fields

Another great plugin is More Fields (`http://wordpress.org/extend/plugins/more-fields`), which is basically a GUI to create custom fields (see Figure 11-16). It makes them look good, as well as make sense to your users. You still use them as you always have, so it's really just a way to make them a bit easier on both developers and, mainly, end-users. Bonus: You might also want to check out More Types and More Taxonomies from the same developers as More Fields.

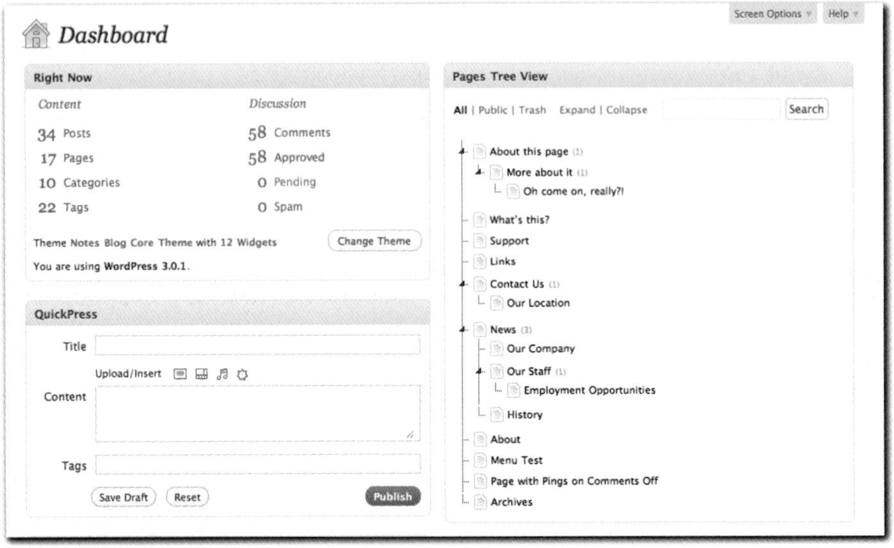

Figure 11-15: CMS Tree Page View

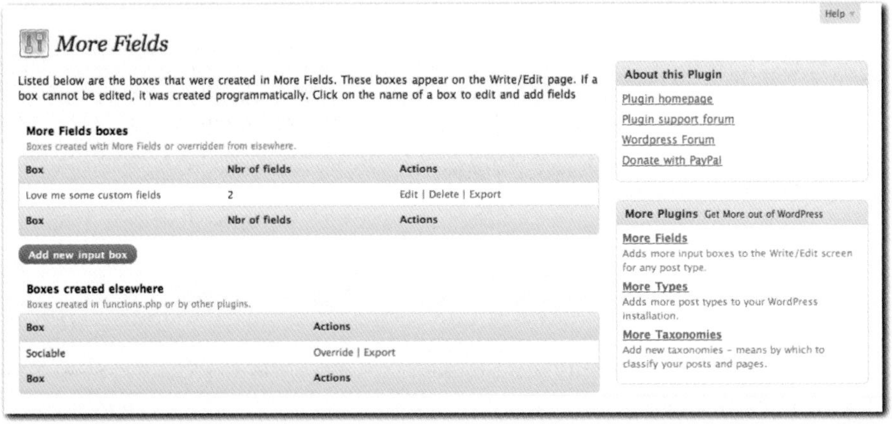

Figure 11-16: More Fields

All in One SEO Pack

Search engine optimization might not be CMS related per se, but then again it depends on what kind of site you're building. There are several plugins that will help you optimize your content for search engines, which is like adding super-turbo-nitro to a muscle car since WordPress already works perfectly well with search engines out of the box. All in One SEO Pack (http://wordpress.org/extend/plugins/all-in-one-seo-pack) is probably the most popular solution, and it does the job well enough by adding custom settings for your posts so that you can target them better and so on.

Google XML Sitemaps

You might also want to check out Google XML Sitemaps (`http://wordpress.org/extend/plugins/google-sitemap-generator`) for your sitemapping needs.

Widgets Reloaded

Don't think that the default widgets that ship with WordPress cuts it? Neither do I; they are a bit dated and lack a bunch of features. Widgets Reloaded (`http://wordpress.org/extend/plugins/widgets-reloaded`) aims to solve this problem by offering updated widgets for things like showing Pages, search box, category listings, and so on (see Figure 11-17). It is a nifty way to spice up the widgets functionality.

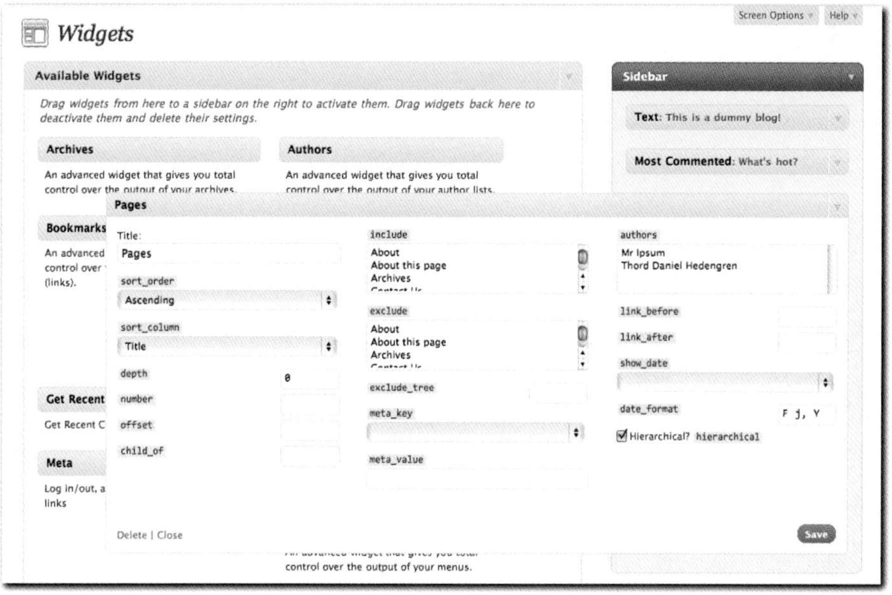

Figure 11-17: Widgets Reloaded

SEMI-ADVANCED MISCELLANEOUS PLUGINS

There are a ton of plugins, and some of them are only interesting in very special cases. Here are some gems you may have missed.

WP No Category Base

WP No Category Base(`http://wordpress.org/extend/plugins/wp-no-category-base`) only applies to sites where you don't want the automatic "category" addition (or whatever you've changed it to in your permalink settings) in your URLs. In most cases it is redundant, or just not necessary, but sometimes it makes a lot of sense.

Redirections

If you have old links you want to take into account, Redirection (http://wordpress. org/extend/plugins/redirections) is the plugin for you. It lets you set up redirects from one URL to another, which means that you can make sure that logical URLs work as well as the one you actually went with. Let's say you have domain.com/msp as your URL, but some people might type in, remember, or whatever, the old URL, which is domain.com/ my-super-product. With Redirection, you can make sure that people end up in the right place, using search engine friendly redirects. Figure 11-18 shows Redirections in action.

Figure 11-18: Redirections

Activate Update Services

Activate Update Services (http://wordpress.org/extend/plugins/activate- update-services) is a multi-site only plugin. It adds the ping box to multi-site installs, which means that you can control the pinging services on a per-blog basis, just like you do with separate installs.

No Self Pings

No Self Pings (http://wordpress.org/extend/plugins/no-self-ping) is another nifty little thing that makes sure the links within your domain aren't registered as a trackback, hence not showing up in the comments. Handy.

WP Mail SMTP

Moving on, WP Mail SMTP (http://wordpress.org/extend/plugins/wp-mail- smtp) is an excellent solution when you're on servers where you don't want to send e-mails. You can, for example, use it to let your Google Apps account act as the e-mail service instead of the server itself. Figure 11-19 displays the Advanced Email Options.

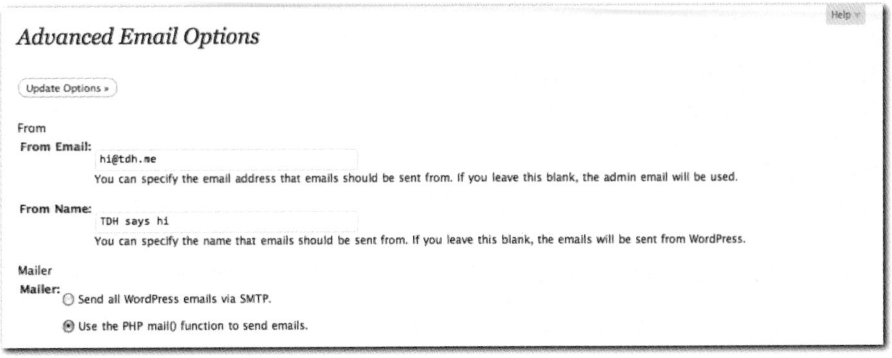

Figure 11-19: WP Mail SMTP

WP Super Cache

Wrapping up this list of plugins is none other than the savior of a ton of traffic, WP Super Cache (`http://wordpress.org/extend/plugins/wp-super-cache`), shown in Figure 11-20. This caching plugin basically creates HTML files of your site, which is a lot lighter on the server than the constant database queries WordPress relies on. Proper server hardware and software, along with PHP accelerators, will help, obviously, but the fastest solution to problems with slow or too heavily loaded sites is WP Super Cache. There are other caching plugins as well, but this is the most widely used and probably the best one, although that might very well change over time. Consult your needs and the server environment, and go with one if you expect some decent traffic. One thing is for sure though: WP Super Cache will help your site stay online.

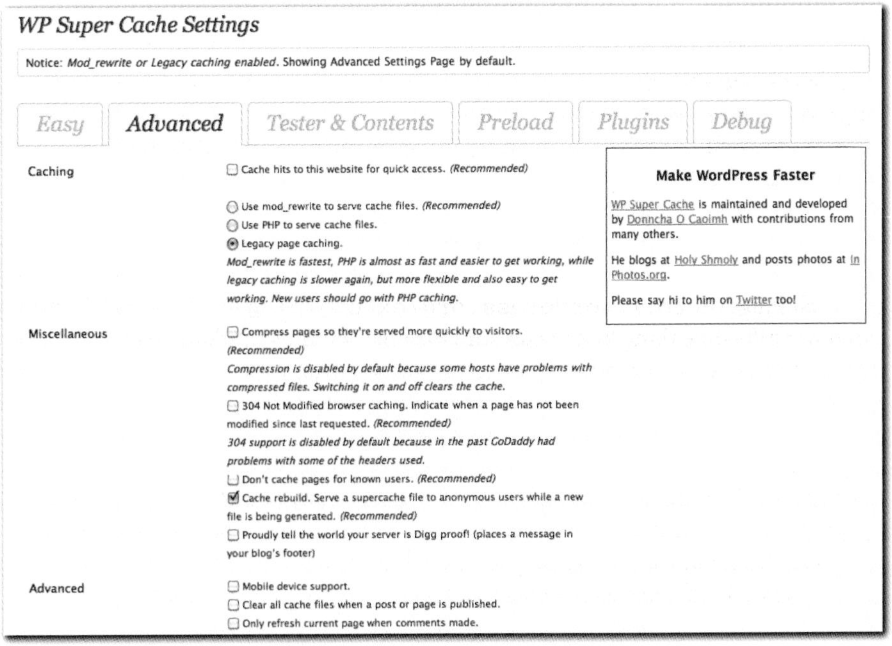

345

Figure 11-20: WP Super Cache

If you're having problems with WP Super Cache you might want to check out W3 Total Cache (`http://wordpress.org/extend/plugins/w3-total-cache/`) as an alternative. Caching is complicated stuff and your mileage will vary depending on your Web host and possibly other things in your WordPress setup as well.

WRITING YOUR OWN PLUGINS

If you know your way around with PHP, you can write your own plugins, should the community not already have done the work for you. Getting started with plugin development isn't hard at all, but it is a step up from working with themes since you create everything yourself from scratch.

That's not entirely true, though, since WordPress gives you a bunch of hooks and functions you'll no doubt want to use (for more information on action hooks, see Chapter 10). The action hooks are where you get into WordPress itself. For example, if you want to make something happen when a page loads, you'll most likely attach your plugin's PHP function for it to the `wp_head` hook.

This book is not about plugin development, so you're on your own here. As usual, the Codex is a good way to start, the Plugin API page (shown in Figure 11-21) in particular: `http://codex.wordpress.org/Plugin_API`.

You can also get some pointers from my other book, *Smashing WordPress: Beyond the Blog*, (Wiley Publishing, Inc.), although it is a more general beast about doing cool, non-bloggish things with WordPress overall, and not just with themes or plugins.

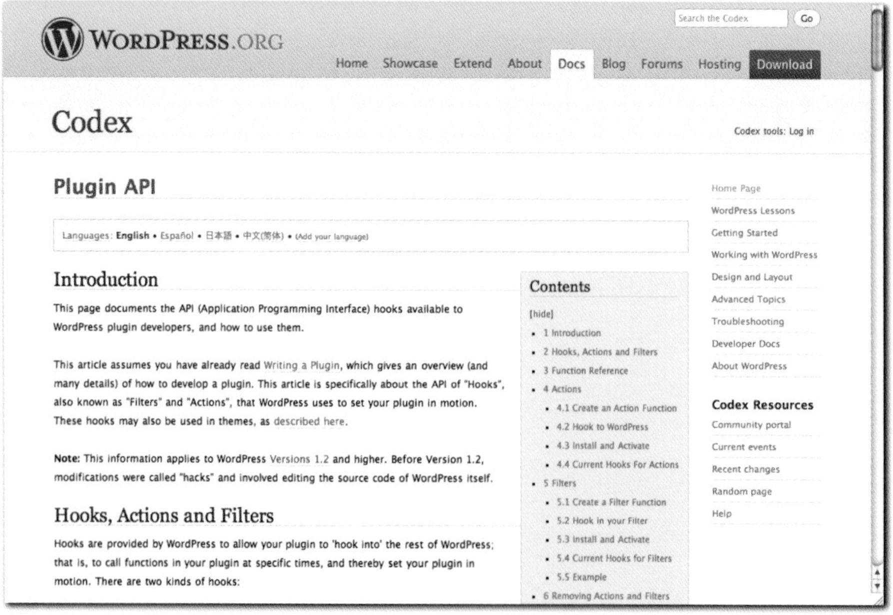

Figure 11-21: The Codex plugin API page

WRAPPING IT UP

Plugins are great when used with caution. They can solve a lot of your problems, but even though they may seem like an easy way out, they can also add overhead and be a nuisance in the future. The lesson here is to use plugins with caution, not to overload your site with unnecessary functionality just because you can and because it sits there in the `wordpress.org` plugin directory.

But again, plugins are great, and even in theme development, you should utilize the power of plugins to lift your WordPress site to new heights.

Index

355